GLOBALIZATION

The face of the world is changing. The past century has seen the incredible growth of international institutions. How does the fact that the world is becoming more inter-connected change institutions' duties to people beyond borders? Does globalization alone engender any ethical obligations? In *Globalization and Global Justice* Nicole Hassoun addresses these questions and advances a new argument for the conclusion that there are many coercive international institutions. She argues that such institutions must enable their subjects to avoid severe poverty. She considers the case for aid and trade in light of these obligations, and concludes with a new proposal for Fair Trade in pharmaceuticals and biotechnology. Her book will appeal to readers in philosophy, politics, economics, and public policy.

NICOLE HASSOUN is Assistant Professor in Philosophy at Carnegie Mellon University. She has published articles in journals including the *American Philosophical Quarterly*, *The Journal of Applied Ethics*, *Public Affairs Quarterly*, *Environmental Ethics*, and *Utilitas*.

GLOBALIZATION AND GLOBAL JUSTICE

Shrinking Distance, Expanding Obligations

NICOLE HASSOUN

CAMBRIDGE
UNIVERSITY PRESS

University Printing House, Cambridge CB2 8BS, United Kingdom

Published in the United States of America by Cambridge University Press, New York

Cambridge University Press is part of the University of Cambridge.

It furthers the University's mission by disseminating knowledge in the pursuit of
education, learning and research at the highest international levels of excellence.

www.cambridge.org
Information on this title: www.cambridge.org/9781107424920

First published 2012
First paperback edition 2014

A catalogue record for this publication is available from the British Library

Library of Congress Cataloguing in Publication data
Hassoun, Nicole.
Globalization and global justice : shrinking distance, expanding
obligations / Nicole Hassoun.
pages   cm
Includes bibliographical references and index.
ISBN 978-1-107-01030-7
1. Globalization–Social aspects.   2. Globalization–Economic aspects.
3. Social justice.   I. Title.
JZ1318.H3835 2012
303.48′2–dc23
2011051231

ISBN 978-1-107-01030-7 Hardback
ISBN 978-1-107-42492-0 Paperback

To Tamil and the memory of Hecky Villanuava – may your children light up the world.

Contents

Figures

viii

Acknowledgments

I owe many thanks to those who have supported, encouraged, and helped me throughout the writing of this book. I hope that I will be forgiven for leaving this list vastly incomplete as I do not have the space to list by name all of the people who have generously advised me, even in very significant ways.

First, I am sure I never could have completed the manuscript without the help, encouragement, and friendship of Thomas Christiano, Gillian Brock, Michael Blake, Alex London, Dale Dorsey, Jerry Gaus, Thomas Pogge, and Michael Gill, who kindly read (and, in Jerry's case, translated) many rough drafts. Thom Brooks, Allen Buchanan, Darrel Moellendorf, Luc Bovens, Jeffery Brennan, Mathias Risse, Leif Wenar, Debra Satz, Jim Nickel, Aaron James, Sarah Wright, Peter Spirtes, Richard Schienes, Clark Glymour, and Teddy Seidenfeld also earned my sincere gratitude.

Second, I would like to thank audiences and, especially, commentators at the conferences, colloquia, and workshops that contributed to the development of ideas in the book, especially: the London School of Economics; University College London; the Workshop in Social and Political Theory at Vanderbilt University; the VI Simposio Internacional De Economía Y Filosofía at the Universidad De Antioquia; the Bay Area Forum For Law & Ethics; the Joint Sessions; the AMINTAPHIL conferences; the American Society for Bioethics and Humanities Annual Meeting; the Morris Colloquium; the Rocky Mountain Ethics Conference; the American Philosophical Association Meetings; the Ethics and Africa conference; Newcastle University; the Conference on Global Justice in the 21st Century; the University of Alberta; Georgetown University; the University of North Florida; the University of Rochester; The Katedra Studiów Europejskich; the University of Washington, Seattle; Dickinson College; Leeds University; Johns Hopkins University; Santa Clara University; the IAPRS Annual Conference; the University of Manitoba; and the Academics Stand Against Poverty North American Conference at Yale University.

Third, I would also like to thank those who attended the colloquia, workshops and works in progress series at Carnegie Mellon University, Stanford University, the University of North Carolina Chapel Hill, Duke University, and the University of Arizona for their help with the project. I am especially grateful for comments from: Thomas Hill, Keith Lehrer, James Sterba, Kevin Zollman, Larry Temkin, Rachana Kamtekar, Josh Knobe, Michael Woolcock, David Copp, Bill Talbott, John Simmons, Roderick Long, Bertil Tungodden, Randall Curren, Robert Keohane, Peter Vallentyne, Matt Frank, Subbu Submaranian, Avram Hiller, Michael Goodheart, Jan Narveson, David Barnard, David Boonin, Don Ross, Gerald Dworkin, Orsolya Reich, Eric Hattleback, Orlin Vakarelov, Win-Chiat Lee, Dale Jamieson, Ralf Grahn, Jonathan Wolff, Garrett Cullity, Rex Martin, Julian Culp, Deen Chatterjee, Carol Gould, David Reidy, Kevin Kelly, Donald Light, Aleksander Surdej, John Weymark, Larry May, Marylin Freedman, Kevin Vallier, Brad Monton, Eran Ben-David, Paul Wise, Mark Roberts, Jerry McLean, Pilvi Toppinen, Nathan Lubchenco, Michael Otsuka, Michael Humer, Efthymios Athanasiou, Elizabeth O'Neill, Robert Cavalier, Bill Oberdick, Chris Brown, Lee Shepski, Cara Nine, Matt Zwolinski, Jason Matteson, Will Braynen, Joel Press, Josh Cohen, Rob Reich, Barbara Fried, Kieran Oberman, Manuel Vargas, Paul Gowder, Daniel Halliday, Eamonn Callan, Peter Stone, and Allegra McLeod.

I owe special thanks to my editor Hilary Gaskin and the students who have helped in the process of preparing the manuscript and with background research, especially Yomei Shaw and Dominic Cerminara.

I deeply appreciate the support I received during this project from the American Association of University Women, the Falk Foundation, the Earhart Foundation, the Berkman Foundation, the University of North Carolina at Chapel Hill, Duke University, Stanford's Center for Ethics in Society, the United Nations University World Institute for Development Economics Research in Helsinki, Finland, The Center for Poverty Research in Salzburg, Austria, and especially the University of Arizona and Carnegie Mellon University. The Philippine Community Organizers Society kindly provided an office and assistance during the summer of 2004 and I am incredibly indebted to Rowel Candelaria, Ariel Joseph, Norman Jaravata, and the Villanueva family, who took me in, took me around, and kept me from being killed by bandits.

I can never repay my friends and family who helped me in innumerable ways, primarily by putting up with me when it seemed that I would never finish. I owe special thanks to my mom who was convinced I should be here, to my father for his undying support, and to Max for finding me wandering the streets of Helsinki. You are all amazing!

Finally, I am greatly indebted to all those who kindly answered my questions about their lives in the Philippines, especially to the woman I call *Tamil* to whom I partially dedicate this work. I am sure she does not know that her brief interview inspired a book and it is for her and others like her that I write this. All of the royalties from this book will go to Partners In Health.

Abbreviations

DALY	Disability-adjusted life-year
EU	European Union
GATT	General Agreement on Tariffs and Trade
GBD	Global burden of disease
GDP	Gross domestic product
GNP	Gross national product
HDI	Human Development Index
HIPIC	Heavily Indebted Poor Countries Initiative
IBRD	International Bank for Reconstruction and Development
IDA	Inter-American Development Association
IFI	International financial institution
IMF	International Monetary Fund
NAFTA	North American Free Trade Agreement
NGO	Non-governmental organization
OECD	Organisation for Economic Co-operation and Development
R&D	Research and development
SAP	Structural adjustment program
UN	United Nations
USA	United States
WB	World Bank
WHO	World Health Organization
WTO	World Trade Organization

PART I

Introduction: Shrinking distance

Tamil shivers on the floor. Her youngest child holds her hand and her husband puts a cold cloth on her forehead. She has been up all night, delirious. At first, she had a high fever but then seemed to have difficulty following conversation and became extremely agitated. At one point, her husband said, she was hallucinating and thrashed about so much she had to be restrained. Now she is unconscious in a coma. If Tamil had had access to a doctor, better medicine, or was not so malnourished, she might be more likely to survive. If she had anti-malarial prophylaxis or a bed net, she might not have caught malaria in the first place. Tamil is too poor to afford a bed, never mind a bed net or proper medical care.

Tamil got malaria when her family moved to the provinces from the city to try to work on her parents' rice farm. Unfortunately, after a few years, they realized they could not make ends meet. They had to move back to the city. The Philippines had to increase rice imports to join the World Trade Organization (WTO). This greatly decreased the demand for local rice. Few of the agricultural extension offices that provided fertilizers and technical support when Tamil was a child were operating. They could not get help from the government or non-governmental organizations (NGOs). Tamil's family now lives in one of the Smokey Mountain temporary housing units in Metro Manila.[1]

Before she got sick, Tamil's family said their lives were better in Manila than it was in the province. Farming is seasonal; after the crops

---

[1] This story is intended to illustrate some of the problems poor people face that can undermine their ability to reason and plan. Although I did not discuss their health problems with the people I met at Smokey Mountain and Pyatas in 2004, the rest of the story comes primarily from interviews with people living in these places. For another example of some of the problems malaria can cause, see: Flower et al., "Blind, Breathless, and Paralysed from Benign Malaria," 438.

were harvested, there was little to eat. When they lived on the farm, Tamil's family suffered from malnourishment-related health problems. Tamil's eldest daughter probably suffered from iodine deficiency which caused severe hypothyroidism. She has the distorted facial features of cretinism. Her physical development was quite slow and she may not ever be competent to live on her own. There is some chance that the rice Tamil's family gets now will be fortified with iodine or vitamin A (lack of which can also cause retardation). The government distributes rice for free to the residents of Smokey Mountain. Tamil's children can also get vitamin supplements from a local aid organization: The Philippine Community Fund.

Living on Smokey Mountain is difficult, though. Smokey Mountain is one of the world's most infamous garbage dumps. The towering stories of garbage have been burning for decades. The stench is unbelievable. The living conditions in the temporary housing units are poor, even by standards in the Philippines. Tamil's family buys clean water, but they bathe in a leaching pool that is created by the run-off from the garbage.

Though Tamil's family is less likely to get malaria in the city, they are exposed to many other debilitating diseases in the dump. Partly because of the poor living conditions and lack of basic sanitation, they are likely to suffer from dysentery and typhoid. Dysentery and typhoid, if untreated, can lead to fever, shock or listlessness, and delirium. The dump also contains many heavy metals and other toxic substances that can lead to mental disabilities, severe emotional problems, or even autism. Other poverty-related diseases like dengue and tuberculosis can cause mental and physical disabilities as well.

Before she got sick Tamil started a business selling comote (a root crop) in the local market. Her husband used to work as a construction worker. The Asian financial crisis, brought about partly by bad lending in an already over-inflated real-estate market, brought an end to that.[2] There are few jobs in construction. He now works as a pedicab driver.

Fortunately, Tamil's other children help by working every day, though they have had to drop out of school. They are "scavengers" – they pick up garbage and sell it to the recyclers. Sadly, even when the kids of Smokey Mountain (and most of the rest of the Philippines) do go to school, they

---

[2] Blustein, *The Chastening.*

usually do not get far. Tamil's 16-year-old, for instance, only completed first grade.

Tamil's family lives in the temporary housing, partly, because people started paying attention to the horrible living conditions within Smokey Mountain itself after another Manila dump collapsed. The collapse at the Pyatas dump killed hundreds of people. It was not an everyday disaster of the kind that regularly happens on a dump (e.g. when a child, because it is hard to see amongst the refuse, is run over by a garbage truck). So, the government decided to move the 21 stories of waste from the similarly dangerous Smokey Mountain to a safer location. President Ramos also wanted to provide people living on the dump with houses and employment.

In 1997, Mr. Ramos hired a company called RII to build permanent (concrete) and temporary (wooden) housing, to move the mountain, and to provide the people with jobs. In exchange, RII got to reclaim and sell land in Manila bay (where the US embassy is located). RII reclaimed over 70 hectares of land in the bay. They only built 21 of the 30 planned permanent housing buildings. Worse, they did a poor job. Now many of the permanent buildings are sinking. Further renovations are necessary. Otherwise, the National Housing Authority will not approve the buildings for habitation. No one is willing to pay for fixing the units.[3] After the Asian financial crisis, no one bought the land RII reclaimed. Now RII refuses to fix the units unless the government comes through with its part of the bargain. Even though the bureaucratic wheels were greased when the new president Joseph Estrada was elected,[4] RII's taxes remain high.

The only people who have moved into the permanent housing were transferred there three years ago because of a fire in the temporary housing complex.[5] Tamil's family was not lucky enough to move into the permanent housing.

[3] Hassoun, Nicole, unpublished interview with Arthur Pasqua Jr., Manila, Philippines, 2004. Hassoun, Nicole, unpublished interview with Chito Nombres, Manila, Philippines, 2004.

[4] As the company official in charge of handling bribes reported, "somewhere around 30–50 people were bribed, up to Estrada." Hassoun, Nicole, unpublished interview with PhilECO representatives, Manila, Philippines, 2004. The bribes ranged from 55,000 pesos to 45 million pesos and were given at the going rate of 10 percent for each of the requested favors – "anything below 10 percent is an insult." Hassoun, Nicole, unpublished interview with PhilECO representatives, Manila, Philippines, 2004.

[5] Hassoun, Nicole, unpublished interview with PhilECO Representatives, Manila, Philippines, 2004.

Still, Tamil's family is luckier than most of the families who work at Smokey Mountain. They live next to, rather than in, the garbage. Only a few years have passed since Pyatas collapsed and the residents of Smokey Mountain were moved into the temporary housing. Migration to the city continues. Both Pyatas and Smokey Mountain have new tenants.

Tamil's husband hopes that one day they can transfer to the permanent housing. They are saving the money to move. In order to do so, they must be able to pay the mortgage. There is also a seven-year waiting list for the permanent housing. Tamil's family has some money from her kids who are working. Right now, however, her family is still trying to save the 1,000 pesos (US$20) needed to join the local cooperative "Precious Jewels." If Tamil recovers, this will be their first priority. If Tamil's family can join the cooperative, she can take out loans of up to 2,000 pesos to expand her business or if someone in her family gets sick.

Joining the local cooperative is about the only way that Tamil's family can get credit. They have no collateral. The banks charge incredibly high interest rates. Structural adjustment programs (SAPs), designed by international financial institutions (IFIs) like the International Monetary Fund (IMF), often require countries to liberalize interest rates. In countries like the Philippines, with inadequate banking regulatory frameworks and fragile business sectors, liberalization can lead banks to raise rates.[6] The IFIs require countries to adopt SAPs when they need loans. When I visited, the Philippines had had 19 such loans.[7]

Despite their difficulties, Tamil's family will continue to work hard to overcome the obstacles they face. If Tamil recovers, her children will probably have a brighter future.

Many families are like Tamil's.

Some 831 million human beings are undernourished, 1197 million lack access to safe water and 2747 million lack access to standard sanitation … About 2000 million lack access to essential drugs … Some 1000 million have no adequate shelter and 2000 million lack electricity … Some 876 million adults are illiterate … and 250 million children between 5 and 14 do wage work outside their household – often under harsh or cruel conditions: as soldiers, prostitutes, or domestic servants, or in agriculture, construction, textile or carpet production.[8]

---

[6] Villanueva and Mirakhor, "Interest Rate Policies in Developing Countries."

[7] Hassoun, Nicole, unpublished interview with Vikram Haksar, Manila, Philippines, 2004. For current statistics, see: World Bank, "Country Lending Summaries – Philippines."

[8] The UN International Labor Organization (ILO) says that 215 million children between the ages of 5 and 17 are working (ILO, "Accelerating Action Against Child Labour," 9). Of these, 115 million children are doing "hazardous work" a proxy for the number involved in the "worst forms"

The poor characteristically lack the resources or capabilities necessary to secure adequate food, water, shelter, education, health care, social support, and emotional goods.

Tamil's story illustrates how the global poor are likely to suffer from diseases that undermine even their basic capacities. Some of these people will become so seriously ill that they cannot even make important decisions for themselves. Others will die. In 2004 about a third of all deaths, 18 million a year or 50,000 every day, were poverty-related.[9] The 18 million who died in 2004 were joined by another 18 million in 2005 and another 18 million in 2006 and so on.[10] For comparison: Imagine a plane flying over 18 mid-sized US cities and killing all of their inhabitants every year. This book is concerned with the kind of severe deprivation that leads to so much suffering and death.

GLOBALIZATION AND GLOBAL JUSTICE

Tamil's story also illustrates that even the world's poorest members are not living in utter isolation. When the WTO requires countries like the Philippines to increase imports or decrease tariffs, it can transform poor people's lives. When the IMF or World Bank (WB) requires countries like the Philippines to implement SAPs, the poorest often feel the effects. Sometimes these programs impact individuals' access to even basic public services and social support programs.[11] Sometimes they impact access to loans or jobs.

With globalization distance is shrinking. Decisions made in one country often affect others and the poor people living in them. International institutions also impact the poor in many ways besides those mentioned above. Both national and international policies can, for instance, exacerbate financial or food crises.[12] Sometimes international organizations apply economic sanctions, air traffic controls, and arms embargoes on rogue countries and groups within them that threaten international security.[13] Sometimes they intervene militarily.[14] Globalization is reaching its fingers into even the most remote corners of the earth. Few escape its grasp.

---

of child labor, which include bonded labor, forced participation in armed conflict, prostitution, and the trafficking or production of illegal drugs (ibid., 22, 56–60).

[9] World Health Organization, *World Health Report 2004*, Annex Table 2.

[10] In 2009, there were 4,099,679 cases of *Plasmodium falciparum* malaria alone. World Health Organization, *World Malaria Report 2009*.

[11] IMF and World Bank, "ESAF Policy Framework Paper."

[12] Headey and Fan, "Reflections on the Global Food Crisis."

[13] Roberts, "United Nations."

[14] United Nations, "Security Council Seeks Expansion of Role."

This does not mean that globalization is a bad thing. But globalization raises important questions of global justice. The face of the world
is changing. The past 100 years have seen the incredible growth of international institutions, norms, rules, and procedures. Today 192 countries
are members of the United Nations (UN). The UN has programs promoting everything from international peace, trade, and development to
good environmental policy.[15] There are 187 country members of the WB
and IMF. The WB and IMF encourage macroeconomic stability and provide advice and help to developing countries.[16] There are 153 countries in
the WTO. The WTO oversees 97 percent of world trade.[17] There are also
many international treaties, customary laws, and international conven-
tions. They apply to everything from human rights to the global environment – from the depths of the seas to outer space. Does the fact that
the world is becoming more inter-connected change institutions' duties
to people beyond borders? Does globalization alone engender any ethical
obligations?

Historically social and political philosophy has focused on intra-
national issues and institutions. But, as more people, goods, and money
flow across state lines, it is increasingly important to consider what, if any,
obligations extend beyond borders.

A new ground for obligations to the poor

The first half of this book provides some new arguments for significant
obligations to the global poor that are intended to address liberals of
many persuasions. Those who endorse liberalism care about individual
freedom and believe the relationship between rulers and ruled must be
free in some sense. Liberalism can be contrasted with certain varieties
of consequentialism. On the relevant versions of consequentialism, the
only reason to preserve individuals' freedom is if doing so brings about
the best results on some other metric (e.g. utility). Liberalism can also be
contrasted with totalitarianism in which governments need not protect
basic freedoms at all. Subsequent chapters say more about the kind of
liberalism to which this book's arguments appeal, as well as several other
important concepts like *libertarianism, coercion, legitimacy, autonomy, liberty, basic capacities,* and *institutional system.*

---

[15] United Nations, "United Nations Member States."
[16] World Bank, "About Us." IMF, "About the IMF."
[17] World Trade Organization, "Members and Observers."

The key idea behind the first half of this book's main argument is this: There are many coercive international institutions. These institutions contain rules that are backed by sanction. Coercive institutions must be legitimate; they must have a justification-right to subject people to coercive rules. For such institutions to be legitimate, they must ensure that their subjects secure sufficient autonomy to autonomously agree to their rules. For most people to secure this basic minimum of autonomy they must be able to reason and plan. To reason and plan, everyone needs some food and water and most require some shelter, education, health care, social support, and emotional goods. Since everyone is subject to some coercive international institutions, these institutions must ensure that these people secure these things. This is an important conclusion in a world where over 2.7 billion people live on less than what US$2 a day buys in the USA.[18]

In making this argument, this book defends some kind of "capability" or "needs" theory, but not on the familiar grounds of humanity or justice suggested by authors like Amartya Sen, Martha Nussbaum, Simon Caney, and Gillian Brock. Its main claim is not that concern for our shared humanity requires ensuring that people secure basic human capacities. Nor does this book rely on this obligation being a requirement of justice (although it starts from an idea implicit in the social contract tradition – focusing upon what social arrangements people could freely accept). Rather, this book argues, roughly, that legitimacy requires coercive institutions to ensure that their subjects secure basic capacities. Whether or not concern for humanity or justice requires that these people secure these capabilities, coercive institutions must ensure that their subjects secure this much because they are *coercive*. Autonomy-undermining poverty is incompatible with the legitimate exercise of coercive power. Ending such poverty is not (just?) a general requirement of morality or justice.

This book engages with the literature on cosmopolitanism and statism in a new way.[19] Statists – like Thomas Nagel and Richard Miller – believe that those within states have stronger obligations to their compatriots than to outsiders. They usually grant that there are obligations of humanity, but deny that there are obligations of distributive justice to the global poor. This book argues, however, that legitimacy is closely connected with justice. So, statists have a reason to take its arguments seriously. Further, statists accept some obligations besides obligations of humanity and

---

[18] Chen and Ravallion, "How Have the World's Poorest Fared since the Early 1980s?" 141–69.

[19] I would like to thank Aaron James and Josh Cohen for discussion on this point. I also owe thanks to Dale Dorsey, Alex London, and James Nickel for extensive comments on this chapter.

(limited obligations of) justice. Consider, for instance, how John Rawls holds that there are duties – though not duties of humanity or justice – to respect a short list of human rights in the *Law of Peoples*. So, even if legitimacy and justice are unrelated, statists have reason to respond to the first half of this book's conclusion. Namely the claim that, for coercive institutions to be legitimate, they must ensure their subjects secure what they need to avoid autonomy-undermining poverty.

Furthermore, the argument sketched above is, in some respects, similar to the "coercion-based theories" defended by Nagel and Miller. It just denies that only coercion exercised by the domestic state requires justification. This book argues that there are many coercive international institutions. At least statists who, like Michael Blake, start from a concern with legitimacy to argue for some priority to compatriots should engage with this book's argument.[20] In making this case, this book defends a cosmopolitan concern with what is necessary for people, independent of where they live, to agree to be subject to coercive institutions.

Yet cosmopolitan theories are often defended on quite different grounds. In some ways, this book's argument is similar to Thomas Pogge's argument in *World Poverty and Human Rights*. This book starts from a concern for individual freedom to defend some significant obligations to the global poor. Pogge argues, however, that we have such obligations because those of us in the developed world are harming the global poor. His argument may, ultimately, be successful. Still, there are significant reasons to worry about whether he has established his crucial premise in a way that everyone who is concerned about individual freedom can accept. Mathias Risse and Alan Patten argue, for instance, that libertarians may reject Pogge's baseline for harm. So it is noteworthy that this book's argument proceeds from entirely different premises (and reaches a slightly different conclusion). It suggests that international institutions are *coercing*, not necessarily harming, the global poor. So, these institutions have significant obligations to these people. This book argues that this is something even those least likely to believe there are significant obligations to the global poor are likely to accept. Furthermore, this book suggests that coercive institutions bear a corresponding obligation to ensure their subjects secure food, water, shelter, and so forth. (Though Pogge may be right to hold that, ultimately, the buck stops with those of us in the developed world who have helped implement, and uphold these institutions.)[21]

---

[20] Blake, "Distributive Justice, State Coercion, and Autonomy," 257–96.

[21] This book's novel argument is intended to appeal to liberals of many sorts. Such liberals need only agree that people must be able to object to being subject to coercive rule. This book's

This book's argument is modest. Unlike Nussbaum and Caney, this book does not defend an egalitarian theory of global justice that requires that everyone have equal opportunities or capabilities.[22] Nor does this book defend another version of global egalitarianism. Rather, subsequent chapters defend one necessary condition for *legitimacy* that requires helping the global poor.

In our world, arguments about world poverty may be more important than arguments about global egalitarianism. Many people alive today cannot secure even basic things like adequate nutrition, education, and health care. About half of the world's population lives below the US$2 a day WB poverty line;[23] 18 million die every year from easily preventable poverty related causes.[24] It may be more important to argue that these people should secure adequate nutrition, education, and health care than that they should have the opportunity to become bankers or circus performers (like those of us in the developed world).[25] We are not likely to achieve even this more modest goal anytime soon.

Valuable philosophical argument

This book's arguments are controversial. Most people know that the extent of world poverty is staggering. Unfortunately, many believe that no one must do anything about it. Some of these people are only concerned about individuals' ability to live their lives free from interference. They believe that no one should have to sacrifice their freedom for another person. This book argues that it is precisely because no one should have to sacrifice their freedom for others that coercive institutions must ensure that all of their subjects secure food and water and most secure shelter, education, health care, social support, and emotional goods. This does not mean that most people should get these things for free. Rather, this book argues that coercive institutions must ensure that their subjects secure these things on their own.

---

main argument does not require readers to accept a Rawlsian hypothetical consent theory. Nevertheless, it should appeal to Rawlsians who believe people should have basic freedoms under coercive institutions. This book's argument is, therefore, different from Thomas Pogge's earlier work as well as Charles Beitz's and Darrel Moellendorf's arguments. Pogge, *Realizing Rawls*. Beitz, *Political Theory and International Relations*, 149–50. Moellendorf, *Cosmopolitan Justice*.

[22] Beitz, *Political Theory and International Relations*, 149–50. Nussbaum, *Women and Human Development*. Caney, "Cosmopolitan Justice and Equalizing Opportunities," 113–34.

[23] World Bank, "Povcalnet."

[24] World Health Organization, *World Health Report 2004*, Annex Table 2.

[25] Caney, *Justice Beyond Borders*.

This book's arguments are primarily intended to address an audience which embraces an individualistic, freedom-based (i.e. liberal) view. They will not appeal to everyone who is concerned about freedom. They will not appeal to those who believe that coercive institutions can be perfectly legitimate even if no one can object to being subject to their rule. It is important, however, to address those who believe everyone should have some *basic freedoms*. For most of those who take on leadership roles in international institutions that greatly influence the lives of the poor accept this much.

Arguments sometimes have a powerful impact on individuals and society. Most people do not change their mind, never mind their behavior, because of philosophical argument – advertising may be a better strategy. Nevertheless, some of those who have yet to make up their minds about a particular issue may be helped to do so by philosophical inquiry. Furthermore, good ideas, when they make their way by a long and winding road into contemporary culture, can be quite powerful. Today about one out of ten young people in the USA is a vegetarian.[26] Few were vegetarians before Peter Singer's *Animal Liberation* and a handful of other important books on the topic were published. They may have had a significant impact. I know of no one who denies that Karl Marx's *Manifesto* changed the world. Ideas have led us to walk on the moon and bring down the Berlin Wall. Much less radical and revolutionary ideas have probably also seeped into the public culture combining with hundreds of thousands of other reasonably good ideas to create much slower, though perhaps equally important, change. This book may help extend the consensus on some important obligations to the poor.

This book's aim is more philosophical, however, than strategic or practical. Some good arguments do not attempt to establish particularly controversial conclusions. The value of a philosophical argument often lies in its details – in the novel, interesting, or broadly compelling way that it attempts to establish its conclusion. While many will agree that there are significant obligations to the poor, the reasons they accept this conclusion are very different. It is important to get clear on the appropriate grounds for these obligations. Different ways of understanding these grounds may lead to different ways of understanding the corresponding obligations' content. Duties of legitimacy may, for instance, be more stringent than duties of justice.

---

[26] Mangels, "How Many Vegetarians Are There?"

Readers might wonder, however, about the book's third chapter in particular. It argues that libertarians should agree that there are significant obligations to the global poor. Why bother considering libertarianism as few accept this view and many find it to be radically implausible?

There are a few good answers to this challenge. First, philosophical libertarianism is perhaps the best worked theory on which one can deny this book's conclusion. Second, considering the view should be intrinsically interesting, especially since the relevant chapter provides new reasons to question the view's coherence. If anarchism plays the role in political philosophy that brains in vats play in epistemology, libertarianism plays the role of idealism. Libertarianism may strike most people as implausible, but it is not obvious how to discredit the view. Examining the foundations for libertarianism may be an important part of the philosophical enterprise's slow but steady crawl towards truth. As John Stuart Mill said, let philosophers give voice to all views true and false for it is only by exposing the false that we can be certain of the true.[27]

Practical proposals for reform

A concern for individual freedom motivates this book's second half as well as its first: In its second half, this book considers ways of modifying, or working around international rules and institutions to better protect individual autonomy. It considers the case for free trade and foreign aid and suggests that it is possible to greatly improve international rules and institutions. In doing so, it addresses those of a skeptical bent who worry about obligations to the global poor for, primarily, practical reasons. It argues against some of the IFIs and trade agreements' policies. (For a brief overview of these institutions and policies see the second and third sections of the Introduction to Part II.)

This book's second half considers some important philosophical work on aid and trade. It connects with the large literature on the nature and limits of our obligations to the poor including the literature in moral philosophy by authors like Peter Singer, Dale Jamieson, and Leif Wenar on obligations to aid.[28] It also engages with the literature on free trade by authors

---

[27] Mill, *On Liberty*, 1909–14.

[28] Singer, "Famine, Affluence, and Morality," 229–43. Cullity, *The Moral Demands of Affluence*. Aiken and La Follette (eds.), *World Hunger and Moral Obligation*. Chatterjee (ed.), *The Ethics of Assistance*. Schmidtz, "Islands in a Sea of Obligation," 683–705. Jamieson, "Duties to the Distant," 151–70. Kuper, "More Than Charity," 107–20. Wenar, "The Basic Structure as Object," 253–78. Wenar, "Accountability in International Development Aid." Wenar, "Poverty is No Pond."

like Christian Barry, Sanjay Reddy, Fernando Teson, and Jonathan Klick. Finally, this book provides a new proposal for promoting global health, in particular, that engages critically with work by authors like Aiden Hollis and Thomas Pogge. In doing so, this book's second half helps fill a pressing need for reflection on practical ways of fulfilling obligations to the poor. It is novel and potentially quite important because it helps fill a neglected gap between high level philosophical argument and empirical examination of institutional arrangements. It offers concrete and practical policy-relevant suggestions for how we might make trade a bit more responsive to the needs of the poor.

Mid-level theory is important for addressing the pressing problems of world poverty. Most moral arguments (including some of the arguments in this book) are pitched at an extremely theoretical level. On the other hand, most empirical research is focused on particular details of institutional design. It is not enough to know that there are obligations to the global poor or which ways of modifying institutions are possible, in isolation. It is important to integrate this information; keeping our heads out of the clouds and the sand.

The proposal with which this book concludes is related to, but different from, some other practical proposals in the literature. It is, in some ways, similar to Pogge's work on achieving democracy, Brock's work on taxation, and Wenar's work on property rights and the resource curse.[29] It explores, at an intermediate level, important features of our world and how it can be improved. Its details differ significantly from existing proposals in the literature, most notably, Pogge's Health Impact Fund. The Health Impact Fund would offer a second (voluntary) patent system for essential drugs and technologies. Under this system, companies would not be given a limited monopoly for their inventions. Rather, inventors would be rewarded based on how much their inventions contribute to ameliorating the global burden of disease (GBD). This book proposes, instead, to rate pharmaceutical and biotechnology companies based on how their policies impact poor people's health and to give the best companies something akin to a "Fair Trade" label to use on all their products. Universities may also make it a condition of the sale of their licenses that companies holding their technology have to be "Fair Trade" certified. This book's last substantive chapter argues that the proposals could create a significant incentive for companies to ameliorate the GBD. Unlike Pogge's proposal, however, this one is relatively inexpensive.

---

[29] Pogge, *World Poverty and Human Rights*. Brock, *Global Justice*. Wenar, "Property Rights and the Resource Curse," 2–32.

Empirical evidence and interdisciplinary approach

This book is unusual as a philosophical work in emphasizing empirical evidence. Globalization raises some of the most important issues that confront the world today. Any work on this subject that ignores how things really are fails in an important way; to come to sound ethical conclusions about the real world, it is important to take into account the capabilities and capacities of agents, the strengths and weaknesses of institutions. Theory should not be made hostage to current practice but, to provide useful guidance, it must be realistic. This book aims to provide concrete policy advice based on sound moral principles.[30]

The assumption that good principles must be compatible with sound practice makes it natural to come to philosophical conclusions from two directions simultaneously: working down from theoretical considerations and working up from empirical evidence. This approach to global justice is similar to the approach of philosophers in other interdisciplinary domains like cognitive science and philosophy of science. Just as philosophers of science often appeal to scientific theories and evidence in considering the nature of space-time, this book will appeal to economic theories and evidence in considering the nature of (and justification for) moral principles and public policies.[31]

The questions addressed in this book span disciplines. What ethical principles should govern the structure of coercive institutions? What are the economic consequences for the poor of different public policies? Is globalization benefiting the global poor? This book examines these and similar questions by looking at the work of philosophers, economists, political scientists, sociologists, and others writing about international development. Though most of the book proceeds via philosophical argument, it also relies on statistical data, theoretical models, and case studies to make important points about, for instance, the efficacy of free trade and foreign aid in ameliorating poverty.

This is not to say that the book attempts to do social science or provide new results in disciplines other than philosophy. It does not provide new data or even new statistical analyses of others' data.

---

[30] This book does not provide the complete set of moral principles institutions must satisfy. Nor does it present principles with which all people are expected to fully comply. It suggests a few principles that constrain the form any acceptable institution can take. On this basis, it suggests a few policies that can, realistically, be implemented in the foreseeable future. Buchanan, *Justice, Legitimacy, and Self-Determination*. Rawls, *A Theory of Justice*.

[31] Healey, *Gauging What's Real*.

Rather, this book relies on and evaluates evidence from other disciplines using a standard available to every discipline – critical analysis. Just as theoretical arguments can be better or worse, so can empirical arguments. Simply asserting empirical conclusions will not suffice to establish them. Nor is it generally acceptable to cite a single source, or even several sources, to support an empirical claim (though that depends to some extent on whether the claim is controversial amongst social scientists and its importance in a larger argument). Still, one need not do new meta-analyses of empirical studies to provide reasonable grounds for empirical hypotheses. Citing such studies may suffice. Critical analysis can provide reasons to attend to certain kinds of studies or point to methodological or data problems underlying them.

Relying on any empirical evidence will open the door to new ways in which one's conclusions can be questioned. It is sometimes best to simply make arguments conditional on factual assumptions holding. When data exists to support its empirical claims, however, this book will take the argument one step further and try to establish its conclusions unconditionally.

Philosophers have a lot to offer those working on development. Philosophers are good at drawing out and examining the justifications offered for policies. They are good at exposing hidden value assumptions. They are also good at identifying alternative ethical frameworks that can guide development. Philosophers can, for instance, help policy makers come to a deeper understanding of what is at stake in debates about aid and trade. Hopefully, this will help policy makers reach better conclusions.

Philosophy, too, can profit from examining work in other areas. Insight in the moral realm sometimes comes from paying attention to facts whose moral significance has been overlooked. Those engaged in different domains of inquiry look at problems from different perspectives. They consider different data. They examine the data in different ways. This book argues that, just as those doing practical work benefit from considering their normative presuppositions, those doing normative work benefit from examining their practical presuppositions. It suggests, for instance, that debates about obligations to aid often hinge on unstated empirical presumptions. To come to sound conclusions about political obligations in the real world, it is important to do moral theory in a way that is responsive to empirical reality.

Theory and practice can inform each other in interesting and often overlooked ways. Theories about our moral obligations may, for instance, guide the development of political and economic institutions. What political and economic institutions exist also partly determine what theories should say about our obligations. What political and economic institutions exist help determine what obligations remain unmet and what means are available to address these obligations.

This book suggests that there is a lot to learn from interdisciplinary study. So, it should be of interest to those focused on methodological questions as well as anyone concerned with the substantive and important problems of poverty, development, and globalization.

OVERVIEW

There are many straightforward arguments for the conclusion that there are significant obligations to the global poor. On these accounts, most people have a right to secure adequate food, water, shelter, education, health care, social support, and emotional goods. Following authors like James Nickel and James Griffin, the first chapter starts from the idea that everyone has a right to the necessary conditions for autonomy. It then argues that, to secure the relevant sort of autonomy, everyone must secure some food and water, and most require some shelter, education, health care, social support, and emotional goods. Authors like Tibor Machan, Jan Narveson, and Loren Lomasky would object, however, that this argument requires some to sacrifice their freedom for others.[32] Others like Onora O'Neill argue that there is indeterminacy in the notion of a positive right (that is, a right to aid).[33] Yet others, like Joseph Raz, suggest that there is no right to autonomy because that would require the demanding provision of collective goods (e.g. institutions).[34] There are plausible responses to some such criticisms.[35] It is possible to avoid indeterminacy in the notion of positive rights by appeal to international law, for instance. Nevertheless, some will probably remain unconvinced. Some (e.g. libertarians and actual consent theorists) only believe people have negative rights that others not do certain kinds of things. Others might maintain that whatever positive rights exist have little force. So, the first chapter suggests that a new argument for obligations

---

[32] See, for instance: Narveson, *The Libertarian Idea*; Lomasky, *Persons, Rights, and the Moral Community*; Machan, "The Perils of Positive Rights"; Nozick, *Anarchy, State, and Utopia*. For further discussion of this line of thought, see: Feinberg, *Social Philosophy*; O'Neill, *Bounds of Justice*; Shue, *Basic Rights: Subsistence, Affluence, and U.S. Foreign Policy*.

[33] O'Neill, "The Dark Side of Human Rights," 427–39.

[34] Raz, The Morality of Freedom, ch. 10.

[35] Hassoun, "Raz on the Right to Autonomy".

to the poor is needed. This lays the groundwork for the arguments in the second and third chapters in two ways. First, this chapter explains and defends some of the crucial concepts and claims relied upon in subsequent chapters. It describes the kind of autonomy necessary to consent to coercive rules and institutions and argues that most people need food, water, shelter, education, health care, social support, and emotional goods to secure it. Second, this chapter makes the case that we need new arguments for significant obligations to the global poor. Subsequent chapters are intended to *extend* the consensus on the conclusion that there are such obligations.

Chapter 2 defends this book's main argument. It suggests that a negative right against coercion actually entails positive rights to things like basic food, water, shelter, and so forth. The second chapter defends, roughly, this claim: To be legitimate, coercive institutions must not merely refrain from interfering with individuals' ability to secure things like basic food, water, shelter, and so forth but actually ensure that they do so. Legitimacy, it suggests, is just a justification-right to exercise coercive force. Coercive institutions must have this right because their subjects have a natural right to freedom. A coercive institution, the chapter argues, can only be legitimate if it ensures that its subjects secure sufficient autonomy to consent to its rules. Next, the second chapter argues that everyone is subject to many coercive international institutions. Since most people must secure basic food, water, shelter, and so forth to secure sufficient autonomy, coercive international institutions must ensure that these people secure these things. The second chapter concludes by considering how its argument might be extended to generate properly global obligations. It argues that international institutions and rules have enough in common that it makes sense to talk about them as a system that can coerce and is liable for doing so.[36]

The third chapter suggests that even those most resistant to accepting any significant obligations to the global poor (i.e. libertarians and actual consent theorists) have compelling reason to endorse these obligations. Most libertarians and actual consent theorists accept the second chapter's argument that coercive institutions must be legitimate. So, the third chapter starts from this conclusion. It then addresses libertarians who accept something like the following proposition: It is only legitimate to exercise coercive force over rights-respecting individuals to protect those individuals' liberty. The third chapter follows authors like John Simmons

---

[36] Although many statists accept the claim that there is a global institutional system, it is controversial.

in arguing that libertarians who accept this much should accept actual consent theory; they should agree that coercive institutions are legitimate only if they secure their subjects' actual autonomous consent. Next, the third chapter suggests actual consent theorists, and hence these libertarians, should agree to the following claim: legitimate coercive institutions have to ensure that most of their subjects secure some food, water, shelter, education, health care, social support, and emotional goods. Libertarians have to agree that states, and perhaps many international institutions, must ensure that their subjects secure food and water and whatever else they need for autonomy.

The second part of this book examines some of the institutions and rules guiding international development. It is clear that many people cannot even secure basic food, water, shelter, medicine and so forth, and most of the global poor live in the developing world. This book's second half considers the case for foreign aid and free trade in light of the moral obligations defended in the first part. It argues that the case for some foreign aid and free trade is strong. Nevertheless, it suggests that some ways of modifying the rules of trade or working around them – encouraging some trade barriers, trade-related adjustment assistance programs, linkage, and the Fair Trade movement – may be necessary and desirable.

Perhaps the biggest challenge to arguments for helping the global poor is the skeptical worry that there is nothing anyone can do to ameliorate poverty. Several philosophers, including David Schmidtz, Andrew Kuper, and Dale Jamieson, have questioned the claim that aid can ameliorate poverty.[37] Most of these critics have questioned this conclusion (at least in part) by discussing particular case studies that have not been rigorously evaluated. The fourth chapter argues that this is a mistake. It considers the kind of empirical evidence that is necessary to make the case for or against aid. In doing so, it defends the book's use of empirical data (that is particularly evident in the last chapters). When one looks at rigorous data regarding aid's efficacy, it is clear that the case for giving some aid is strong. Importantly, it suggests that there are rigorous ways of figuring out when aid works and when it does not. As long as one does not fail to see the trees for the forest, as long as one can see the good that comes from helping some, even if it is impossible to completely ameliorate poverty, there is little basis for the skeptical worries.

---

[37] Schmidtz, "Islands in a Sea of Obligation," 683–705. Jamieson, "Duties to the Distant," 151–70. Kuper, "More Than Charity," 107–20.

Advocates of globalization argue that free trade is a better way of helping the global poor than aid. Most people are familiar with *The Economist*'s, WB's, and IMF's claims to this effect.[38] Even philosophers and lawyers like Teson and Klick argue that the case for free trade is strong because it will reduce poverty. So, Chapter 5 examines the case for the kind of free trade the IFIs and trade agreements advocate. It finds that there is no theoretical guarantee that free trade will ameliorate poverty. In theory, the most such reforms guarantee is that liberalized markets will reach a Pareto optimal state, that is, a state in which it is impossible to make anyone better off without making someone else worse off. Pareto optimality (under the relevant interpretation) tells us little about distribution. Even a situation in which one person has everything, and everyone else is poor, can be Pareto optimal. In practice, the case for free trade is even less clear. Even if the aggregate benefits of free trade for the poor are large, there may be no reason to support free trade. Free trade reforms often have mixed effects. This chapter concludes that some trade barriers, linkage, trade-related adjustment assistance programs, and the Fair Trade movement may provide ways of capturing the benefits of free trade for the poor, while avoiding the costs.

Chapter 6, thus, makes a preliminary case for one kind of Fair Trade in particular. It proposes and defends a package of Fair Trade strategies to encourage pharmaceutical and biotechnology companies to improve poor people's access to essential drugs and technologies. In doing so, it does not suggest a general strategy for addressing poverty. There is not a single problem to solve. Rather, it tries to illustrate one way of addressing some of the problems poor people face. It suggests rating pharmaceutical and biotechnology companies based on how their policies impact poor people's access to essential drugs and technologies. The best companies, in a given year, can then be Fair Trade certified and be allowed to use a Fair Trade label on their products. Highly rated companies will have an incentive to use the label to garner a larger share of the market as those engaged in trade and investment often prefer to purchase Fair Trade goods and invest in Fair Trade companies.[39] If even a small percentage of consumers or doctors prefer Fair Trade products, the incentive to use this label could be substantial. Further, socially responsible investment

---

[38] See, for instance: World Bank, *Globalization, Growth, and Poverty.*

[39] Ruben, *The Impact of Fair Trade.* Raynolds, "Poverty Alleviation Through Participation in Fair Trade Coffee Networks." In fact, ethics-based consumption of all sorts is on the rise: Doane, "Taking Flight."

companies could include in their portfolio Fair Trade certified companies. Finally, having a Fair Trade certification system for pharmaceutical and biotechnology companies would open the door to all kinds of fruitful social activism including boycotts of poorly rated companies, lobbying of insurance companies to include Fair Trade products in their formularies, and so forth. After considering some of the details of the Fair Trade certification scheme, Chapter 6 considers one kind of activism using the scheme that might benefit the poor – a Fair Trade licensing campaign. Pharmaceutical and biotechnology companies rely, to a large extent, on university research and development. So, if universities only allow companies that agree to use Fair Trade practices to benefit from their technology, companies have an incentive to abide by Fair Trade standards. If universities are reluctant to require this much of their clients, however, researchers and students might have an impact. Researchers sign agreements to allow universities to license patents resulting from research they create and students have been successful in convincing their campuses to participate in other Fair Trade licensing campaigns.

In short, the second half of this book argues that there is no contest between free trade, Fair Trade, and foreign aid, each is appropriate in some cases. Even if aid and trade together do not solve all of the poor's problems, this book argues, there is a lot coercive institutions can and must do to help the global poor. This is a significant conclusion in a world where so many suffer and die from easily preventable poverty related causes every year.

CHAPTER I

Human rights, autonomy, and poverty

I.I INTRODUCTION

There are many straightforward arguments for the conclusion that there are significant obligations to the global poor. On these accounts, most people have a right to secure adequate food, water, shelter, education, health care, social support, and emotional goods. Many believe these rights are practically self-evident.[1] The claims of the hungry, thirsty, and sick are just that, claims upon us. We cannot ignore others' needs without (significant) reason. Lack of food, water, shelter, and so forth poses a serious threat to individuals' interests and autonomy. As this chapter will explain, however, many liberals who are deeply concerned about individual freedom do not believe people have positive rights to food, water, shelter, and so forth. Libertarians like Machan and Lomasky argue, for instance, that people only have negative rights to be free from interference by others.[2] Even more mainstream liberals might maintain that this chapter's argument does not go through.[3] So, this chapter starts by defending one version of the above argument for positive rights to secure adequate food, water, and so forth. It then examines objections to this argument. Finally, it suggests that a new way of defending obligations to the global poor is needed. The next chapter provides this book's new argument for these obligations.

This chapter's argument is, however, primarily positive. It cashes out and defends some of the crucial concepts and claims relied upon in

---

[1] Although Henry Shue gives extensive argument in defense of basic rights to sustenance, he also seems to think that the fact that people have these rights should be self-evident. Shue, *Basic Rights*. As he suggests, it is clear that these rights are important for protecting individuals against significant suffering and exploitation. I owe thanks to James Nickel and Dale Dorsey for their particularly helpful comments on this chapter.

[2] Narveson, *The Libertarian Idea*. Lomasky, *Persons, Rights, and the Moral Community*. Machan, "The Perils of Positive Rights." Nozick, *Anarchy, State, and Utopia*.

[3] See, for instance: Raz, *The Morality of Freedom*. I engage with the details of Raz's sophisticated argument in: Hassoun, "Raz on the Right to Autonomy."

subsequent chapters. It, first, describes the kind of autonomy necessary to consent to coercive rules and institutions. It then argues that, to secure this autonomy, everyone needs some food and water and most need some shelter, education, health care, social support, and emotional goods. Next, it highlights and responds to some worries about human rights arguments. Only then does it suggest that we have arrived at a stalemate in the attempt to justify or reject human rights arguments. So, this chapter concludes that we need new arguments for significant obligations to the global poor to *extend* the consensus on this conclusion.

1.2 ARGUING FOR POSITIVE RIGHTS

There are many ways of arguing that people have positive rights to secure some food, water, and so forth.[4] James Nickel and Allen Buchanan suggest, for instance, that people have a human right to fulfill their basic interests.[5] James Griffin and Alan Gewirth argue that people have a human right to secure agency or autonomy.[6] On such accounts, people possess human rights in virtue of their humanity.[7] Furthermore, these accounts usually support derivative rights *to* the things that are necessary to protect basic interests or autonomy.[8] If one accepts this much, it is easy to argue that everyone has a right to some food and water, and most people have a right to some shelter, education, health care, social support, and emotional goods.[9] For most people have a basic interest in these things and they are necessary for most people to secure and maintain autonomy.[10]

---

[4] It does not matter for present purposes whether the rights this chapter defends are better classified as (justified) legal rights or moral rights. It is only trying to establish an obligation to ensure that people secure the food, water, shelter, and so forth they need for autonomy.

[5] Both Nickel and Buchanan restrict this claim in some ways; e.g. they say people have a right to protection against standard threats. See discussion that follows. Also see: Nickel, *Making Sense of Human Rights*; Nickel, "A Human Rights Approach to World Hunger"; Buchanan, *Justice, Legitimacy, and Self-Determination*.

[6] Gewirth, *The Community of Rights*. Nickel, *Making Sense of Human Rights*. Buchanan, *Justice, Legitimacy, and Self-Determination*. Pogge, "Severe Poverty as a Human Rights Violation."

[7] See: Nickel, *Making Sense of Human Rights*. Also see: Nickel, "A Human Rights Approach to World Hunger"; Buchanan, *Justice, Legitimacy, and Self-Determination*.

[8] More precisely, these authors might say that rights are grounded in interests, agency, or autonomy. Nevertheless, they believe that people have rights to whatever protects interests, agency, or autonomy. The account that follows will try to stay neutral on which of these is the proper account of rights' basis. Shue, *Basic Rights*.

[9] Exceptions might be made, for instance, in cases where rights conflict. Still the burden of proof for most restrictions should probably lie on those advocating them as long one can show that being unable to secure the object of a purported right provides a standard threat to individuals' basic interests or autonomy.

[10] Buchanan, *Justice, Legitimacy, and Self-Determination*.

Often those who defend interest or autonomy-based accounts of rights restrict their accounts in some ways.[11] On Nickel's, John Tasioulas', and Allen Buchanan's accounts, for instance, people only have a right to protection against standard threats.[12] This kind of constraint goes beyond the claim that it must be feasible to fulfill the duties correlative to rights. It may be feasible to protect everyone against some non-standard threats to their interests and autonomy. Nevertheless, there may be practical reasons for restricting accounts of rights in these ways. If an account of rights is to play important roles in international law, for instance, it may be good to constrain the account. One might argue that Allen Buchanan is right to constrain his account of rights in the context of his argument that severe human rights violations justify humanitarian intervention.[13] Alternately, there could be other practical reasons for constraining an account of rights in this way. It is not clear, however, that such accounts should be constrained in the absence of good practical reasons for constraining them. Suppose autonomy grounds the importance of human rights. Then, perhaps, rights should protect individuals' ability to secure whatever they need for autonomy, unless there are equally strong considerations that justify exceptions (e.g. other rights cannot be met if rights to some components of autonomy receive protection). Nevertheless, this chapter's account of rights can be constrained where there are good reasons for constraining it.[14]

The rest of this section will illustrate how a traditional argument for positive rights to food, water, shelter, and so forth might go – adopting an account on which people have a right to autonomy. First, this section will consider what autonomy requires. Next, it will argue that everyone, to secure this autonomy, needs some food and water and most need shelter, education, health care, social support, and emotional goods. Those who believe people have a right to autonomy should, thus, agree that these people have a right to secure these things. People may have rights to much more than autonomy. Further, it may require much more than food, water, shelter, and so forth for many people to secure autonomy. To

---

[11] Nickel, *Making Sense of Human Rights*. Buchanan, *Justice, Legitimacy, and Self-Determination*. Tasioulas, "The Moral Reality of Human Rights."

[12] Nickel, *Making Sense of Human Rights*. Buchanan, *Justice, Legitimacy, and Self-Determination*. Tasioulas, "The Moral Reality of Human Rights."

[13] Buchanan, *Justice, Legitimacy, and Self-Determination*.

[14] Any such constraints will be left implicit in what follows.

secure broad agreement on its conclusions, however, this book will start from a very minimal conception of this right.[15]

There are other ways of trying to ground rights to food, water, shelter, and so forth. These things are often necessary for individuals' other important interests, even in remaining alive. This chapter will, however, only explore one way of grounding these rights for a few reasons. First, this will suffice to illustrate some common objections to traditional arguments for such rights. The objections this chapter will consider also apply to interest-based arguments for human rights. Second, skeptics about significant obligations to the poor are often deeply concerned about individual freedom. One might thus expect them to be more amenable to autonomy-based grounds for rights than interest-based grounds. (As should become clear below, however, libertarians and actual consent theorists will probably reject both accounts.) Finally, subsequent chapters will rely on this chapter's account of the connection between autonomy and food, water, shelter, and so forth.

1.2.1 Autonomy

There are many conceptions of autonomy. Some define autonomy in terms of freedom from external control, agency, self-governance, or moral perfection.[16] At the heart of most autonomy-based accounts of rights, however, is a minimal conception of *autonomy* on which people only need to be able to reason about, make, and carry out significant plans on the basis of their commitments.[17]

To secure broad agreement on its conclusions, this book will rely on just this minimal conception of autonomy.[18] Few will reject subsequent chapters' arguments because this conception is too demanding. The arguments in this and subsequent chapters can be extended by those who endorse more robust conceptions of autonomy on which people must have the capacity for moral agency, for instance. This section will just consider

---

[15] Joseph Raz rejects a right to autonomy because he thinks it would be much too demanding. See: Raz, *The Morality of Freedom*. For critique of his argument, see: Hassoun, "Raz on the Right to Autonomy."

[16] Bratman, "Planning Agency, Autonomous Agency." Hill Jr., "The Kantian Conception of Autonomy." Also see: O'Neill, *Faces of Hunger*.

[17] Nothing here presupposes an answer to the free will debate – one may lack free will and yet be able to reason and plan. See, however: Susan Wolf, *Freedom within Reason*.

[18] This section draws on some conditions for Joseph Raz's conception of autonomy as explicated here: Nicole Hassoun, "Raz on the Right to Autonomy". This discussion also draws on: Hassoun, "World Poverty and Individual Freedom." Also see: Raz, *The Morality of Freedom*.

what the abilities to reason about, make, and carry out the relevant plans on the basis of one's commitments require.

For one to reason on the basis of one's commitments, one just needs basic instrumental reasoning ability. On this account, one can rationally decide to become a slave or to have one's left foot burned off. As Hume said, "'Tis not contrary to reason to prefer the destruction of the whole world to the scratching of my finger."[19] Some hold much more demanding conceptions of reasoning on which saying that autonomy requires the ability to reason would be controversial. Kant, for instance, thinks that reason requires everyone to acknowledge the categorical imperative as unconditionally required.[20] This much is not necessary to secure the basic minimum of autonomy at issue, however. The idea is just that one needs adequate instrumental reasoning ability to evaluate and decide to pursue the projects that one values.

To make the relevant plans on the basis of one's commitments one need not plan one's whole life or every detail of one's day. Rather, one must be able to navigate through one's day without too much difficulty and make general plans for the future.[21] Though one might not choose to exercise this ability, one must have the planning ability necessary to pursue the projects one values, to pursue a good life as one sees it. This ability requires a kind of internal freedom – or self-control – one can have even if subject to external constraint. Internal freedom is roughly the capacity to decide "for oneself what is worth doing"; one must be able to make "the decisions of a normative agent," to recognize and respond to value as one sees it.[22] One must be able to form significant plans that would work if implemented. One must be able to make significant plans that one could carry through if free from external constraint.[23]

Finally, to carry out significant plans one must have some external as well as internal freedom.[24] External freedom – or liberty – is roughly freedom from interference in one's pursuit of a worthwhile life.[25] One must

---

[19] Hume, *A Treatise of Human Nature*, 463.
[20] See: Hill Jr., "The Kantian Conception of Autonomy." Also see: O'Neill, *Faces of Hunger*.
[21] See: Raz, *The Morality of Freedom*.
[22] Griffin, *Human Rights*, 150.
[23] There are many ways of making sense of this idea. One possibility is to analyze the ability to make some significant plans on the basis of one's commitments in terms of the ability to make one's motivating commitments generally coherent. Alternately, it is possible to give a decision-theoretic analysis of planning in terms of a consistent preference ordering. Yet another option is to explain what it means to be able to make some significant plans on the basis of one's commitments in terms of ordering one's ends perhaps by drawing on John Rawls' work on plans of life. See, for instance: Rawls, *A Theory of Justice*. Also see: Bratman, "Planning Agency, Autonomous Agency."
[24] Griffin, *Human Rights*.   [25] Ibid.

have enough freedom from coercion and constraint to carry out those actions necessary to bring significant plans to fruition.

On this book's conception, autonomy is different than liberty and freedom. *Liberty* is just external freedom or freedom from external constraint. *Autonomy*, as this book uses the term, requires basic internal *and* external freedoms. There are, however, other freedoms autonomy does not require. People need not be free to do literally anything they want. They need not be free, for instance, to violate others' rights. So, autonomy includes some liberties and internal freedoms but there are some liberties and internal freedoms autonomy does not require. One must be able to reason about, make, and carry out significant plans in one's pursuit of a worthwhile life.

To put the basic idea slightly differently, to have a basic minimum of autonomy, an individual's capacity to reason and plan must remain intact over the course of a normal or healthy life.[26] Reasoning and planning capacities come in degrees, but people must exceed at least a minimal threshold on these capacities to qualify as autonomous.

To fully defend a human right to autonomy, one would have to precisely specify and defend the relevant threshold on the reasoning and planning capacities. It may be hard to specify a fully worked out theory. There may be room for reasonable disagreement about which ways of drawing the threshold are best.

Because this chapter's aim is limited, however, it is not necessary to precisely specify the threshold on basic reasoning and planning capacities here. This chapter just suggests that there are some difficult objections to the right to autonomy, so a new argument for significant obligations to the global poor is required. These objections are relatively independent of how this threshold is specified.

Subsequent chapters will only require that people have sufficiently good reasoning and planning ability to consent to, or dissent from, the rule of their coercive institutions (henceforth *sufficient autonomy*).[27] In other words, subjects must have the reasoning and planning capacities they need to determine their actions and shape the nature of their relationships with the coercive institutions to which they are subject. How

---

[26] It is somewhat difficult to say what qualifies as a normal life. The phrase is intended to signify something, roughly, equivalent to "a healthy life." Even in the international context, a normal life should probably be at least as long as the median life in a developed country. One way of trying to get at exactly what people need is by appeal to a perfectionist theory. For an interesting discussion of perfectionism, see: Dorsey, "Three Arguments for Perfectionism."

[27] Buchanan and Brock, *Deciding for Others*.

much this book's arguments will show will depend on how robust are these capacities.

Although nothing in subsequent chapters will depend on this, one might appeal to legal definitions of competency to decide when people are capable of consenting to, or dissenting from the rule of their coercive institutions.[28] US courts have specified, for instance, that to make other important decisions for themselves people must be "capable of appreciating the nature, extent and probable consequences" of their decisions.[29] People also have to see themselves as agents acting over time and form and act on their own commitments. Competency is, to some degree, a task relative notion.[30] Nevertheless, these are also plausible conditions for consent or dissent from the rule of coercive institutions. Presumably, competence to consent to a coercive institution requires, more specifically, that people be able to understand the general features of the institutions to which they are consenting or from which they are dissenting. They must also understand the major consequences of consenting or refusing to do so. They must be able to appreciate, for instance, that these institutions affect their basic life prospects. They must also be able to understand what rights and obligations consenting entails and what penalties dissenting carries with it.

On the some accounts of competency, agreeing to be subject to coercive institutions, or protesting against them, may be very difficult. People may need robust capacities to evaluate information about the coercive institutions to which they are subject. They may need to be able to process a lot of information to be able to consent to, or dissent from, the rule of many (extremely complicated) coercive institutions.[31]

This book's argument will go through, however, even if the threshold is set very low. Subjects may need to be able to process some information for autonomy, but they do not have to be able to agree to every single coercive rule to which they are subject. Subjects may only need to be able to autonomously agree to the general principles underlying their coercive institutions. Alternately, consent may require only that individuals autonomously agree to the general structure of coercive rules to which they are subject, not every subsidiary rule.[32]

---

[28] I owe thanks to Alex London and Allen Buchanan for their help with this point.

[29] Stenger, "Exclusive or Concurrent Competence to Make Medical Decisions."

[30] Ibid.

[31] If the correct conception of competence to consent is very demanding, additional constraints on the obligations the next chapter's argument entails may be necessary.

[32] The interested reader may refer to Kant's and Rawls' discussions that are relevant to this issue. See: Kant, *On the Common Saying*. Alternately, see Rawls, *Political Liberalism*.

On even the most minimal thresholds for competence, many people are clearly capable of consenting to coercive rules, but some are not. If the threshold is low, people do not have to be experts in international law or economics to consent. Nevertheless, many people lack the capacity to agree to be subject to coercive institutions, though this lack is remediable. This includes very young children and people who are ill or mentally disabled to such a degree that their ability to reason and plan is compromised. Those who, like Tamil, are suffering from malaria-induced delusions may lack the necessary reasoning and planning capacities for autonomy. Similarly, those who, like Tamil's daughter, are severely cognitively or emotionally disabled because of iodine deficiency lack the requisite autonomy. These people lack the basic reasoning and planning capacities necessary to freely agree to be subject to coercive institutions. They are not really able to make any difficult decisions for themselves.

More and less robust accounts of the appropriate threshold on reasoning and planning ability for autonomy should just issue different judgments about harder cases. This chapter has said enough, however, to clarify what is at stake in the debate over what makes someone autonomous and explain why many people lack autonomy.

A much fuller conception of autonomy might require much more than the instrumental reasoning and planning necessary to consent to, or dissent from, the rule of coercive institutions. To have full autonomy, people may have to recognize the categorical imperative as self-imposed as Kant suggests.[33] More generally, people may need a capacity for moral evaluation and moral responsibility.[34] Some suggest that, for full autonomy, people must shape a unique identity, they must be self-creators. Others believe full autonomy requires a unified life. People may have to have the ability to engage in self-evaluation, self-criticism, and self-reform.[36] Some kind of equality may even be necessary for a conception of *full* autonomy. One might expand this books argument using these more robust conceptions of autonomy.

Nevertheless, subsequent chapters will work only with the very minimal conception of autonomy suggested above. Only basic instrumental reasoning and planning abilities and the ability to evaluate some information are necessary for this kind of autonomy. Relying on this

---

[33] Of course, one could insist on using the term "autonomy" to indicate only what this chapter has called full autonomy, but the disagreement is only semantic.

[34] Rawls, *Law of Peoples*.

[36] Gewirth, *The Community of Rights*.

conception of autonomy will help secure agreement even from those who reject more robust liberal conceptions of autonomy. Even some of those who believe there are significant constraints on what public morality can require of us seem to hold that people must have this much under decent institutions.[37]

Still, this conception of autonomy is, in some ways, a traditional liberal one. So perhaps one could object that the kind of autonomy at issue is only valuable from a Western perspective. One might argue that it is incompatible with the kind of concern for community and care central to many non-Western countries. So, one might conclude, it is inappropriate for evaluating non-Western institutions.

The conception of autonomy at issue here, however, is not particularly Western. It is compatible with concern for community and care. People can reason about and carry out plans to follow the crowd (or, for that matter, the whims of fancy). They can become monks or ascetics or follow other hierarchical social orders. So there is little reason to suppose the relevant kind of autonomy is inappropriate for evaluating non-Western institutions. To see this, suppose Emal is a devout Muslim. He wants to live his whole life according to his faith. Occasionally he wants to drink with the other young men who live in his neighborhood. Fortunately, he is able to reason about, make, and carry out significant plans on the basis of his competing commitments. Emal might autonomously decide, for instance, that his commitment to being a good Muslim is much stronger than his desire to drink and, so, never drink at all. Alternately, Emal might decide not to drink because he needs to remain sober to care for his aging parents. In either case, Emal has the components of autonomy at issue.[38]

The rest of this chapter will consider what people need to secure sufficient autonomy. It argues that everyone needs some food and water to pursue a worthwhile life, whether or not they decide to consent to coercive institutions. Further, it suggests that *most* people need some shelter, education, health care, social support, and emotional goods as well. This will lay the groundwork for subsequent chapters' arguments. It should also establish significant human rights obligations if the rest of this chapter's argument is defensible.

---

[37] See, for instance: Gaus, "The Place of Autonomy within Liberalism." Furthermore, subsequent chapters will argue that even libertarians cannot reasonably deny that this much is necessary for free consent.

[38] The conditions for autonomy this chapter has set out do not prevent one from acting from poor reasons (e.g. wishful thinking). If one thinks this is not compatible with autonomy, additional criteria for autonomy will be necessary to rule out this possibility.

1.2.2 Conditions for autonomy

It should be obvious that everyone needs some food and water to secure sufficient autonomy. Without food and water no one can survive. Even those with some food and water are likely to suffer from autonomy-undermining disabilities if they do not have enough.[39] Malnutrition inhibits one's immune system's ability to fight infection and poor nutrition is linked even more directly to many non-infectious illnesses.[40] It is an underlying cause in about half of all children's deaths in developing countries.[41]

Those without basic preventative health care (e.g. immunizations) are at risk for many severe illnesses. Those who cannot secure essential medications (e.g. dehydration salts and antibiotics) are likely to be disabled by these diseases. Often the diseases those who lack food, water, and health care acquire result in severe disabilities.[42] Often the very sick are incapable of securing sufficient autonomy.[43]

Similarly, if people lack decent shelter they are likely to suffer from autonomy-undermining disabilities. Those without decent shelter may be exposed to environmental hazards including disasters, pollutants, parasites, and bacteria (e.g. in flood water or unsanitary living conditions).[44] These "hazards are responsible for about a quarter of the total burden of disease worldwide, and nearly 35% in regions such as sub-Saharan Africa."[45] Bed nets alone could prevent a lot of autonomy-undermining illness.[46]

Less obviously, those without basic education, emotional and social goods may suffer from autonomy-undermining disabilities.[47] Basic education,

---

[39] I sketch a similar line of argument in: Hassoun, "World Poverty and Individual Freedom."

[40] Scurvy results from a lack of vitamin C, beri-beri from a lack of thiamine, pellagra from niacin deficiency, and macrocytic and microcytic anemia from folic acid and iron deficiencies, for instance. There is also a lot of evidence that decent nourishment is important for good cognitive functioning. Children's mental functioning may even be impaired if their mothers do not receive proper nourishment during pregnancy. Keratomalacia, which results from vitamin A deficiency, kwashiorkor, which results from protein deficiency, and iodine deficiencies can all lead to severe disabilities and death. See: Leathers and Foster, *The World Food Problem.*

[41] Blossner and de Onis, *Malnutrition.*

[42] Ibid.

[43] The feedback loop between malnutrition and illness also goes in the other direction – illness can promote dietary deficiencies just as dietary deficiencies can promote illness. Ibid.

[44] Those who must live in unsanitary conditions are likely to contract diseases like dysentery, tetanus, typhoid, cholera, or hepatitis. Red Cross, "American Red Cross Urges Public Health Precautions."

[45] World Health Organization, "10 Facts on Preventing Disease Through Healthy Environments."

[46] Bed nets can prevent many cases of dengue fever and malaria, for instance. Centers for Disease Control and Prevention, "Vector Control."

[47] See: Woolcock, "The Place of Social Capital in Understanding Social and Economic Outcomes." Also see: Doyle, "Calculus of Happiness."

emotional, and social goods are often necessary for securing decent living conditions, health care, livelihood opportunities, and earning power.[48] Most children gain the information and analytic skills they need to reason and make significant plans through formal education. At least some informal elementary education, however, is probably required for most people to acquire this information and these skills. People must be able to communicate with others to get the information they need to make many complex decisions. Those who lack basic emotional and social goods are at high risk for mental and physical illness, suicide, and early death from other causes.[49] "Fear, insecurity, dependency, depression, anxiety, intranquility, shame, hopelessness, isolation and powerlessness ... such experiential elements of a bad life ... [often impact] ... agency."[50] Most people must secure basic education, emotional, and social goods to secure sufficient autonomy.[51]

On the conditions for autonomy defended here, most people can secure sufficient autonomy as long as their minds do not become clouded. It is true that some people can secure sufficient autonomy without being able to obtain very much food, water, shelter, education, health care, social support, and emotional goods. Still, severe deprivation will undermine most people's ability to reason about, make, and carry out significant plans on the basis of their commitments. People have a right to secure the food, water, shelter, and so forth they need for autonomy.

People may have rights to much more than this. There are plausible ways of expanding the accounts of autonomy and rights with which we started. Nevertheless, the people this chapter is concerned to address are likely to think the account too robust, not too minimal.[52] Many do

---

[48] Marmot, *Status Syndrome*. Stress may contribute to a host of autonomy-undermining mental disorders. Stress can, for instance, cause panic attacks and depression. Psychological disorders can reduce the ability of one's immune system to fight infection. See: Beaton, "Effects of Stress and Psychological Disorders on the Immune System." The causal evidence suggests that perception of low social standing may increase stress which reduces immune functioning and can harm health in other ways as well.

[49] See: Cullen and Whiteford, "Inter-relations of Social Capital with Health and Mental Health." See also: Woolcock, "The Place of Social Capital in Understanding Social and Economic Outcomes." Finally, see: Hudson, "Socioeconomic Status and Mental Illness."

[50] Those who lack self-esteem are more likely to develop some devastating psychological problems. Karen Brock, "'It's Not Only Wealth that Matters it's Peace of Mind Too'".

[51] It is worth noting that people may not need to obtain an education sufficient to secure a decent job if they can secure other things that they require for sufficient autonomy, e.g. food stamps and free health care. In our world, however, most people will have to secure this much education to secure sufficient autonomy.

[52] As noted above, this conclusion is in some ways more robust than many human rights arguments endorse – people have a right to whatever they need for autonomy. Subsequent chapters will discuss this aspect of this chapter's conclusion.

not believe anyone has a right, simply in virtue of their humanity, to the things necessary to protect autonomy.[53] So, the next section will consider how these people are likely to object to the above argument.

1.3 POSITIVE AND NEGATIVE RIGHTS: UNEQUAL MORAL FORCE?

Many libertarians and actual consent theorists do not believe that individuals' autonomy grounds positive rights with correlative positive duties.[54] Machan, Narveson, and Lomasky argue, for instance, that people only have negative rights with correlative negative duties. Positive rights, they suggest, are rights to certain kinds of assistance.[55] Positive duties require people to provide this assistance. Negative rights, they claim, are rights that others not do certain kinds of things.[56] Negative duties only require people to refrain from doing these things. So, for instance, I may have a negative right that others not interfere with my autonomy and others may have a negative duty not to interfere. Still, libertarians and actual consent theorists might argue that individuals' autonomy does not have enough moral force to ground a positive right to everything that is necessary for autonomy.[57]

Even some of those with more moderate views might agree, at least regarding whether autonomy can ground positive rights that generate demanding duties.[58] Even Raz seems to hold something like this view. He says that no one has a right to autonomy (or all of the things that protect autonomy) because no one is under the demanding obligation to provide the necessary collective goods (e.g. institutions).[59]

Defenders of basic rights might follow Henry Shue, James Nickel, and Allen Buchanan in arguing that, even if it is *usually* harder to fulfill the rights typically characterized as positive than to respect those

---

[53] Machan, "The Perils of Positive Rights." Nozick, *Anarchy, State, and Utopia.*

[54] Narveson, *The Libertarian Idea.* Lomasky, *Persons, Rights, and the Moral Community.* Machan, "The Perils of Positive Rights." Nozick, *Anarchy, State, and Utopia.*

[55] Ibid.   [56] Ibid.

[57] Nozick, *Anarchy, State, and Utopia.* One promising response that this chapter does not consider is that important negative freedoms may fail to be respected and may even be violated by side constraints. Side constraints do not protect the freedom to take food from those who have more than enough in order to survive, for example. For discussion see: Sterba, *From Liberty to Equality: Justice for Here and Now.*

[58] See, for instance: Raz, *The Morality of Freedom.*

[59] Ibid.

typically characterized as negative, this is not always so.[60] Many of the rights typically characterized as negative (and endorsed even by libertarians) have correlative positive duties requiring the demanding provision of collective goods. In some instances, of course, these rights could be respected without positive action. People might simply refrain from violating them. Sometimes positive rights to things like food, water, and shelter can also be fulfilled easily. So, even if it is *usually* harder to fulfill the rights typically characterized as positive than to respect those typically characterized as negative, this is not always so. In the real world, ensuring that someone secures the food, water, shelter, and so forth they need for autonomy may even be less demanding than not violating their right to bodily integrity, for instance. It is worth making these points in some detail.

Many of the rights typically characterized as negative and embraced by liberals of many sorts, even libertarians and actual consent theorists, have correlative positive duties. Fulfilling the duties generated by rights typically characterized as negative may, for instance, require great institutional change. Shue and Buchanan illustrate with the right not to have one's bodily integrity violated. Without police officers, courts, and jails – they point out – many individuals' bodily integrity would be violated.[61] Decent institutions may not be necessary to protect the right to bodily integrity in a state of nature or in areas with low population density. In most modern states, however, police officers, courts, and jails are necessary to prevent crimes that violate bodily integrity.[62]

Sometimes, institutional protection is not necessary to protect rights typically characterized as negative. If people simply refrain from violating others' bodily integrity, for instance, institutional protection is not necessary.

Sometimes, however, it is also possible to fulfill positive rights easily – without the provision of any collective goods. Consider an illustration. On the island of Balbac off the southern tip of Palawan (not far from where Tamil was raised) in the Philippines, many of the local tribespeople have lost their fishing rights. They are now desperately poor. Some have become migrant workers in Malaysia. Others are trying to farm on marginal lands. Still others have turned to increasingly destructive fishing

---

[60] Shue, *Basic Rights*. Nickel, *Making Sense of Human Rights*. Buchanan, *Justice, Legitimacy, and Self-Determination*.

[61] Buchanan, *Justice, Legitimacy, and Self-Determination*.

[62] Shue, *Basic Rights*.

techniques or to denuding the mangrove resources to survive. Their story is complicated. Part of the reason they have been running out of food is pressure put on scarce fishing resources by population growth and migration. They have other problems too. A large portion of the tribes' traditional fishing grounds has been leased to a pearl farming corporation by the government of the Philippines. The Jewelmer Corporation was originally granted a lease to the property by the Marcos government. Now Jewelmer has a long-term lease from the local mayor. If the migrants had not come to Balbac, there would have been more fish. There would be more food if the corporation stopped operating. If Marcos had not given Jewelmer the lease to start with, many people would have been able to secure adequate food, water, shelter, and so forth who were prohibited from doing so by the corporation. By simply not offering to lease the land, the government would not have interfered with the ability of the fishermen to secure these things. By not requesting the lease, or policing the area, the corporation would not have interfered with the ability of the fishermen to secure food, water, shelter, and so forth.[63] Simple restraint is often sufficient to protect individuals' rights to secure these things.

In the real world protecting rights typically characterized as negative (*so-called* negative rights) may even require more demanding institutional change than protecting the rights typically characterized as positive (*so-called* positive rights). To respect the rights of the Palawan people to bodily integrity someone may have to pay for voting booths, courts, and a host of other goods and institutions. It may require little for the Jewelmer Corporation to stop policing and let the Palawan people fish. The point holds even if this is not a fair example. It holds even if the government would have to make the Jewelmer Corporation let the people fish, this required *difficult* institutional change. Even if positive action is necessary to protect so-called positive rights, it may be easier to protect these rights than to avoid violating so-called negative rights. Individuals may secure sustenance, for instance, with food voucher programs. Food voucher programs may be easier to implement than police or military programs. Police and military programs may be necessary to ensure that people do not interfere with others' bodily integrity.

---

[63] Perhaps changes would still need to be made to ensure that people can continue to secure food, water, shelter, and so forth even without the fishing restrictions or migration. Part of the fishing community's problem may be that, since contraception is difficult to acquire, people continue to have large families. What seems pretty clear, though, is that the people would have had fewer years of hunger had the lease never been given. Ibid.

The above remarks will probably not convince everyone. Some people might maintain that so-called negative rights really are negative and only require people to refrain from certain acts. Individuals *can* fulfill their negative duties by simply abstaining from acts that violate the corresponding rights. A police force or court system is not necessary to respect rights to bodily integrity. People must merely refrain from abrogating them. It is only when people violate these rights that they bear a positive duty; they are responsible for compensating the victims of their action. People do not violate such rights if they do not help support the police or maintain a court system. On the other hand, libertarians and actual consent theorists will probably argue that so-called positive rights are objectionable because they sometimes require positive action even when no one has interfered with others' freedoms. Perhaps they can argue that this is what makes the duties correlative to positive rights more demanding than negative ones.

The notion of demandingness at work in (at least some version of) this critique of positive rights is implausible. Non-interference can be very demanding. One's very survival may require one to violate negative rights. Hutus in the Rwandan civil war were often forced, on pain of death, to kill or rape Tutsis.[64] One might maintain, however, that people are not always permitted to violate others' rights even in such dire circumstances. Sometimes it is simply impermissible to violate others' rights (e.g. when they are just as vulnerable and innocent as the potential violator). If this is so, the mere fact that fulfilling a duty is demanding is not always an objection to the claim that one has an obligation to fulfill it. In any case, in our world, the duties correlative to the rights traditionally characterized as positive may be no more demanding than the duties correlative to the rights traditionally characterized as negative. The demandingness objection to positive rights does not go through. Even if critics of positive rights accept this argument, however, they might defend the idea that people only have negative rights in another way.

Critics of positive rights might follow Onora O'Neill, for instance, in arguing that there is ineliminable indeterminacy in the notion of positive rights.[65] The obligations correlative to positive rights do not provide clear and definite requirements on particular others. Who is supposed to preserve Tamil's ability to secure the food, water, shelter, and so forth she needs for autonomy? Many people might make sure she can do so,

[64] United Human Rights Council, "Genocide in Rwanda."
[65] O'Neill, "The Dark Side of Human Rights."

but the fact that she has a right to such things does not tell us who must ensure that she is able to secure them. O'Neill is probably right that there is nothing in the concept of a positive right (as this chapter has characterized it) that assigns responsibility to particular parties for fulfilling correlative positive obligations.

There are, however, many ways of eliminating the indeterminacy in positive rights. One might argue, for instance, that international institutions are responsible for fulfilling the obligations correlative to these rights.[66] Then, one could argue that, in the first instance, those who have inaugurated and upheld these institutions bear derivative responsibility for bringing about institutional change. Pogge even suggests that this is one way of looking at the standard account of responsibility for fulfilling the obligations correlative to human rights.[67]

Another way of eliminating the indeterminacy in positive rights is to specify that states have primary responsibility for ensuring that their subjects secure the objects of their human rights. Individuals and other institutions have secondary obligations to ensure that people secure these things if states fail in their obligations. James Nickel, for instance, explains the obligations correlative to human rights in this way:

> Governments are the primary addressees of the human rights of their residents … individuals have responsibilities as voters and citizens to promote human rights in their own country; and … governments, international organizations and individuals have back-up responsibilities for the fulfillment of human rights around the world.[68]

On this account, positive duties begin as domestic duties and, if necessary, end up being international duties.[69] It is the *primary* duty of Zimbabwe – not (say) the USA – to take actions, implement policies, and support institutions that secure the human rights of Zimbabweans. Similarly, it is the primary duty of the USA – not (say) Zimbabwe – to take actions, implement policies, and support institutions that secure the human rights of US citizens. When a country is unable to secure the human rights of its people,

---

[66] Buchanan, *Justice, Legitimacy, and Self-Determination.* Wenar, "Responsibility for Severe Poverty."

[67] Pogge, *World Poverty and Human Rights.*

[68] Nickel, "A Defense of Welfare Rights as Human Rights," 442. For an expanded discussion of this, see: Nickel, "How Human Rights Generate Duties to Protect and Provide."

[69] This paragraph is adapted from Hassoun and Frank, "Are Debt-for-Nature Swaps Morally Permissible?" Also see: Nickel, "A Human Rights Approach to World Hunger." For the standard view, see: Nickel, *Making Sense of Human Rights.* The plausibility of this account is, of course, a matter of some dispute. For a very different account of human rights see, for instance: Rawls, *Law of Peoples.*

however, the international community has a *secondary* (positive) duty to do so. Not just states but individuals and international institutions must assist. If, for example, Zimbabwe is unable to secure the human rights of its people, then it becomes the responsibility of the USA – along with similarly capable members of the international community and international institutions – to assist in securing the human rights of Zimbabweans.[70]

This is all expressed in the international covenant on economic and social rights, part of the United Nations' (UN's) Universal Declaration of Human Rights as explicated in the general comments.[71] The International Covenant on Economic, Social and Cultural Rights' Article 2(1) says that to fulfill rights:

Each State Party to the present Covenant …[must undertake]… steps, individually and through international assistance and cooperation, especially economic and technical, to the maximum of its available resources, with a view to achieving progressively the full realization of the rights recognized in the present Covenant by all appropriate means, including particularly the adoption of legislative measures.

The third general comment states:

The Committee notes that the phrase [in Article 2(1)] "to the maximum of its available resources" was intended by the drafters of the Covenant to refer to both the resources existing within a State and those available from the international community through international cooperation and assistance. The Committee wishes to emphasize that in accordance with Articles 55 and 56 of the Charter of the United Nations, with well-established principles of international law, and with the provisions of the Covenant itself, international cooperation for development and thus for the realization of economic, social and cultural rights is an obligation of all States. It is particularly incumbent upon those States which are in a position to assist others in this regard.[72]

---

[70] Individuals and non-state institutions also have secondary obligations to assist in protecting human rights. Citizens, for instance, have obligations to vote or campaign for appropriate protections.

[71] "[O]ver time the general comment has become a distinct juridical instrument, enabling the [Human Rights Committee] to announce its interpretations of different provisions of the [ICCPR] in a form that bears some resemblance to the advisory opinion practice of international tribunals. These general comments or 'advisory opinions' are relied upon by the Committee in evaluating the compliance of states with their obligations under the Covenant, be it in examining State reports or 'adjudicating' individual communications under the Optional Protocol … General comments consequently have gradually become important instruments in the law-making process of the Committee, independent of the reporting system." Steiner and Alston, *International Human Rights in Context*, 732.

[72] From: Committee on Economic, Social and Cultural Rights, "The nature of States parties' obligations." Furthermore, the charter of the UN also expresses this understanding of the obligation to ameliorate poverty and secure other conditions for stability and wellbeing. Consider articles 55 and 56 of Chapter IX of this charter, for instance. Article 55 says: "With a view to the creation

In other words, although states have the primary obligation to ensure that their subjects' human rights are secure, other states and international institutions that are well placed to do so must provide assistance if necessary.[73]

Certainly, much more is required to cash out and defend any particular account of the obligations correlative to human rights.[74] How should the failure of others to do their part in ensuring people secure food, water, shelter, and so forth alter obligations to assist the global poor? It seems plausible to suppose that there will be some situations in which this will increase the strength of the obligation. It does not seem plausible to suppose that all unfair burdens are excessive. Fully cashing out and defending a plausible account of responsibility for fulfilling obligations to the poor is beyond the scope of this book, however. The important point here is just that there are ways to eliminate any indeterminacy in positive rights.

Critics of positive rights might object that this response misunderstands the problem of indeterminacy. The problem is not that it is impossible to create institutional arrangements that will protect human rights. The problem is that, without specifying such arrangements, there are no positive duties to ensure that people secure the objects of their positive rights. So, there is no corresponding positive right.[75]

of conditions of stability and well-being which are necessary for peaceful and friendly relations among nations based on respect for the principle of equal rights and self-determination of peoples, the United Nations shall promote: a. higher standards of living, full employment, and conditions of economic and social progress and development; b. solutions of international economic, social, health, and related problems; and international cultural and educational co-operation; and c. universal respect for, and observance of, human rights and fundamental freedoms for all without distinction as to race, sex, language, or religion." Article 56 says: "All Members pledge themselves to take joint and separate action in co-operation with the Organization for the achievement of the purposes set forth in Article 55." United Nations, "Article 56."

[73] One way of justifying this account of the obligations correlative to human rights is to suggest that these obligations are truly universal because autonomy is important enough to generate obligations on all. Pragmatic considerations might then suggest that states are the primary duty bearers. States are usually best placed to assist individuals in securing autonomy. It is only when states fail that other individuals and institutions that are well placed to help must do so.

[74] O'Neill worries, for instance, about the traditional way of resolving the indeterminacy in positive rights. She worries that the responsibilities this resolution implies are unjustifiable. States, she suggests, may not be well placed to protect rights (NGOs or voluntary contributions may be better). There may also be reason to assign obligations to the people who must actually pay the costs of protecting rights (e.g. farmers and doctors). But it is not clear that this is justifiable for two reasons: (1) The costs to those people may not outweigh the benefits to others; (2) Assigning obligations to those who must bear their costs might crowd out good intentions. O'Neill, "The Dark Side of Human Rights," 427–39. Although these may be significant considerations in designing a good account of responsibility for protecting positive rights, they do not undermine the claim, relied upon here, that there are many possible accounts.

[75] O'Neill also worries that if these rights are not just noble aspirations, they lack a point without determinate obligation bearers. Ibid. This is not clearly true. Rights might help us point out

There are a few ways advocates of positive rights might respond. Advocates might distinguish between those who bear the duties correlative to positive rights in principle and in practice. If it is possible to specify who bears the duties correlative to positive rights in principle, then one cannot object that the claim that such rights exist is incoherent. Perhaps everyone bears the duties correlative to positive rights, in principle.[76] Who will bear the burden of fulfilling the associated duties in practice depends on a mix of pragmatic and moral considerations. Many people believe this is how it works with negative rights.[77] In principle, everyone is obligated to refrain from doing certain kinds of actions; the obligations correlative to negative rights are universal. In practice, not everyone bears the burden of restraint. Some people never come into contact with each other at all.

This kind of reply may go through even if there are not universal obligations correlative to *all* rights. As long as individuals' right to secure what they need for autonomy carries universal correlative obligations, the indeterminacy objection will not apply to this right.

Critics of positive rights might reject this response. The real difference of opinion, however, is probably deeper than either a concern about what rights require or the proper interpretation of the duties corresponding to different rights. At base, those most skeptical of positive rights are probably concerned only about prohibiting certain kinds of actions. This, at least, is what motivates Lomasky, Narveson, and Machan to reject positive rights.[78] They believe that what is wrong with violating negative rights is not merely that violations imperil people's freedom, but that someone is imperiling this freedom; certain kinds of actions are illegitimate. Negative rights ensure that others not do certain kinds of things. These skeptics about positive rights might, thus, argue that people do not have a positive right even to secure adequate food and water. People only have negative rights that others refrain from doing certain kinds of things.

---

injustice, for instance, even if we cannot say who caused the injustice. We know that a woman's right to life was violated if she is hanged for a crime she did not commit, even if we do not know who was responsible for preventing this injustice.

[76] This may also help make sense of the claim that states are justified, in part, because they make the satisfaction of positive rights possible. Perhaps that is how states come to possess the obligations correlative to these rights. I would like to thank Alex London for this suggestion and members of the Center for Ethics and Public Policy for helping me clarify the threshold for autonomy relied upon in this chapter.

[77] See, for instance: Nozick, *Anarchy, State, and Utopia*.

[78] Narveson, *The Libertarian Idea*. Lomasky, *Persons, Rights, and the Moral Community*. Machan, "The Perils of Positive Rights." Nozick, *Anarchy, State, and Utopia*.

This disagreement is persistent, but need not block all attempts to extend the consensus on significant obligations to the poor. The conviction that people must only refrain from (unjustifiably) interfering with others' external freedom is unlikely to convince advocates of positive rights. Nor is the conviction that the importance of autonomy is, in itself, sufficient to ground positive duties likely to convince those who believe there are only negative rights. So, this book will not continue with this dialectic. Rather, the next chapter defends a new argument for the conclusion that there are positive obligations to the poor. It derives these obligations from a common strand in liberal thought. The third chapter argues that many libertarians and actual consent theorists, in particular, should agree that the poor have a right to secure what they need for autonomy. Disagreement about some things may be irresolvable but this book will try to extend the consensus on at least this much.

1.4 EXTENDING THE CONSENSUS

Before providing a new argument, however, it is worth noting that there are many other arguments for positive duties to the poor in the global justice literature. Perhaps some of these other arguments can address the skeptics. There are three main lines of argument for positive obligations to the poor. First, authors like Charles Beitz, Darrel Moellendorf, and Gillian Brock offer contractualist arguments along the lines of John Rawls' *Theory of Justice* writ large.[79] They argue that reasonable people who are appropriately impartial would not agree to any global order in which they could not secure the food, water, shelter, and so forth they need for autonomy. The global order, they conclude, is obligated to ensure that most people secure these things. Second, authors like Amartya Sen and Martha Nussbaum argue that justice requires structuring both national and international institutions so that they secure basic capabilities for people.[80] Finally, authors like Onora O'Neill argue that to secure the kind of autonomy at issue for a Kantian theory, people must secure some food, water, shelter, and so forth.[81]

---

[79] Pogge, *World Poverty and Human Rights*. Beitz, *Political Theory and International Relations*. Moellendorf, *Cosmopolitan Justice*. Gillian Brock, "Liberal Nationalism versus Cosmopolitanism," 307–27.
[80] Sen, *Development as Freedom*. Sen, "Global Justice: Beyond International Equity." Nussbaum, *Women and Human Development*.
[81] O'Neill, *Bounds of Justice*.

Unfortunately, none of the traditional arguments fare better than most human rights theories in addressing those who believe there are no positive obligations to the poor. So, a new argument is needed. In providing such an argument, this book does not follow any of the traditional tracks, though it does start from an idea implicit in the social contract tradition, that people must have basic freedoms under coercive rule, to argue that there are positive obligations to ensure that people are capable of avoiding severe poverty. Nevertheless, it does not take commitment to providing these capabilities as basic. Nor does its argument appeal exclusively to those who accept hypothetical consent or Kantian accounts of what freedom requires. Rather, its argument is intended to appeal to everyone who takes a particularly liberal commitment to freedom seriously.[82]

Still, one might suggest, there is at least one other argument in the global justice literature for obligations to the poor that is intended to appeal to liberals of many sorts. Pogge argues that the global order harms the global poor and concludes that there are duties of restorative justice to help these people.

There are some potential problems with Pogge's argument, however. Risse suggests that Pogge considers three baselines relative to which a deprivation counts as harm – human rights, state of nature, and absence of historical injustice baselines.[83] Risse argues that the only baselines for harm that libertarians, in particular, will accept are the state of nature and absence of historical injustice baselines.[84] He argues that Pogge has not done enough to make the case that the global order harms the poor using these baselines. Risse agrees with Alan Patten, who suggests that further evidence is necessary to conclude that the poor are worse off than they would be in a state of nature.[85] Risse does not think that it is clear that the poor would be better off in the absence of historical injustices perpetrated by international institutions.[86] Contra Risse, some libertarians might accept a negative-(human)-rights baseline for harm. Still, Risse is probably right to think that Pogge's argument is unlikely to convince

---

[82] Furthermore, the traditional theories are often intended to provide full accounts of global justice. This book does not give a full account of global justice. Its first part merely defends one minimal condition for the legitimacy of coercive international institutions.

[83] Risse, "Do We Owe the Poor Assistance or Rectification?" 9–18. Pogge might respond that only the human rights baseline is at issue, but Risse might reply there are at least three different ways one might understand a human rights baseline and run his critique from there. Pogge, "Introduction," 9–18.

[84] Risse, "Do We Owe the Poor Assistance or Rectification?"

[85] Patten, "Should We Stop Thinking about Poverty in Terms of Helping the Poor?"

[86] Risse, "Do We Owe the Poor Assistance or Rectification?"

many libertarians. So, while Pogge's claims are compelling, and his argument may ultimately be correct, it is important to find other ways of arguing that liberals should agree that there are significant obligations to the global poor.

Although the next chapter's argument is different from Pogge's, it is potentially very powerful. It does not rely on the premise that international institutions are harming the poor.[87] Still, it suggests that they are doing something to poor people – coercing them – that make many of them partly responsible for the plight of the poor. It is one thing not to benefit the poor; it is another to coerce them.

There are many interesting arguments for positive duties to the poor in the global justice literature, but this book's arguments are novel. They rely neither on traditional (e.g. autonomy-based) accounts of rights nor on these more recent accounts of our obligations. Rather they provide a new way of establishing the conclusion that there are significant obligations to the poor that should engage and challenge readers of many different persuasions.

---

[87] One might argue, however, that international institutions harm the poor when their coercion undermines autonomy. Coercion is also an affront to one's dignity and independence.

CHAPTER 2

Legitimacy and global justice

2.1 INTRODUCTION

Many of those who resist traditional arguments for positive rights against poverty are liberals. Liberals are concerned about the freedom of individuals to live their lives. They believe that no one should be required to sacrifice their freedom for another person. The first half of this book suggests that it is *because* no one should be required to sacrifice their freedom for others that there are significant obligations to the global poor. Subject to a few qualifications, this chapter defends the following *Autonomy Argument:*[1]

(1) Coercive institutions must be legitimate.
(2) For a coercive institution to be legitimate it must ensure that its subjects secure sufficient autonomy to autonomously consent to, or dissent from, its rules (henceforth *sufficient autonomy*).
(3) Everyone, to secure this autonomy, must secure some food and water, and most require some shelter, education, health care, social support, and emotional goods.
(4) There are many coercive international institutions.
(C) So, these institutions must ensure that their subjects secure food, water, and whatever else they need for sufficient autonomy.

The first chapter defended the third premise of this argument. This chapter defends the remaining premises. Subject to a few qualifications, it argues that coercive international institutions must ensure that their subjects secure sufficient autonomy. The conclusion of the Autonomy Argument follows: These institutions must (roughly) ensure that their subjects secure food, water, and whatever else they need for sufficient autonomy. The next section considers how this argument, if successful, engages with an important debate in the global justice literature. It

---

[1] I sketch a similar argument in: Hassoun, "World Poverty and Individual Freedom," 191–8.

considers the connection between justice and legitimacy. Subsequent sections defend the remaining premises of the Autonomy Argument. The penultimate section considers how this argument might be extended to apply to a properly global institutional system composed of a set of rules and institutions that shape, at the global level, individuals' basic life prospects. The final section concludes. The next chapter addresses some of those least likely to accept significant obligations to the global poor – libertarians and actual consent theorists.

This chapter's argument is different from traditional human rights arguments for obligations to the poor. It does not suggest that the value of autonomy can, on its own, ground rights to those things that are necessary for people to secure it. Rather, this chapter argues that liberals of many sorts should agree that the relationship between rulers and those who are ruled must be free. It claims that, for this reason, coercive institutions must ensure that their subjects secure sufficient autonomy. This claim is obviously controversial.

This chapter should be interesting even to those who grant that there are significant obligations to the global poor. Some of those who endorse these obligations believe that they are purely humanitarian; these people deny that there are any obligations of justice to aid the poor.[2] This chapter suggests that the same relation some statists have argued gives rise to obligations of justice within states obtains internationally. It argues that there are many coercive international institutions.[3] So, it not only provides a new argument for significant obligations to the poor, it challenges the claim that obligations of justice do not extend beyond borders.[4]

2.2 THE NATURE OF LEGITIMACY AND ITS RELATION TO JUSTICE

Subsequent sections defend a "capability" or "needs" theory. They suggest that coercive institutions are obligated to ensure that their subjects are capable of securing what they need for autonomy.

---

[2] For statist theories on which there are no obligations of justice to aid the poor, see: Nagel, "The Problem of Global Justice," 113–47; Richard Miller, "Cosmopolitan Respect and Patriotic Concern," 202–24; Blake, "Distributive Justice, State Coercion, and Autonomy," 257–96. For cosmopolitan accounts of global justice that endorse such obligations, see: Moellendorf, *Global Inequality Matters*; Tan, *Justice Without Borders: Cosmopolitanism, Nationalism, and Patriotism*; Caney, *Justice Beyond Borders*.

[3] For an account on which only states exercise coercion that requires justification see, for instance: Blake, "Distributive Justice, State Coercion, and Autonomy," 257–96.

[4] For some examples of arguments that make this claim, see: Nagel, "The Problem of Global Justice," 113–47; Richard Miller, "Cosmopolitan Respect and Patriotic Concern," 202–24.

The obligation to ensure that those subject to coercive rules secure sufficient autonomy does not rest on the familiar grounds of humanity or justice suggested by authors like Sen, Nussbaum, Brock, and Caney. The claim is not that concern for humanity requires ensuring that people secure basic human capabilities. Nor do subsequent sections suggest that this is a requirement of justice (or fairness), though some of the arguments in subsequent sections start from an idea implicit in the social contract tradition – focusing upon what social arrangements people could freely accept.

Rather, subsequent sections suggest that *legitimacy* requires coercive institutions to ensure that their subjects secure basic capacities. Whether or not concern for humanity or justice requires ensuring that people secure these capabilities, coercive institutions must ensure that their subjects secure this much because they *coerce* them. Poverty is incompatible with the legitimate exercise of coercive power.

Before making this argument, it is therefore necessary to consider (1) the nature of legitimacy and its relation to related concepts like justified authority and justice and (2) why coercive institutions must be legitimate. This section will take on the first task. The next section will take on the second.

There are different conceptions of legitimacy in the global justice literature. On one conception, a coercive institution is *legitimate* if, and only if, the institution has the justification-right to use coercive force.[5] An institution has a *justification-right* to make coercive rules and give coercive commands if it is morally permissible for it to do so.[6] Claim rights, like those generated by promises, carry with them correlative duties.[7] Liberty rights do not carry with them correlative duties. I may have a right to dance, but no one is under any obligation to help me do so. On the above account, the justification-right to rule is a liberty right. So, knowing that an institution has a justification-right to rule does not tell us whether or not it is permissible for others to interfere with its rule. *Legitimacy*, on this conception, is different from *justified*

---

[5] *Legitimacy*, as this chapter will use the term, comes in degrees. Some people believe legitimacy is an all or none affair. This is not a substantive disagreement. Those who hold a binary theory of legitimacy can specify that an institution is legitimate in the binary sense if it surpasses a threshold of legitimacy in the degree sense. Understanding *legitimacy* as a degree term allows one to specify different thresholds on legitimacy for different purposes. Rebellion against very illegitimate institutions may be justified. For the purpose of what follows, one need only suppose that imperfectly legitimate institutions require reform. See: Buchanan, *Justice, Legitimacy, and Self-Determination.*

[6] Landenson, "In Defense of a Hobbesian Conception of Law," 134–59.

[7] Simmons, *Moral Principles and Political Obligations.*

authority.[8] An institution has *justified authority* if, and only if, individuals have a moral duty to comply with its rules.[9]

Some believe that legitimacy, in the sense above, yields justified authority. Perhaps this is because they hold that the same features that give an institution a right to rule ground a correlative obligation to obey its dictates. These people might argue that a unified account of legitimacy and justified authority is simpler and, so, better, than a disparate account.

This book does not need to resolve this debate. Nothing in its argument is intended to establish, or rides on, the claim that there is an obligation to obey coercive institutions. So this book does not need to suppose that if a coercive institution has a right to rule through force, its subjects are obligated to obey its dictates, though that may be so. This book is only trying to show that certain conditions must be met before institutions have the (liberty) right to rule through force.

Different ways of understanding legitimacy, however, lend themselves to different ways of thinking about the relationship between legitimacy and justice. (There are many accounts of justice, but it is often supposed to be equivalent to some kind of fairness.[10]) Legitimacy may be a necessary condition of justice (or vice versa), they may be equivalent, or legitimacy may simply be different than justice.

Charles Beitz seems to hold that justice is a necessary condition of legitimacy, though this is doubtful. He seems to think that individuals have an obligation to obey legitimate institutions and that they do not have an obligation to obey unjust institutions.[11] Those who do not believe the right to rule carries with it correlative obligations to obey cannot, however, accept this argument. (These people might hold that even if there is no obligation to obey unjust institutions, they may be legitimate.) Moreover, even some of those who hold that legitimacy entails justified authority might question the conclusion that justice is a precondition of legitimacy. Suppose, for instance, that full justice requires preserving full religious freedom. Suppose, further, a coercive institution does not pre-

---

[8] See: Christiano, "Authority."   [9] Ibid.

[10] Rawls, *Justice as Fairness: A Restatement.*

[11] This seems to be one of the premises underlying *Political Theory and International Relations.* For instance, Beitz says "Assuming that it is part of the justice of institutions that they treat their members in some sense as autonomous persons, then the claim that unjust states should not be accorded the respect demanded by the principle of state autonomy follows from the claim that it is only considerations of personal autonomy, appropriately interpreted, that constitute the moral personality of the state." Beitz, *Political Theory and International Relations,* 81. I would like to thank Josh Cohen for this point and the example below.

serve full religious freedom. It, say, bans headscarves. Nevertheless, the institution might have the right to rule through force.

Understood as a justification-right to rule, it is more plausible that perfect justice requires full legitimacy rather than the other way around. It is not clear that an institution can be perfectly just if it is illegitimate (i.e. if it does not even have the right to rule through force). Other things may be necessary for an institution to be fully just. Nevertheless, one might maintain, a coercive institution must at least meet the minimal conditions necessary to be justified in exercising coercive force over its subjects to be fully just.

If this is right, this chapter offers a "coercion-based theory" that goes beyond the coercion-based theories defended by Michael Blake, Thomas Nagel, and Richard Miller. This chapter denies that the relevant sort of coercion is only exercised by the domestic state. Subsequent sections argue that all coercive institutions require justification to subject people to their rules. They suggest that many international institutions exercise coercion.

Perhaps statists can resist the idea that perfect justice requires full legitimacy. They might think, for instance, that perfect justice is unobtainable. So, they might argue that it is an open question whether there can be conflicts between justice and legitimacy.

Even if statists are right on this count, however, this book's arguments may still address them. Legitimacy may just be different than justice and statists accept some obligations besides obligations of humanity and justice. Consider, for instance, Rawls' argument that there are duties – though not duties of humanity or justice – to respect the short list of human rights in the *Law of Peoples*. Even if there are good arguments for the view that obligations of justice should have priority over humanitarian obligations, they do not tell us whether obligations of justice have priority over other sorts of obligations.[12] In any case, this chapter's argument addresses statists like Michael Blake. Such statists argue that coercion generates obligations of legitimacy but believe legitimacy grounds giving priority to compatriots.[13]

---

[12] Richard Miller, "Cosmopolitan Respect and Patriotic Concern," 202–24.
[13] Blake, "Distributive Justice, State Coercion, and Autonomy," 257–96. If Blake's argument goes through, and many international institutions exercise the kind of coercion that generates obligations of legitimacy, there may even be much more extensive obligations in the international realm than those this book defends. These international institutions may have to be structured so that everyone subject to their rules is treated equally and differences in things like income and wealth benefit the least well off.

2.3 THE FIRST PREMISE: COERCION
AND LEGITIMACY

To make the case that coercive institutions must be legitimate it is necessary to say a few words about institutions and coercion. Very roughly, an *institution* is an organization that creates, enforces, and/or arbitrates between rules that regulate interaction between individuals or groups.[14] This book will primarily focus on treaty organizations, like the UN, the WTO, and the North Atlantic Treaty Organization (NATO). The UN creates rules, the WTO arbitrates between rules, and NATO enforces rules. These organizations have clear governance structures and lines of command. This chapter's penultimate section considers ways of expanding the scope of its argument so that it applies to more than individual institutions.

For an institution to be *coercive* individuals or groups violating its rules must be likely to face sanctions for the violation.[15] A *sanction* is a punishment or penalty. Coercion usually creates conditions under which the coerced have no good alternative except to do what their coercer wants them to do. This is usually explained by the fact that the coerced are threatened by sanctions.[16]

As this book will use the term, coercion can include the use of brute force. This is the "mainstream view of coercion that is more or less continuous with the view found in Aquinas, Hobbes, Locke, Kant, and some of the things Bentham and Mill say.[17] "This view identifies coercion with the use of force or violence, as well as to threats of the same."[18] Those who do not believe the use of brute force constitutes coercion can read "coercion" throughout as "coercion or use of force."

Depending on the kind and amount of coercion and so forth, coercion may or may not undermine autonomy. Usually, it engages the will of the coerced.[19] Consider a paradigmatic case of coercion. Suppose a homeless woman threatens a man with a gun saying "your money or your life." The man does not literally have to give over his money. He just has no good alternative and will face severe sanctions if he resists. Rather, the man has

---

[14] Because institutions create, enforce, and/or arbitrate between norms, rules, or procedures regulating interaction between individuals or groups, they are not mere practices.
[15] For further discussion of coercion and its moral significance, see: Gaus, "Liberal Neutrality."
[16] Risse, "What to Say about the State."
[17] Scott Anderson, "Coercion."   [18] Ibid.
[19] Frankfurt, "Coercion and Moral Responsibility," 65–86. Fowler, "Coercion and Practical Reason," 329–55.

to choose to hand over his money. Since, however, coercion can include the use of brute force, even those who completely lack autonomy can be coerced.[20]

Further, people can be coerced into doing what they would otherwise do freely. Perhaps the man the homeless woman threatens would have charitably donated money to the woman if he had not been coerced into doing so.

There is certainly more to say. A lot hangs on what counts as a violation, a punishment or penalty, and a good alternative in this analysis.[21] Some believe, for instance, that only threats can be coercive while others want to say sanctions can include withholding an offered good.[22] There is also disagreement about the appropriate baseline relative to which something counts as a threat.[23] On one account, coercion must be backed by a threat to (or use of force that) make(s) someone worse off than they can otherwise (reasonably) expect to be. On another account, coercion must be backed by a threat (or use of force that) make(s) someone worse off than they deserve to be. Perhaps the most demanding account of coercion suggests that coercion must be backed by a threat to (or use of force that) violate(s) rights.[24] It is impossible to resolve all of the debates about coercion here.

What is important for this book is that any coercive institution must be legitimate (i.e. justified in exercising coercive force). This is because coercion requires justification. This point is relatively uncontroversial.[25] Still,

---

[20] Wertheimer, *Coercion*. There are also important questions about the relationship between coercion and freedom. See: Fowler, "Coercion and Practical Reason."

[21] Scott Anderson, "Coercion." I find the following papers quite reasonable: Haksar, "Coercive Proposals." Lyons, "Welcome Threats and Coercive Offers." Benditt, "Threats and Offers." Although I think coercion is not always successful, I might endorse a disjunctive account of coercion on which some threats and offers that do not violate rights, but that are exploitative, are coercive. As Benditt notes, "It is sometimes said that everyone has his or her price. This may be true, but there is nevertheless all the difference between being prepared to give in (or sell out) when the price is right, and not at all being ready to do so but finding that one must because the alternatives are so awful." Benditt, "Threats and Offers," 384. Although no one may be to blame for making coercive offers, even knowingly, some justification is necessary. Nothing in this book will hang on this being so, however.

[22] See: Scott Anderson, "Coercion"; Stevens, "Coercive Offers."

[23] For criticism, see: Nozick, "Coercion," 440–72; Zimmerman, "Coercive Wage Offers," 121–45. For a critique of Zimmerman, see: Alexander, "Zimmerman on Coercive Wage Offers." Also see: Gorr, "Toward a Theory of Coercion," 383–406; McGregor, "Bargaining Advantages and Coercion in the Market," 23–50; Virginia Held, "Coercion and Coercive Offers"; Van De Veer, "Coercion, Seduction, and Rights."

[24] Wertheimer, *Coercion*.

[25] Nozick, "Coercion," 440–72. Zimmerman, "Coercive Wage Offers," 121–45. Alexander, "Zimmerman on Coercive Wage Offers." Gorr, "Toward a Theory of Coercion,"

consider a quick argument in its defense that might appeal to liberals deeply concerned about coercion that violates rights. Adapting an argument by John Locke, one might assert that each person has a natural right to freedom; hence, people cannot be subject to others' commands without justification.[26] One might hold that people are "naturally in ... a state of perfect freedom to order their actions, and dispose of their possessions and persons, as they think fit, within the bounds of the law of nature, without asking leave, or depending upon the will of any other ..."[27] The constraint that all are subject to the law of nature can be explained in terms of being subject to reason, which "teaches all mankind, who will but consult it, that being all equal and independent, no one ought to harm another in his life, health, liberty, or possessions ..."[28] So, as long as one does not violate another's rights, justification is necessary to abridge one's natural right to freedom. Those who are concerned about individual freedom should agree that institutions require justification to use coercive force; they must have the right to use such force. If this argument goes through, it follows that institutions must be justified in exercising coercive force; they must be legitimate.

H.L.A. Hart provides one possible way of defending a natural right to freedom. Hart argues that if there are any natural rights, there is a natural right to freedom.[29] His argument is, roughly, this:

(1) All rights are either special or general.
(2) Special rights are claims that others have authorized a particular act which would otherwise violate a fundamental right to freedom.
(3) General rights are claims that a particular act is covered by a fundamental right to freedom.

383–406. McGregor, "Bargaining Advantages and Coercion in the Market," 23–50. Virginia Held, "Coercion and Coercive Offers." Van De Veer, "Coercion, Seduction, and Rights."

[26] Locke, *Second Treatise on Civil Government.*

[27] Ibid., Section 4. Locke only holds that sane adults have a natural right to freedom which is given by reason, but this cannot be the basis for all our obligations to others. Locke seems to believe that the non-autonomous have some positive rights and governments should provide for those who lack reason and other means of sustenance. Ibid., Sections 59–60. He says these people lack natural rights because those who lack reason cannot be free subjects under the law. Those who deny that there are positive obligations to these people should, however, at least hold that they have some negative rights. Moreover, only by enabling people to secure reason can they become free subjects under the law. For plausible constraints on the rights of potentially autonomous people, see: Lipson and Vallentyne, "Libertarianism, Autonomy, and Children"; Lipson and Vallentyne, "Child Liberationism and Legitimate Interference." See also Chapter 3.

[28] Locke, *Second Treatise on Civil Government*, Section 6.

[29] Hart, "Are There Any Natural Rights?" 175–91.

(4) A fundamental right to freedom is a right to freedom from coercion or constraint except where it is necessary to prevent coercion or constraint.

(5) This just is a natural right to freedom.[30]

Alternately, one might try to ground the concern for freedom in another way, perhaps in a concern for individuals' interests. Recall, however, that the Autonomy Argument is only intended to appeal to liberals who are deeply concerned about individual freedom. Most of these people will probably accept the claim that everyone has a natural right to freedom.

Those who hold very weak accounts of coercion might say that coercion does not require justification. They might hold that trade relationships are coercive because some are excluded from trading with those who exchange with others. Yet these people might not think that this kind of coercion requires justification.

Some also believe an institution that only protects individuals' rights does not exercise the kind of coercion that requires (additional) legitimation. John Simmons says, for instance, that even "the Third Reich was justified in prohibiting rape and punishing rapists."[31] Some believe acts that impermissibly violate individual liberty can be legitimately prevented by any person or institution even if prevention requires coercion.

Here, however, I think we need only restrict our attention to those kinds of coercion that do require justification. Subsequent sections argue that many international institutions are coercive even on the most demanding accounts. Furthermore, even those who accept weaker accounts of coercion tend to hold that coercion requires justification.[32] So it should not imperil the Autonomy Argument to limit our attention to forms of coercion that require justification.

Some will argue that only states need to be justified in exercising coercive force (i.e. legitimate). Some things that fundamentally shape individuals' basic life prospects need not be legitimate. Hurricanes, typhoons, and earthquakes have significant impacts on individuals. They do not need justification. Perhaps non-state institutions are more like natural disasters than like states.

Although natural disasters are often inescapable and significant, natural disasters are different from (all) institutions in some important

---

[30] Ibid. For a similar outline of Hart's argument, see: Hoekema, *Rights and Wrongs*, 91.
[31] Simmons, "Justification and Legitimacy," 770.
[32] Haksar, "Coercive Proposals." Lyons, "Welcome Threats and Coercive Offers." Benditt, "Threats and Offers."

respects. Institutions are created and upheld by humans.[33] Hurricanes are not. Partly for this reason, hurricanes and other natural disasters cannot be coercive, though they may fundamentally shape individuals' basic life prospects. That is why it does not make sense to ask "Are hurricanes and other natural disasters legitimate?" Even non-state institutions, on the other hand, can be coercive. When they are, they must be legitimate.[34]

Statists might argue that only states must be legitimate because only they claim a right to exercise coercive force in the name of their subjects. They might suggest that only if coercive non-state institutions amounted to something like a world government or global sovereign would they have to be legitimate.[35] Thomas Nagel holds something like this view in "The Problem of Global Justice," although he is concerned about equality and justice rather than autonomy and legitimacy. He believes that there is a duty of humanitarian assistance on the part of states. Nagel argues that there is no sufficiently developed global institutional system that can have egalitarian distributive obligations.

The claim that there is no world government or global sovereign does not entail, however, that coercive institutions need not be legitimate.[36] Furthermore, Nagel does not argue that only an institution, or institutional system, that claims a right to exercise coercive force in the name of its subjects must be just (never mind legitimate). At best he argues that *if* (not *only if*) an institution, or institutional system, imposes coercive rules on its subjects in their name, it has to be just. He merely asserts the view that it is *only if* an institution, or institutional system, imposes coercive rules on its subjects in their name that it has to be just. So his argument cannot be used to support the claim that only states must be legitimate because only they claim a right to exercise coercive force in the name of their subjects. Perhaps Nagel's insight is that some justification is necessary even to *claim* a right to exercise coercion over someone. This may be so, even if the claim is not backed by effective coercive force. Perhaps it is worse for rulers to say they are coercing me in my name than it is for them to say they are coercing me in someone else's name. The main reason institutions must be justified in coercing me "in my name," however,

---

[33] Pogge, *Realizing Rawls*.
[34] One might say that hurricanes and other natural disasters can present coercive situations.
[35] Nagel, "The Problem of Global Justice."
[36] It is not entirely clear what it means for an institutional system to impose coercive rules on its subjects in their name. Eric Cavellero suggests that this might amount to the claim that institutional systems must be norm-guided in Hart's sense. Cavellero, "Coercion, Inequality and the International Property Regime," 29. This chapter will suggest, however, that the global institutional system is norm-guided. Those within individual institutions might be as well.

is that they must be justified in coercing me at all (assuming that I respect others' rights etc.). If the preceding arguments are correct, coercive institutions must be justified in exercising coercive force over their subjects whether or not they exercise this force in the name of anyone at all.

Nagel does say that "the newer forms of international governance share with the old a markedly indirect relation to individual citizens and that this is morally significant."[37] So maybe one could argue that non-state institutions need not be justified in coercing individuals because they have secured states' consent to coerce their citizens.

There are several problems with this suggestion. One is that most international institutions have not secured the consent of all states to whose citizens their rules apply.[38] Another problem is that state consent does not clearly justify international institutions in coercing individuals especially since many states are not legitimate on any liberal theory. Many states are totalitarian. Finally, even if all states were legitimate and consented to international institutions coercing their citizens, that may not legitimize these institutions. States may be undermining their own legitimacy in consenting to some international institutions' rules. This worry is especially pressing if these institutions prevent some states from fulfilling their obligations to their citizens (as this chapter will suggest below). Finally, one could argue that all coercive institutions must themselves be legitimated by their individual subjects. There may be a way around these problems. Even so, those who are deeply concerned about individual freedom should agree to this much: all institutions must be *justified* in exercising coercive force over their subjects, though these institutions may *be* so justified (where, for example, they have secured states' consent).

2.4 THE SECOND PREMISE: LEGITIMACY AND OBLIGATION

The previous section defended the first premise of the Autonomy Argument; this section defends the second. The previous section argued that coercive institutions must be legitimate because coercion requires justification. It said nothing about what is necessary for legitimacy. This section defends the Autonomy Argument's condition for legitimacy by appeal to a commitment implicit in many liberal theories.

---

37 Nagel, "The Problem of Global Justice," 132.
38 The Financial Action Task Force (FATF), for instance, threatens even non-member jurisdictions. See: FATF, "High-risk and Non-Cooperative Jurisdictions." NATO does not restrict its security operations to member states.

Philosophers advance many conditions for legitimacy. Legitimate institutions might need to treat people equally. They might need to embody a commitment to reciprocity, publicity, free speech, or due process. Legitimate institutions might have to protect the disadvantaged.[39] They might even need to give all people equal status, respect, consideration, resources, or opportunity for welfare.[40]

Subject to a few constraints, this section will defend the following thesis: To be legitimate, coercive institutions must ensure that their subjects secure sufficient autonomy. Some of its discussion will apply to the analogous premise in the next chapter.[41] Consider some of the components of the proposed condition for legitimacy.

First, the kind of autonomy at issue is just the kind of autonomy discussed in the first chapter. Recall that, to secure this autonomy, people must at least be able to reason about, make, and carry out *some* significant plans on the basis of their commitments (see Chapter 1, Section 1.2). This was spelled out in terms of what is necessary for people to consent to, or dissent from, the rule of coercive institutions. Because this conception of autonomy is so minimal, few should deny that to freely dissent, people must have at least this kind of autonomy.

Next, what does *ensuring* that someone secures sufficient autonomy require? Institutions must do whatever is necessary to help their subjects *secure and maintain sufficient autonomy until, and unless, these people autonomously relinquish their ability to do so*. Again, the idea is not that people must be able to reason and plan at every second to have sufficient autonomy. Rather the idea is, roughly, that an individual's capacity to reason and plan must remain intact over the course of a normal or healthy life.[42]

There may be an implicit possibility constraint here. If so, what is *possible* here is what is achievable in the real world. Perhaps an institution does not lose legitimacy if it does not ensure that someone secures the reasoning and planning components of autonomy if there is no implementable institution which could ensure that this person secures this

---

[39] See: Hurrell, "Global Inequality and International Institutions."

[40] For different accounts of legitimacy, see: Brock, *Global Justice*; Buchanan, "Justice as Reciprocity vs. Subject-Centered Justice," 227–52; Caney, "Survey Article," 95–133; Pogge, "Severe Poverty as a Human Rights Violation."

[41] The next chapter will argue that libertarians must agree that people have to be able to freely consent to this rule and that people must have sufficient autonomy to enter into legitimate contracts. Again, few should deny that this is so. The consequences of doing so, the next chapter will suggest, are intolerable.

[42] See discussion in Chapter 1.

autonomy.[43] Some are in permanent comas. That need not mean the coercive institutions to which they are subject are less legitimate.[44]

Because this chapter's account of *ensuring* plays a large role in the Autonomy Argument, it is worth emphasizing that what is necessary for people to secure the relevant components of autonomy will vary with the case. It depends on how close people are to securing such autonomy and what resources one already has. In cold climates, for instance, heat may be necessary. In the tropics, heat is usually unnecessary. Some will secure sufficient autonomy as long as they are free from interference. Others, however, need assistance to do so. The coercive institutions to which these people are subject may have to supply this assistance. Suppose, for instance, someone falls into a coma from which that person could recover with proper medical care. If that person is not receiving such care from friends, family, or benefactors, subsequent sections will argue the coercive institutions to which that person is subject must provide it.

2.4.1 Initial defense of the Autonomy Argument's second premise

There are two parts to the above condition for legitimacy.[45] First, it embodies the claim that coercive institutions can only be legitimate if their subjects secure sufficient autonomy (assuming this is possible). Second, it embodies the claim that such institutions must ensure that their subjects secure this much autonomy. It is possible to defend the first claim by appeal to one strand in liberal thought (leaving the qualifications discussed above implicit where their importance is minor). The second claim follows from the first and some observations about the nature of ensuring and coercive institutions.

At the heart of liberalism is concern for individual freedom. Recently liberals have focused primarily on arguing that whatever coercive

---

[43] For further discussion, see: Hassoun, "Meeting Need," 250–75.

[44] Note: There may be a similar possibility constraint on many of the theories of legitimacy from which this chapter will derive the obligation to ensure that subjects secure sufficient autonomy. It is debatable whether it is possible for international institutions to be legitimate on any of the main liberal theories of legitimacy. I see little basis for this worry if a possibility constraint is included. It is obviously possible for an institution to, for instance, secure as much (actual or tacit) consent as possible. There are, however, hard questions about what we should do if we do not know what is possible. The introduction to the second part of this book discusses this last point.

[45] I owe thanks to Alex London for comments on many drafts of these chapters and, in particular, for his help in this section.

institutions are imposed upon people must be decent, if not fully just.[46] An equally powerful strand in liberal thought, however, expresses the idea that the *actual* relationship between the rulers and *each person* who is ruled must be voluntary in some way. Still, those who are concerned about individual freedom disagree about what makes this relationship voluntary. On liberal communitarian theories, for instance, this relationship is voluntary if the rulers allow or support communities of appropriate kinds that need not be explicitly consensual. Other liberal theories make consent central to legitimacy. On hypothetical consent theories, for instance, the relationship between rulers and ruled is only voluntary if (reasonable) people *would* agree to be subject to the rulers' dictates *were* they asked.[47] Democratic theory requires more. On democratic theory, legitimacy arises through the democratic process where the majority must actually consent to the institutions to which they are subject. Perhaps the most demanding theory of this type is actual consent theory. On actual consent theory, coercive institutions are legitimate only if they secure their subjects' actual consent.

Although those who are concerned about individual freedom disagree about what makes the relationship between the rulers and ruled voluntary, they agree that this relationship can only be voluntary if the ruled possess at least some freedom. The kind of freedom at issue here is not overly expansive or limited. This freedom is not constituted by the social order but it is compatible with significant constraints on social life.[48] The key idea is that subjects must be free to determine their actions and shape the nature of their relationship with the institutions to which they are subject.[49] Although individuals may not get to decide whether or not they are subject to coercive institutions, they must be able to control the way they react to their subjection. Subjects should be able to decide whether or not to abide by, dissent from, or consent to coercive institutions for themselves.[50] Political liberals almost unanimously agree, for instance, that people have a right to dissent from the rule of coercive institutions by conscientious objection, non-violent protest, passive resistance, and so forth. To react to their institutions' rules in these ways, people must be able to reason about, make, and carry out some significant plans in

---

[46] See: Rawls, *Political Liberalism*. Also see: Pogge, *Realizing Rawls*.
[47] See: Pogge, *Realizing Rawls*. Also see: Beitz, *Political Theory and International Relations*.
[48] Waldron, "Theoretical Foundations of Liberalism," 133.
[49] Ibid., 132.   [50] Ibid., 146.

light of their beliefs, desires, values, and goals.[51] So these liberals implicitly accept the first claim embodied in this chapter's condition for legitimacy; as many of those living under a coercive institution as possible must secure the relevant components of autonomy for that institution to be legitimate.

To make this case, this section will first argue that communitarians, democratic, hypothetical, and actual consent theorists have to agree to this much: Legitimacy requires that subjects be free to determine their actions and shape the nature of their relationships to coercive institutions. It will then explain why reasoning and planning are necessary for this freedom.

Consider communitarianism first. Communitarians believe that legitimacy vests in relationships of various kinds that need not rely on consent. Some communitarians follow Will Kymlicka in holding that communities are valuable because they support, promote, or give rise to individual identity or autonomy.[52] To do these things, communities must at least protect individuals' right to dissent from their rule. So these communitarians have to agree that subjects must be able to decide whether or not to abide by, dissent from, or consent to coercive institutions for themselves. Perhaps communitarians can hold that communities are independently valuable; they need not think communities are valuable, in the first place, because they support, promote, or give rise to individual identity or autonomy.[53] Rather, their primary concern might be that communities and relationships themselves flourish. To keep communities and relationships strong and vibrant, however, orthodoxies have to be open to challenge at least from within.[54] People must at least have a right to dissent from the rule of coercive institutions by voicing their disagreement with, if not exiting, these institutions. As Charles Taylor puts it, these sorts of freedoms protect the "crucial moral interest that each one of us has in the authentic development of the other."[55] Even if communities do not want to hear heretics or reformers, communities cannot

---

[51] This does not mean that freedom cannot be shaped by society in important ways. Society can have a great influence on individuals' preferences, for instance, without undermining individuals' ability to reason about, make, and carry out some significant plans.

[52] Kymlicka, "The Rights of Minority Cultures," 140–46. Parekh, *Rethinking Multiculturalism*.

[53] It is not clear that anyone holds this view, though some communitarians seem to think communities are independently valuable. See, for instance: Blum, *Moral Perception and Particularity*; MacIntyre, *Whose Justice, Which Rationality?*; Charles Taylor, *Sources of the Self*.

[54] MacIntyre, *Whose Justice, Which Rationality?* Charles Taylor, *Philosophy and Human Sciences*, Ch. 7.

[55] Charles Taylor, "The Dynamics of Democratic Exclusion," 153.

remain strong unless their members inhabit their traditions in a way that keeps these traditions alive and responsive. So even this kind of liberal communitarian has to agree that subjects must be able to decide whether or not to abide by, dissent from, or consent to coercive communities for themselves.

Some communitarians might believe they are liberals and yet not think individuals need any substantive freedoms at all under coercive institutions.[56] They may just be committed to the liberal principle of toleration and believe that toleration only requires respecting individuals' right to exit from their community.[57] Chandran Kukathas argues, for instance, that people must only have freedom of conscience under coercive institutions. He believes that the right to freedom of exit is sufficient to preserve freedom of conscience.[58]

Still, individuals have to be able to decide whether or not to abide by, dissent from, or consent to the coercive institutions to which they are subject to have a real right to exit.[59] If communitarian theories deny this, they deny an important strand in liberal thought.[60] William Kymlicka puts the point this way:

Liberalism is committed to (and perhaps even defined by) the view that individuals should have the freedom and capacity to question and possibly revise the traditional practices of their community, should they come to see them as no longer worthy of their allegiance.[61]

On communitarian theories that do embrace this liberal commitment, the relationship between legitimate coercive institutions and their subjects must be free.

---

[56] Kukathas, *The Liberal Archipelago.*
[57] Ibid.   [58] Ibid.
[59] Furthermore, if it exists, there is no exit from the global institutional system discussed below. So, if there is such a system, either Kukathas' argument must be rejected or the global institutional system must be eliminated. Freedom of exit might be created by establishing self-sufficient societies subject to no jurisdiction other than their own rules. Still, it would be extremely difficult, if not impossible, to establish self-sufficient societies that do not affect each other. Many of those most concerned about individual freedom do not find the idea of dissolving many international institutions appealing. Libertarians, for instance, often argue that such institutions are desirable. Most want to establish liberal property law internationally. They cite global collective action problems, externalities, and efficiency arguments for international institutions. It requires a less radical revision of the traditional libertarian view to accept the minimal freedom-based requirements for legitimacy defended here than it does to dissolve the global institutional system, if one exists. See, for instance: Lomasky, "Liberalism Beyond Borders," 206.
[60] Kymlicka, "The Rights of Minority Cultures," 140–46.
[61] Ibid., 142.

Hypothetical consent theorists should agree that subjects must have basic freedoms under coercive institutions.[62] Obviously, many hypothetical consent theorists are statists. Still, if hypothetical consent is what legitimizes coercive institutions, in general, people must have basic freedoms under them. On hypothetical consent theory, legitimacy requires that coercive institutions be organized according to those principles that would be chosen in an appropriately specified original position. Reasonable people in a liberally construed original position would only agree to be subject to coercive institutions if they are able to abide by, dissent from, or consent to their rule.[63] On John Rawls' theory, for instance, people would choose principles of justice on which they would be fully autonomous and people living under these principles would be able to understand and embrace them. Full autonomy and the ability to understand and embrace Rawls' principles of justice require the ability to abide by, dissent from, or consent to the rule of coercive institutions.[64]

One might object that people, even in a liberally construed original position, would accept some risk of not being able to shape their relationship to coercive institutions to reduce other risks or secure other benefits. In Rawls' original position, for instance, the deliberators are heads of families and might be more concerned to ensure that their family members can abide by, consent to, and dissent from these institutions' rule. This is especially likely if there are not enough resources to ensure that everyone secures these freedoms.

Hypothetical consent theorists are, however, committed to the idea that for coercive institutions to be *fully* legitimate, all of their subjects must be able to abide by, consent to, and dissent from their rule. Full legitimacy may be impossible. Still, hypothetical consent theorists must agree to this much: *Insofar as possible* subjects have to be able to shape the nature of their relationships to their coercive institutions *for these institutions to be fully legitimate.*

Some believe democratic theory cannot be applied usefully beyond states.[65] Like hypothetical consent theorists, many democratic theorists are statists. Further, it may be very difficult to democratize non-state

---

[62] For global hypothetical consent theories, see: Pogge, *Realizing Rawls*; Beitz, *Political Theory and International Relations.*

[63] Rawls, *Political Liberalism*, 68–81.

[64] Rawls, "Kantian Constructivism in Moral Theory," 520–32.

[65] See: Buchanan and Keohane "The Legitimacy of Global Governance Institutions." Also see: Hassoun, "Ideal Theory and Practice."

institutions, never mind a global institutional system (if, as this chapter will suggest below, one exists).

Nevertheless, there is reason to consider democratic theories of legitimacy insofar as they can be applied to international institutions. Some even argue for global democratic reforms. David Held, for instance, defends a theory of global democracy. On his theory, a voluntary confederation of states that secure the consent of their peoples should establish cosmopolitan democratic political structures. Over time, he believes, nation-states should "wither-away" so that they are no longer the "sole centers of legitimate power."[66] Rather, he argues for a system of subsidiarity with dispersed decision-making at the lowest effective levels.[67] Democratic (and other) conditions for legitimacy may be necessary (only) insofar as they are possible. Moreover, even if it is impossible to democratize all international institutions, it may be possible to democratize some of them.

At least insofar as democracy can be required to legitimize coercion, people must be able to decide whether or not to abide by, dissent from, or consent to their coercive institutions to be able to participate in the democratic process.[68] On democratic theory, everyone must be free to participate in the democratic process.[69] Most democratic theorists also accept important institutional constraints on the exercise of coercive force that protect individuals' basic freedoms.[70] Written or unwritten constitutions often form the basis of democratic societies and protect individuals' rights to dissent from the rule of their coercive institutions by conscientious objection, non-violent protest, or passive resistance.

Finally, the idea that subjects must be free to determine their actions and shape the nature of their relationships with coercive institutions is implicit in actual consent theory.[71] Recall that, on actual consent theory, coercive institutions are *legitimate* only if they secure their subjects' autonomous consent. The ability to determine one's actions and shape the nature of one's relationship to the institutions to which one is subject is a precondition for autonomous consent. For subjects to actually

[66] David Held, *Democracy and the Global Order*, 233.
[67] Held allows that there are many possible democratic forms from direct to representative democracy.
[68] Knight and Johnson, "What Sort of Political Equality Does Deliberative Democracy Require?"
[69] David Held, *Democracy and the Global Order*.
[70] Christiano, *The Rule of the Many*.
[71] The next chapter argues at more length that libertarians should accept this premise, in part, because they should be actual consent theorists. It also responds to obvious objections to this claim. See: Simmons, "Consent Theory for Libertarians," 330–56.

autonomously consent to a coercive institution, they must be able to do so. Actual consent theorists, like Harry Beran, have to agree that subjects must *be able* to decide whether or not to abide by, dissent from, or consent to their coercive institutions' rule for these institutions to be legitimate.[72]

What would accounts of legitimacy look like that denied that subjects must have basic freedoms under coercive institutions? On such accounts, coercive institutions could be legitimate *even though people living under these institutions could not even freely object to them.* It is hard to see how such institutions would not be totalitarian. After all, some of their subjects would not be able to dissent from their rule by voting, conscientious objection, non-violent protest, or even passive resistance. Even if such institutions provide some formal freedoms, and are otherwise decent, it is hard to see how these subjects' relationships to these institutions are voluntary.

Liberals should agree that subjects must be free to determine their actions and shape the nature of their relationship with the coercive institutions to which they are subject. They must be able to decide for themselves whether or not to abide by, dissent from, or consent to these institutions. To make this decision for themselves, subjects must be able to reason about, make, and carry out some significant plans on the basis of their commitments. Subjects must not be constrained to making plans only to satisfy their immediate needs. Though they might not exercise this ability, those subject to coercive institutions must be able to decide whether or not to abide by these institutions' rules; they must at least be able to protest against these institutions. In other words, subjects must have sufficient autonomy to be able to determine their actions and shape the nature of their relationship with the coercive institutions to which they are subject.[73] So, liberals should agree that coercive institutions can only be legitimate if their subjects secure sufficient autonomy (assuming this is possible). Further argument is necessary to show that coercive institutions must ensure that their subjects secure sufficient autonomy.

---

[72] For further argument on this point see the next chapter and Beran, *The Consent Theory of Political Obligation.*

[73] On Rawls' theory, full autonomy requires more than the rational autonomy people possess in the original position. Rawls was also quite clear that even the rational autonomy attributed to the agents includes more than the minimal kind of autonomy at issue in the Autonomy Argument. Rawls, "Kantian Constructivism in Moral Theory," 532.

2.4.2 *Concluding the defense of the Autonomy Argument's second premise*

Consider why coercive institutions must ensure that their subjects secure sufficient autonomy. The previous subsection defended the following claim: Because coercive institutions subject people who cannot secure sufficient autonomy to coercive rules, they are illegitimate. This is because coercive institutions are not justified in exercising coercive force over those who could be, but are not, sufficiently autonomous. Yet coercive institutions continue to exercise such force. From here it is a short step to the conclusion that these institutions must ensure that their subjects secure sufficient autonomy.

If coercive institutions continue to exercise coercive force, legitimacy requires that they ensure that their subjects secure sufficient autonomy. Coercive institutions do, necessarily, continue to exercise such force. So, coercive institutions must ensure that their subjects secure sufficient autonomy.

To clarify the basic structure of this argument and put the point another way, this claim follows from the previous subsection's argument: For coercive institutions to be legitimate, they must either (1) stop coercing people or (2) ensure that their subjects secure sufficient autonomy. Because coercive institutions are *coercive*, they will not (1) stop coercing their subjects. So, (2) they must ensure that their subjects secure sufficient autonomy.

One might object that even if a coercive institution wrongly subjects people to coercive rules, it need not ensure that its subjects secure sufficient autonomy. It can just stop coercing them. Consider an analogy. Suppose someone who is not autonomous, let us call her Alea, agrees to give me a large sum of money. I do not thereby have a duty to do what I can to ensure that Alea secures sufficient autonomy. I merely fail to have a contract with her. Alea has not, by agreeing to give me a large sum of money, incurred an enforceable debt to me. If I were to try to enforce the agreement on Alea, I would act wrongly. As long as I do not try to extract any money from her, I have no obligation to her.

This objection does not undercut the argument for the conclusion that coercive institutions must ensure that their subjects secure such autonomy. The objector may be right about Alea's case. If I do not try to extract any money from Alea I may have no obligation to her. Similarly, if an institution stopped subjecting people to coercive rules, it might not need to do anything to ensure that its subjects secure sufficient autonomy. The problem is that the objection does not appreciate the nature of *coercive* institutions. Insofar as *coercive* institutions *continue* to subject people to coercive rules, they can be legitimate *only if* they ensure that their subjects secure sufficient autonomy. Such institutions must ensure that their subjects secure sufficient autonomy because they will not cease subjecting people to their rules (if they did, they would no longer qualify as coercive). Consider a better analogy to illustrate the import of these observations. Suppose I find out Alea is (currently) incapable of autonomously agreeing to give me her money and do not go elsewhere. Rather I continue to coerce her. In this case, I act illegitimately unless I get her free consent to give me the money (which, by supposition, requires ensuring that she can autonomously agree). Similarly, coercive institutions, because they continually subject people to coercive rules, must ensure that their subjects secure sufficient autonomy. Otherwise, they cannot be legitimate. If a (formerly) coercive institution is altered so that it is no longer coercive, then this obligation will not apply. Still, as long as an institution is coercive, it is obligated to ensure that those subject to its coercive rules secure sufficient autonomy.

One might worry that this response relies on a false premise. According to the response, coercive institutions can be legitimate *only if* they ensure that their subjects secure sufficient autonomy. Perhaps relatives or charities can ensure that these people secure these components of autonomy. Sticking with the analogy, the objection would be that Alea may secure sufficient autonomy (and freely consent to the loan) without my ensuring that she can do so. Perhaps her family or others involved in charitable work can do so instead. I may be able to legitimately enforce the contract without ensuring that Alea secures the relevant components of autonomy.

This objection has some truth in it. Others may ensure that those subject to a coercive institution secure sufficient autonomy. Others may even have primary responsibility for doing so. Nevertheless, the objection misunderstands the nature of *ensuring*. Ensuring is like being a lender of last resort. If people secure this autonomy on their own, or with the help of friends and/or benefactors, their coercive institutions can ensure that they secure autonomy without doing anything. Coercive institutions must step into the breach, however, if help is required. It is only if coercive institutions do this that as many of their subjects as possible will secure sufficient autonomy. Coercive institutions must ensure that their subjects secure this autonomy. This is the only way coercive institutions can be legitimate in our imperfect world.

Again, what is necessary here may just be what is realistically achievable.[74] A coercive institution may not lose legitimacy if it does not ensure that someone secure basic reasoning and planning capacities. It may be impossible for this person to secure these capacities under any implementable institution. When they are very young, children will lack basic reasoning and planning capacities no matter what anyone does. Most children who receive proper care will secure basic reasoning and planning capacities as they get older. If no one else does so, the coercive institutions to which these children are subject must help them secure these capacities once they are old enough. (Further constraints may be necessary if the resources to ensure that everyone secures sufficient autonomy do not exist.)[75]

Some ways of trying to ensure that everyone secures sufficient autonomy may not make a coercive institution more legitimate. Suppose, for instance, one such institution gave someone anti-malarial medicine that left them in terrible pain. Suppose, further, that that institution could have given that person another, equally effective, drug that did not have any bad side effects. That institution might not be fully legitimate. Even if the pain does not undermine that individual's freedom, there may be other conditions for legitimacy that are unfulfilled. People may have a human right against avoidable suffering.[76]

The second half of this book will suggest that there are probably many ways of making coercive institutions more legitimate. The important point here is just that everyone must secure sufficient autonomy for the coercive institutions to which they are subject to be legitimate. This is a necessary condition for legitimacy, even if other conditions must be fulfilled as well.

If hard tradeoffs between fulfilling different conditions for legitimacy are required, coercive institutions may be justified in doing other things before, or instead of, ensuring that their subjects secure the reasoning and planning components of autonomy. Suppose, for instance, legitimacy also requires ensuring that everyone receives a minimum wage. In our world, tradeoffs between fulfilling this condition for legitimacy and

---

[74] As is common in political philosophy, I am interested in policies that could be implemented in the real world for (and by) real people in the foreseeable future.

[75] If institutions simply lack the resources to ensure that everyone who has the potential to secure basic reasoning and planning capacities does so, further restrictions will be necessary. I discuss some of these issues in: Hassoun, "Meeting Need."

[76] I owe thanks to Peter Spirtes for this example.

the condition for legitimacy this book defends may be necessary.[77] Even standard protections of autonomy are expensive. Suppose that minimum wage laws are necessary for people to secure a minimum wage but not for reasoning and planning. Suppose that elementary education is essential for reasoning and planning but not for a minimum wage. It might be acceptable to use resources to pass minimum wage laws before, or instead of, hiring teachers.

Though nothing in the Autonomy Argument hangs on this point, standard protections of autonomy should have a good deal of priority. Autonomy is both a precondition for many other things to have value and a component of welfare. A minimum wage, for instance, may do little for the non-autonomous. Autonomy will do a lot for people even if they are underpaid. Autonomous people can seek better jobs and find meaning in other areas of their lives as well as participate in the political process or refuse to do so. Those without even the minimal autonomy described here can do none of these things.[78]

Those who want to deny the conclusion that rulers have an obligation to ensure that their subjects secure sufficient autonomy should deny that legitimate coercion requires this much. (It is radically implausible to deny that coercive institutions must be legitimate. It is better to deny this chapter's claim about what legitimacy requires.) Since the Autonomy Argument is only intended to appeal to those who accept a liberal theory of legitimacy, perhaps it is best to deny this thesis by arguing that one of the liberal theories of legitimacy in the literature does not entail that coercive institutions have significant obligations to their subjects. One might deny, that is, that this chapter's condition for legitimacy can be derived from a concern for freedom implicit in liberalism. One might argue, for instance, that actual consent is required only when it is not too demanding to secure and no one else is responsible for ensuring that the coerced

---

[77] These tradeoffs would be particularly difficult if what fulfills one condition for legitimacy makes it more difficult to fulfill another condition. Inquiry into such matters is left for another time. Before worrying about such tradeoffs, it is important to get clear on just what legitimacy requires in the first place.

[78] On the degree conception of legitimacy, the Autonomy Argument shows that the only way a coercive institution can be perfectly legitimate is if as many of its subjects as *possible* secure sufficient autonomy. If there is more than one condition for legitimacy, then a coercive institution will not be perfectly legitimate unless it fulfills all of the conditions for legitimacy but it can be pretty legitimate if it comes close to fulfilling most of the conditions. A different way of looking at legitimacy is as legitimacy-with-respect-to-individual-subjects. If an institution only ensures that some of the people it coerces secure sufficient autonomy it may be fully-legitimate-with-respect-to-those-individual-subjects but not fully-legitimate-with-respect-to-its-other-individual-subjects.

secure sufficient autonomy. Alternately, one could – contra Rawls – deny that (reasonable) people in a liberally construed original position would only agree to coercive rules under which they are able to abide by, dissent from, or consent to being subject to (at least the general structure of) these rules.[79] One might argue that there is a distinction between natural and social inequalities. Perhaps there is reason not to coerce those who are deprived of basic reasoning and planning capacities due to the working of shared institutions. Nevertheless, one might deny that justification is necessary to coerce those who naturally lack these capacities.

It is impossible to fully defend the claim that this chapter's condition for legitimacy follows from a concern for freedom implicit in liberalism here, but this chapter has provided one argument for this conclusion. Not *all* liberals will agree that respect for persons, autonomous or not, requires refraining from forcing them to do things to which they cannot even object. Still, there is *one* important strand of liberal thought that supports this contention.

Furthermore, a version of liberalism on which people must have some freedom under coercive rule strikes me as utterly plausible. If one rejects this claim, one has to agree that coercion can be legitimately exercised even over those who lack basic reasoning and planning capacities and cannot dissent from rulers' dictates. To deny the claim that people must secure sufficient autonomy under coercive rules, one has to deny what it asserts – that those subject to coercive rules must at least be able to object to these rules. At least those who agree that a charitable construal of liberalism implies a commitment to the claim that everyone must have some basic freedoms (ie sufficient autonomy) under coercive rule should accept this chapter's argument. The next section considers this argument's implications for global justice (or, more properly, legitimacy).

2.5 THE FINAL PREMISE: IMPLICATIONS OF THE ARGUMENT FOR GLOBAL JUSTICE

So far this chapter has argued that coercive international institutions owe their subjects whatever resources and assistance they need to secure sufficient autonomy. So this section defends the Autonomy Argument's final premise. Namely, that there are many coercive international institutions.

While most people assume that only states exercise the kind of coercive power that requires the type of legitimation sketched above, the

---

[79] Rawls, *Political Liberalism*, 68–81.

Autonomy Argument applies quite widely – to whatever institutions continue to coerce people. It focuses on the coercive core of the ruler–ruled relationship. So this section will advance a new argument for the conclusion that there are many coercive international institutions. The next section will set out a tentative argument for the conclusion that these institutions along with states, many NGOs, and some corporations constitute a properly global institutional system.

Once again there are many disputes about what exactly constitutes coercion (that requires justification) such as: What is a sanction? Are all threats coercive? Can offers be coercive? Some hold much more restrictive accounts of coercion than others.

Rather than try to resolve all of the disputes about coercion here, this chapter will try to avoid them. For its primary aim is not to delineate the limits, or try to explicate the precise scope, of its argument. Rather, it tries to explicate a general line of reasoning worth further exploration from a variety of perspectives. What is crucial for the Autonomy Argument is just that what qualifies as coercion requires justification. If it is justified in light of a liberal theory of legitimacy like those discussed above, the Autonomy Argument's conclusion will follow.

The rest of this chapter makes its case by appeal to what I hope will be intuitive examples of coercion. It should be relatively uncontroversial to assume that taxation, law enforcement, and military and economic sanctions are coercive.[80] Furthermore, if law enforcement, for instance, was primarily carried out by volunteer bounty hunters or external armies, most liberals will still agree that law enforcement is coercive.[81] Not everyone will accept the examples of coercive international institutions below but, hopefully, everyone can accept at least some of them. This chapter's argument will only be strengthened if there are other cases of coercion.

The EU illustrates a large range of ways in which international institutions can be coercive. The EU passes regulations which become laws in member states even without states taking action to implement the relevant laws; directives with which member states must comply; and decisions to which individual addressees (e.g. companies or individuals) must submit.[82] The EU also has a criminal intelligence agency (EUROPOL)

---

[80] Gaus, "Liberal Neutrality."
[81] State rules are often enforced indirectly through local police forces, bounty hunters, and, at least historically, by the victims of a crime or the victims' agent. In Viking-age Iceland tribunals sometimes allowed victims to punish the perpetrators of a crime.
[82] McCormick, "A Primer on the European Union and its Legal System."

and commands active military forces; for instance, it deployed troops in Bosnia.[83]

International trade organizations, like the WTO and NAFTA, impose sanctions on member countries that violate their rules. States enforce these sanctions. North American Free Trade Agreement (NAFTA) sanctioned Mexico for prohibiting Metalclad from operating a toxic waste dump in San Luis Potosi, for instance. Mexico had to pay Metalclad US$16 million in damages.[84] The WTO found the USA guilty of violating its rules with the Byrd Amendment. It allowed prosecuting countries to impose import duties on the USA, taxing US consumers, until the USA repealed the act.[85] The WTO sanctioned the EU by allowing the USA to impose tariffs on EU goods, taxing EU producers, because the EU had used import licensing requirements to support Caribbean banana producers.[86] In many cases, laws passed by states as a result of international trade institutions' rulings eventually coerce businesses and individuals into abiding by the rulings. They may be required, for instance, to post a bond for trading subsidized products internationally.[87] Similarly, member countries are coerced into abiding by WB and IMF rules. These countries are threatened with sanctions – like bad credit reports and reduced access to funds in the future – if they do not follow these rules. In many cases, states have to coerce their citizens into abiding by international rules. People may be forced to move from their lands to make way for new infrastructure projects, and so forth.[88]

Or, consider how the UN exercises coercion. The UN Security Council imposes economic sanctions, air traffic controls, and arms embargoes on countries and groups within countries that threaten international security. The UN has sanctioned Rhodesia, Iraq, South Africa, Serbia, Montenegro, Yugoslavia, Somalia, Libya, Haiti, Sudan, Rwanda, Sierra Leone, Ethiopia, Eritrea, and groups within Cambodia, Angola, and Afghanistan.[89] The UN Security Council also authorizes the use of force against countries threatening international peace. When Iraq invaded Kuwait, the UN authorized the use of force to stop the invasion. The

[83] NATO, "What's on NATO's Agenda?"
[84] Wallach, "Slow Motion Coup d'Etat."
[85] European Union, "U.S. Congress Repeals Byrd Amendment."
[86] British Broadcasting Corporation, "WTO Approves Banana Sanctions."
[87] International Trade Administration, "An Introduction to US Trade Remedies."
[88] Charcon et al., "Inter-American Development Bank Megaprojects: Displacement and Forced Migration." Cernea, "Involuntary Resettlement in Development Projects."
[89] Roberts, "United Nations."

UN-mandated International Security Assistance Force, of about 30,000 troops, is currently involved in military action in Afghanistan.[90]

Threats and uses of force may require some justification even if they do not impinge upon (threaten or violate) rights. If they must be justified by appeal to one of the liberal theories of legitimacy above, the Autonomy Argument can rely on such examples alone.

Still, on any plausible account of rights, many of the examples of coercion are backed by threats to (or uses of force that) violate(s) individuals' rights. However not all rights violations are coercive. To see this, it will help to consider two views on opposite sides of the political spectrum:[91] an account on which rights are primarily negative, and one on which there are many positive rights.[92]

Although the next chapter will say more to address those (libertarians) who believe there are only negative rights, consider one example that may appeal to these people. Suppose people have rights in their persons and property and rights-violators can be punished by any person or institution with the power to do so. Many military interventions are coercive in ways that impinge upon rights. These interventions impinge upon individuals'

---

[90] United Nations, "Security Council Seeks Expansion of Role."

[91] People on both sides of the spectrum would probably also hold that intellectual property rights agreements in the WTO and other trade agreements violate rights. Some of these people argue that these agreements violate rights because they make it more difficult for people to secure life-saving drugs and technologies. Others say intellectual property rights should be further extended to provide incentives for (rights-fulfilling) innovation. Some think that there are no natural rights to intellectual property and, so, the WTO and NAFTA violate rights in prohibiting people from using things that are un-owned (ideas). Kinsella, "Against Intellectual Property," 1–53. There is a live contemporary debate about these issues. See, for instance: MailOnline, "Copyright Laws Should Be Extended to Protect Ageing Artists"; Barnard, "In the High Court of South Africa," 159–74.

[92] The preceding argument may not convince realists in international relations who accept the most demanding account of coercion. Realists do not think states can violate rights internationally. So, they may reject the idea that international organizations can violate rights. They may hold that these organizations are just forums for states. It is impossible to adequately address such realists here. Still, the claim that international organizations (and states) cannot violate rights internationally is radically implausible. They do not have a right to do things like frustrate (other) states' attempts to fulfill their obligations to their citizens. (This is so even if states' primary obligations are to their own citizens.) A moment of reflection also undermines the empirical hypothesis that many realists appeal to in support of their view: It is not the case that states only act in their self-interest. They can sometimes afford to accept moral obligations to outsiders. As the fourth chapter suggests, many states have been giving humanitarian aid for decades. Though much aid is clearly strategic, the idea that no states do (or can) give aid unless it is in their self-interest strains credulity. That said, there are many versions of realism and this note does not pretend to adequately address any of them. For an interesting version of realism, on which states cannot afford to do anything but further their interests because that will lead to disaster, see: Morgenthau and Thompson, *Politics Among Nations*. For a great book that engages seriously with realism see: Allen Buchanan, *Justice, Legitimacy, and Self-Determination*. I owe thanks to Alex London for discussion here.

rights to life, constrain their freedom of movement, and so forth. Military interventions do not only protect rights. Moderates who are concerned about negative rights might object that such interventions require no further justification when they protect *many* people's rights and only impinge on the rights of a *few* innocent civilians. Despite good intentions, however, many military interventions do not just result in a few civilian casualties. Sometimes they lead to tragedies like the Srebrenica massacre where Bosnians, whose weapons were taken by UN and NATO troops, were raped and killed in UN safe zones. (When attack seemed imminent and the Bosnians requested their weapons back, their request was not granted despite the fact that the Serbian army had not come through with its part of the demilitarization agreement.)[93] At least coercion that carries with it a non-negligible risk of contributing to such tragedies requires justification. If the justification is via a liberal theory of legitimacy like those above, the Autonomy Argument's conclusion will follow.

Those who grant that there are positive rights to aid, on the other hand, might argue that poor countries, or their inhabitants, have a right to IMF and WB loans on much more concessive terms than they are offered.[94] If so, these countries, and their people, are coerced into abiding by existing IMF and WB terms; they are coerced into accepting them.

Perhaps one can object that international institutions rarely coerce because strong states often refuse to follow their rules.[95] The USA, in particular, is exempt from many international rules. It is hard to imagine the USA facing international military sanctions. International courts do not have jurisdiction over US citizens. It is also hard for small states to sanction the USA and EU for violating the rules of trade or other international laws.

The arguments that follow only depend on the fact that many international institutions coerce some states.[96] Despite the fact that the USA and other strong states are less likely to be coerced than weak states, there

---

[93] United Nations, "Report of the Secretary-General Pursuant to General Assembly Resolution 53/35."

[94] Lucy Baker, "The World Bank and Human Rights."

[95] I owe thanks to Peter Spirtes for making this point.

[96] If one adopts a causal theory of responsibility, one might argue that strong states should bear correspondingly greater responsibility for altering international rules. Perhaps strong states should also bear greater responsibility for enabling those subject to coercive international institutions to secure autonomy. On some accounts, the USA and its allies just use international institutions to coerce other states and individuals. Some argue that the USA and EU largely set the agenda for international institutions. They also choose the heads of the WB and IMF and have majority voting power in these institutions. WTO Watch, "NGOs Call on Trade Ministers to Reject Closed WTO Process." These people might argue that it is only if other states freely

is a lot of international coercion. Strong states are very likely to coerce weak states into abiding by international institutions' rules.[97]

A related objection is that only states are responsible for coercing people in the examples above. Consider an analogy. Suppose that a matriarch wants her family to join a club which requires a membership fee. Even if the club refuses to waive the fee, and the matriarch forces her family to join the club, the club does not coerce the family by its rules. Only the matriarch coerces the family.[98]

Although this move may work against some of the examples above, it misses a few crucial points. First, many countries' participation in international institutions is not voluntary in the way that becoming a member of a club is voluntary. Countries often pay significant penalties if they do not abide by WTO, UN, WB, or IMF rules. Sometimes these countries do not have other decent options and, so, are not free to resist these organizations' conditions. Highly indebted poor countries facing default, for instance, may have to abide by IMF conditionality. The consequences of refusing to do so can be devastating.[99] Many countries have, for example, had to coerce individuals into allowing their public services to be privatized or to accept additional taxes to abide by IMF conditions, despite violent protests.[100]

---

participate in upholding these rules, that they bear some responsibility for ensuring that those subject to these rules secure autonomy. In this way, this book's argument may connect with recent work in global justice on US empire. Richard Miller, *Globalizing Justice: The Ethics of Poverty and Power*. This account of responsibility is obviously different from the accounts of responsibilities correlative to human rights sketched in the first chapter. This book is not concerned to defend any particular account of responsibility, however, so it will not continue with this inquiry. This book is only concerned to argue that liberals of many kinds should agree that there are some significant obligations to the global poor that stem from a concern with international coercion. This will follow as long as there are many coercive international institutions (whether or not states are ultimately responsible for this coercion). I owe thanks to Peter Spirtes and Teddy Seidenfeld for their discussion.

[97] On how the USA exercises its power, see: Richard Miller, *Globalizing Justice: the Ethics of Poverty and Power*.

[98] I owe thanks to Dale Dorsey for suggesting this example.

[99] Consider an example. "For Argentina, the months that followed its 'bankruptcy' were horrendous. The country went into a brutal downward spiral of inflation, currency collapse and the rationing of cash by the banks. In a nation that is a big agricultural exporter, children went hungry and the economy imploded, shrinking by 13 per cent in a year. Unable to borrow to pay its bills, the state was forced to cut public sector wages, slash the state pension and unemployment soared to 20 per cent. Unable to pay for goods with cash, many Argentineans resorted to barter." Mortished, "What Happens When a Country Goes Bust?" Also see: IMF and World Bank, "Heavily Indebted Poor Countries (HIPC) Initiative."

[100] Public Citizen, "Water Privatization Case Study."

Consider three concrete examples that illustrate how states may lack decent options but to abide by international institutions' rules. (These examples also provide further support for the claim that these institutions' conditions threaten or violate positive rights.) In 1998, for instance, the WB and IMF worked with the Bolivian government to privatize its public enterprises – including Bolivia's water company (SEMAPA) – as a condition of giving Bolivia a loan.[101] Subsequently, when the Bechtel Corporation took over the Bolivian water supply, many poor Bolivians saw their water bills triple or quadruple. In March 2000, Bolivians took to the streets in protest – demanding affordable water. In another case, the IMF required Ecuador to privatize its water and sewage system as a condition of giving Ecuador a loan. Although service improved in some respects, poor infrastructure led to an outbreak of hepatitis A, and poor Ecuadorians suffered as prices rose and subsidies were eliminated. As a result, some suggest that, in some parts of Ecuador, the poor were unable to gain access to clean water and sanitation.[102] Finally, in a third case, the IMF pressured Niger to put a 19 percent value-added tax on goods – including foodstuffs – as a condition of giving Niger a loan. The tax was levied even though the price of basic grains had risen by up to 89 percent in the previous five years.[103] The tax was levied even though Niger's nomadic herders' main source of income (livestock) had fallen 25 percent in value.[104] Although causation is notoriously hard to prove, we know there was famine in Niger in 2005. The tax may well have been an aggravating factor in the famine.[105] Bolivia, Ecuador, and Niger may have had to accept the international financial institutions' conditions.

Furthermore, on some accounts, international institutions bear some responsibility for poor countries having no decent options but to abide by their rules.[106] Some argue that the basic reforms international institutions have required countries in crisis – like Russia – to adopt have caused

---

[101] IMF and World Bank, "ESAF Policy Framework Paper." Cited here: Public Citizen, "Water Privatization Case Study."

[102] Expreso de Guayaquil, "Hepatitis," cited in: Joiner, "Murky Waters," 15. Delgado, "Incidencia", cited in: Joiner, "Murky Waters," 15. Also see: Inter-American Development Bank, *Privatization for the Public Good?* 103–108.

[103] Amanthis, "Niger: The IMF and World Bank's Invisible War on Africans."

[104] Ibid.   [105] Ibid.

[106] This condition may not be necessary for coercion. For discussion see: Nozick, "Coercion," 440–72. Zimmerman, "Coercive Wage Offers," 121–45. Alexander, "Zimmerman on Coercive Wage Offers." Gorr, "Toward a Theory of Coercion," 383–406. McGregor, "Bargaining Advantages and Coercion in the Market," 23–50. Virginia Held, "Coercion and Coercive Offers." Van De Veer, "Coercion, Seduction, and Rights."

many of their problems.[107] Others argue that when WB and IMF loans require countries to liberalize financial markets, they make financial crises much more likely.[108] Yet others suggest that the resource or borrowing privileges international institutions grant anyone who has de facto control over territory have led terribly bad dictators to take power in poor countries – contributing to their dire situations.[109] When international institutions cause countries' lack of decent options, the proper analogy is to a man with a gun forcing another to shoot a third. When international institutions play a large enough role in the causal chain that results in states coercing their subjects, these institutions may be like a man who tells the mafia where their suspect is hiding and then offers to save the suspect from the mafia at an exorbitant price.

Even if one does not want to admit that the preceding examples are cases of coercion, it should be plausible that they require justification. It should be plausible that international institutions require justification to subject states to their rules when these states have no decent option but to accept their dictates. This is especially plausible when these institutions bear some responsibility for putting these states in this position. Again, if such justification is via a liberal theory of legitimacy like those above, the Autonomy Argument should go through.

Moreover, many international institutions coerce individuals in ways that threaten or violate rights directly. UN peacekeeping forces and NATO troops coerce individuals by, for instance, taking over territory, patrolling borders, and creating safe havens for refugees. Peacekeeping forces have been deployed in places as diverse as the Democratic Republic of the Congo, Iran, Lebanon, Sinai, Yemen, the Golan Heights, and Cyprus. Between 1988 and 1999 alone, the UN initiated forty peacekeeping missions.[110] International institutions' role in the Balkans provides an interesting case study. As the humanitarian crisis in the Balkans developed, the UN imposed an arms embargo against the former Yugoslavia, a flight ban over Bosnia and Herzegovina, and economic sanctions against

---

[107] Stuckler, King, and McKee, "Mass Privatisation and the Post-Communist Mortality Crisis," 399–407. These kinds of criticisms are often levied by countries' governments at times of crisis. The president of Argentina said, for instance: "International Monetary Fund policies are to blame for impoverishing 15 million people in Argentina." See: British Broadcasting Corporation, "Argentina Blames IMF for Crisis."

[108] Sachs, "Alternative Approaches to Financial Crises in Emerging Markets," 40–52. Ayadi, Adegbite, and Ayadi, 2008. "Structural Adjustment, Financial Sector Development and Economic Prosperity in Nigeria," 318–31.

[109] Pogge, *World Poverty and Human Rights.*

[110] Roberts, "United Nations."

Montenegro and Serbia. NATO enforced these measures. In 1995, when the UN peacekeeping force failed to prevent the Srebrenica massacre, NATO bombed Bosnia. NATO then enforced the Bosnia-Herzegovina peace agreement under the auspices of a UN protectorate and brought individuals accused of war crimes to The Hague. Eventually, NATO ceded command in Bosnia to the EU, which deployed its own troops.[111] These institutions thereby directly coerced, and enabled the court to coerce, individuals. Again, such military and peacekeeping missions often coerce individuals in ways that require justification. The Autonomy Argument addresses those who think the relevant justification must be by appeal to a liberal theory of legitimacy like those discussed above.

One might worry that insofar as coercion is backed by a threat to (or force that) violate(s) individuals' rights or undermines their entitlements, coercion is never legitimate, and the only obligation is to protect rights. So, if there is an obligation to ensure that people secure sufficient autonomy, that obligation follows directly from the account of rights at issue.

If the most demanding account of coercion is plausible, the Autonomy Argument's condition for legitimacy may be necessary to justify it. The biggest objection to theories of coercion on which it must be backed by a threat to (or force that) violate(s) rights is that such coercion cannot be justified.[112] If, however, coercion based on threats to (or force that) violate(s) rights can be justified, it is reasonable to hold that it can only be justified *if the relationship between the rulers and the ruled remains free.* If so, this chapter's argument shows that coercive international institutions have a derivative obligation to ensure that subjects secure what they need for sufficient autonomy.

Moreover, as suggested above, it is plausible that some of the preceding examples show that international institutions require justification even when they do not threaten or violate rights. International institutions may require justification, for instance, to subject states to their rules when these states have no decent option but to accept their dictates and

---

[111] NATO, "What's on NATO's Agenda?"

[112] Some coercion, e.g. to maintain law and order within states, is acceptable. Scott Anderson, "Coercion." Advocates of the account of coercion on which it is necessarily backed by a threat to (or force that) violate(s) rights might say that, though these threats and uses of force are regrettable, they are justified. Alternately, if coercion violates rights, there may just be duties of rectification to the victims of coercion Those who believe some coercion requires no further justification, because it only protects but does not violate rights, cannot accept this account of coercion, however. Furthermore, the account of coercion on which it necessarily violates rights neglects some intuitive examples of coercion. It seems, for instance, that just laws that violate no one's rights are still coercive.

these institutions bear some responsibility for putting these states in this position. If the requisite justification requires that people at least be able to dissent from these institutions' rules, the Autonomy Argument's conclusion follows.

Before considering whether this chapter's line of argument can be extended beyond international institutions, consider one of its advantages over the main alternative for deriving positive obligations from negative rights in the literature. By and large, this Autonomy Argument escapes the baseline worry for Pogge's harm-based argument. Coercion may require a threat and, hence, a baseline relative to which something counts as a threat. Even if coercion must be backed by a threat to violate rights, however, that baseline can be libertarian rights. Furthermore, figuring out what will happen if a threat is carried out is frequently easy. Even when it is difficult, it may not be as difficult as figuring out how things would be now in the absence of "a common and violent history," for instance.[113] One only needs to consider the empirical evidence for hypotheses like this: The Philippines will probably have lower interest rates, or higher trade barriers, if the IMF does not sanction the Philippines for refusing to open its rice market. Subsequent chapters explain how it is possible to argue for such empirical claims. Hard questions may arise if one says that international institutions are coercive because these institutions bear some responsibility for putting countries, or individuals, in a situation where they have no good option but to do as these institutions suggest. One would have to make the case, for instance, that international institutions bear this responsibility because they create and uphold the resource or borrowing privileges. That said, these issues are also subject to empirical study. There is a great deal of empirical literature on the resource curse and how loans impact the quality of institutions.[114] Moreover, the claim that international institutions are responsible for poor countries' plights only strengthens the argument that there is a lot of international coercion on some accounts.

2.6 SYSTEMATIC COERCION

It is possible to extend this chapter's argument further if the rules and institutions discussed above are part of a properly global institutional

---

[113] Pogge, "Severe Poverty as a Human Rights Violation."

[114] See, for instance: Rosser, "The Political Economy of the Resource Curse"; Independent Evaluation Group, "The World Bank's Country Policy and Institutional Assessment."

system. Again, this system is composed of a set of institutions and rules that shape, at the global level, individuals' basic life prospects.[115] The international institutions discussed above along with states, many NGOs, and some corporations may constitute the basic structure of such a (henceforth *the*) global system.[116] Even some of those who reject the Autonomy Argument accept the claim that this system exists.

One reason it makes sense to say there is a properly global institutional system is this: International law regulates the international institutions discussed above along with states, many NGOs, and some corporations. It does not matter whether the rules this book will continue to refer to as international law *are* properly law.[117] What is important is that the relevant rules determine what counts as an act of the global institutional system as opposed to one of its parts in isolation. The majority of institutions discussed above are treaty organizations (e.g. the UN, WTO, WHO, IMF, and WB).[118] So, treaty law embedded, for instance, in the Vienna Convention on the Law of Treaties and these organizations, primarily, determines what counts as an act of these parts of the system.[119] Very roughly, other institutions act as parts of the system when they act in accordance with these or other international laws.[120] So, when a country enters into an agreement with the WB to secure a loan to support its energy industry, and its energy companies fulfill the conditions associated with the loan, these companies are acting as part of this system.[121]

---

[115] See, for instance: Risse, "How Does the Global Order Harm the Poor?" 9–10.

[116] Beitz, *Political Theory and International Relations*, 149–50.

[117] Some deny that there is properly international law because some states are not reliably constrained by international rules. The WTO can sanction the USA but it is often ineffective. A powerful state must be willing to carry out the sanctions. Less powerful states are much more likely to have to abide by international rules.

[118] Pauwelyn, "Bridging Fragmentation and Unity," 903–16. I owe thanks to Aaron James and those who attended the Center for Ethics and Policy reading group on this book for discussion.

[119] The WB Articles of Agreement, for instance, specify its obligations, prerogatives, immunities, and privileges. Consider a few of just the International Development Association's (IDA's) Articles of Agreement. (The IDA is the part of the WB that is supposed to help the poorest countries.) The IDA's fifth Article of Agreement requires it to cooperate with other international development organizations. Its eighth Article of Agreement gives it full "juridical personality" and, in particular, the ability to: (a) contract, (b) acquire and dispose of property, and (c) begin legal proceedings. This article also specifies the immunities and privileges of the organization. This article says the IDA is immune from taxation and can treat communications between all members equally. World Bank, "International Development Association." Pauwelyn, "Bridging Fragmentation and Unity," 903–16.

[120] See discussion of shared norms below as these may play a role in deciding whether or not an institution acts in accordance with international law.

[121] The structure of such loans and the players involved in them can be quite complicated. See the diagram in the following publication, for instance: World Bank, "World Bank Guarantee Catalyzes Private Sector Investment for Uch Power Project in Pakistan." Also see discussion below and: World Bank, "World Bank's Loans to Japan."

On this account, parts of the global institutional system can violate international laws in the way that parts of a corporation can act outside of corporate mandates. When, for instance, a state uses force against another state in contravention of international law, it is not acting as part of this system. When a state uses force with the backing of the UN's Security Council in support of international law, it is acting as part of this system. The USA was acting as part of the global institutional system, after December 2001, when it provided the majority of troops necessary for securing Kabul in Afghanistan under the International Security Assistance Force (ISAF). Before 2003, however, the ISAF's mandate did not extend to the whole of Afghanistan.[122] So it is not clear that the USA was acting as part of the global institutional system in pursuing military action outside of Kabul before 2003.

Perhaps the previous section's argument can be used to show that the global institutional system is coercive. For the previous section suggested that there are many coercive international institutions. It should be relatively uncontroversial that states are also coercive. All of these institutions are part of the global institutional system and much of the coercion they exercise is in accordance with international law. So, perhaps there is a coercive global institutional system?

Many hold that, for there to be an institutional system that coerces (and bears responsibility for doing so), however, it must make sense to say there is a system that *can* coerce (and bear responsibility for doing so). There must be a collective agent of some sort. It is impossible to cash out or defend necessary and sufficient conditions for a group of institutions to act (coerce) and be held responsible here.[123] Nevertheless, it is possible to motivate the claim that the global institutional system can act and bear obligations.

Unlike states, the global institutional system is constituted by a dispersed network of international institutions with no analogue to a head of state. It lacks a single hierarchical structure of courts and administrative bodies with a clear separation of powers and adequate enforcement mechanisms.[124] It just consists of some relatively independent

---

[122] International Security Assistance Force, "About ISAF."

[123] For work on conceptions of agency, see: May, "Symposia Papers," 269–77; List and Koenig-Archibugi, "Can There Be a Global Demos?" 76–110; David Miller, *National Responsibility and Global Justice*; Feinberg, "Collective Responsibility," 674–88; Virginia Held, "Can a Random Collection of Individuals Be Morally Responsible?," 471–81. Also see: Kutz, *Complicity*. For an introduction to the literature, see: Risser, "Collective Responsibility"; Smiley, "Collective Responsibility"; Roth, "Shared Agency."

[124] See, for instance: Risse, "How Does the Global Order Harm the Poor?" 9–10.

institutions backed by a patchwork of poorly enforced international law.[125] Perhaps critics can object that parts of an institutional system act together and can be held responsible only when they have explicitly articulated agreements to do so. Perhaps parts of the global institutional system are like separate terrorist groups that just agree to coordinate some projects together and stay out of each other's way. Although their actions give rise to patterns of behavior, critics might maintain, they are completely separate institutions. It is not acceptable to hold some individual terrorist groups responsible for the actions of others without these agreements.

It is plausible, however, that loosely structured groups can be held liable for their actions and some even suggest that such groups are often morally responsible for what they do.[126] Some things that have almost no structure – like mobs or random collections of individuals (e.g. Nazi sympathizers) – can act and be held responsible.[127] So perhaps it is reasonable to ask whether *the global institutional system* is liable for what it does. Even if it is loosely structured, it forms a fundamental part of the normative and coercively enforced institutional backdrop against which persons interact. It seems acceptable to ask whether the rules of games played in the military, backed by coercive force, are legitimate. On analogy, perhaps it is acceptable to ask whether the global institutional system's components are organized consistently with the demands of the right – whether they are legitimate.[128]

---

[125] Nagel, "The Problem of Global Justice," 113–47.

[126] What conditions for collective agency are appropriate probably depend on the kind of responsibility at issue in the Autonomy Argument. It will suffice for this book's purposes if international institutions are (or the global institutional system is) liable for coercing people. So, one would not need to show that these institutions are (or this system is) morally responsible or at fault for anything. This suggests that strong conditions for action and responsibility, motivated by an analogy to what is necessary for individuals to be morally responsible, are inapplicable. For an individual to be at fault for something, it must be reasonable to expect that person to know what he or she has done. Similarly, many argue, groups of institutions must have adequate decision-making capabilities to be morally responsible. Individuals can be held liable for the fact that other people did things they could never have known about, however. Employers are often liable for their employees' misconduct, for instance, even if there is no way the employers could have known what their employees were doing. Similarly, adults are held liable for having sex with minors, even if they could not have known that their partners were underage. So, there is no reason to think the international institutions (or the global institutional system) must have adequate decision-making procedures to be held liable. Still, see: Freeman, *Justice and the Social Contract*. For further discussion of institutional agency see: Green, "Institutional Responsibility for Global Problems," 79–96. For more on collective responsibility, see: May, "Symposia Papers," 269–77.

[127] May and Hoffman, *Collective Responsibility*.

[128] I owe thanks to David Reidy for discussion here.

Moreover, there is some reason to believe that even those liberals who think some structure is necessary for group action and liability can accept the claim that the global institutional system is a collective agent.[129] To see this, it will help to consider some of the characteristic features of another (e.g. terrorist) network that few will deny has agency. Though, again, the following analogy is not intended to provide (never mind defend) a complete account of corporate agency.

Suppose, first, that a terrorist network's key cells were created at a single conference to pursue a common purpose – e.g. to institute a new Muslim state. Second, suppose that, although these cells' aims have evolved, and there is a division of labor between them, they still pursue common objectives. They may, for instance, try to institute Sharia law in the Muslim world instead of creating a new Muslim state. Third, suppose that individual cells often create new agreements, sometimes with new cells and sometimes with old cells, in pursuit of their common aims. Fourth, suppose that, although individual cells sometimes pursue different goals and fight with each other, they cooperate much of the time. Their commitment to cooperation is reiterated and extended in many places. Fifth, suppose that there are some formal methods for incorporating new cells into the network and shifting groups of cells reaffirm their commitment to cooperation in these subunits. Sixth, suppose cells use many of the same instruments (e.g. suicide bombing) to achieve shared aims and often measure their success in very similar ways; for example, many cells consider the number of mosques built or infidels killed as measures of success. Finally, suppose that parts of the network set up independent committees to coordinate action in pursuit of these aims when necessary. If one cell, or a small group of cells, captures Baghdad and enforces Sharia law in the city, few would object if the network said it had won a small victory. Moreover, those opposed to terrorism might, rightly, condemn the network.

The, first, corresponding feature of the global institutional system that might, arguably, give it agency is this: The basic structure of the global institutional system, now embodied in the UN, IMF, WB, and WTO, was created in 1944 at the Bretton Woods conference for a

---

[129] For work on conceptions of agency, see: May, "Symposia Papers," 269–77; List and Koenig-Archibugi, "Can There Be a Global Demos?" 76–110; David Miller, *National Responsibility and Global Justice*; Feinberg, "Collective Responsibility," 674–88; Virginia Held, "Can a Random Collection of Individuals Be Morally Responsible?," 471–81. Also see: Kutz, *Complicity*. For an introduction to the literature, see: Risser, "Collective Responsibility"; Smiley, "Collective Responsibility"; Roth, "Shared Agency."

common purpose – "to establish a framework for economic cooperation and development that would lead to a more stable and prosperous global economy."[130]

Second, although these institutions' mandates have evolved, and there is a division of labor between them, they still pursue common aims.[131] Talking just about the WB and IMF, the IMF website says, for instance:

The IMF and the World Bank are institutions in the United Nations system. They share the same goal of raising living standards in their member countries. Their approaches to this goal are complementary, with the IMF focusing on macroeconomic issues and the World Bank concentrating on long-term economic development and poverty reduction.[132]

In particular, they work together to reduce poverty and debt, and to promote financial stability and development. Similarly, talking about its relationship with the WTO, the IMF says:

The IMF and the WTO work together on many levels, with the aim of ensuring greater coherence in global economic policymaking. A cooperation agreement between the two organizations [and the WB], covering various aspects of their relationship, was signed shortly after the creation of the WTO ... The work of the IMF and the WTO is complementary. A sound international financial system is needed to support vibrant international trade, while smoothly flowing trade helps reduce the risk of payments imbalances and financial crisis. The two institutions work together to ensure a strong system of international trade and payments that is open to all countries. Such a system is critical for enabling economic growth, raising living standards, and reducing poverty around the globe.[133]

Towards this end, the IMF "participate[s] actively in meetings of certain WTO committees and working groups."[134] "The WTO Agreements require that it consult the IMF when it deals with issues concerning monetary reserves, balance of payments, and foreign exchange arrangements."[135]

Third, parts of the global institutional systems' commitment to cooperation is reiterated and extended in many places. "The WTO Secretariat has working relations with some 200 organizations from all around the

---

[130] IMF, "Factsheet: The IMF and World Bank." Also see Article 1 of: United Nations, "Conference at Bretton Woods."

[131] The Marrakesh Agreement establishing the WTO makes this clear: World Trade Organization, "Marrakesh Agreement Establishing the World Trade Organization." The commitment to cooperation is reiterated in many places: IMF, "Factsheet: The IMF and World Bank." Also see: World Trade Organization, "Heads of International Agencies Agree to Work Together." Finally, see: IMF, "Joint Statement."

[132] IMF, "Factsheet: The IMF and World Bank."

[133] Ibid.

[134] Ibid.   [135] Ibid.

world. The nature of the joint work can range from informal contacts and information sharing to joint projects and programmes."[136] Other key organizations in the global institutional system work with a similar number of other organizations in many other ways.[137]

Fourth, though some parts of the global institutional system, like corporations and states, pursue their own aims and sometimes come into conflict with each other, they cooperate with other parts of the global institutional system much of the time. Many corporations have signed on to the UN's global compact.[138] Many also enter into agreements with countries and international institutions, like the African Development Bank. When they are fulfilling their obligations under these agreements, they are acting as part of this system.[139] They often do things like build dams or take over the administration of public services. Almost every state is a member of the UN, WB, IMF, and WTO.[140] States' commitment to cooperation is continually reaffirmed and extended through these organizations and new treaties. They cooperate on everything from human rights to the use of the seas and outer space.

Fifth, new institutions are often incorporated into the global institutional system via Memorandums of Agreement and treaties. The WB, IMF, and UN Development Program have agreed to work together with many Regional Development Banks, for instance, to promote development and growth. States create new trade agreements all the time and these rules are integrated into the global trade regime. When necessary, the WTO's dispute resolution panel helps in the process.

Sixth, as suggested above, there is a division of labor amongst different organizations, they use many of the same instruments to promote many of the same aims, and they measure results in similar ways. The IMF's programs often focus on macroeconomic stability. The WB often focuses on poverty relief. They both use Poverty Reduction Strategy Papers drafted in consultation with governments to promote pro-poor growth. Such international development organizations, and many countries, also measure results in very similar ways. Many Regional Development Banks and

---

[136] World Trade Organization, "Intergovernmental Organizations Working with the WTO Secretariat."

[137] World Bank, "Partners."

[138] Kuper, "Redistributing Responsibilities: The UN Global Compact." United Nations, "Overview of the UN Global Compact."

[139] For some such requirements see, for instance: World Bank, "World Bank's Loans to Japan." Also see the discussion below.

[140] United Nations, "United Nations Member States." World Bank, "About Us." IMF, "About the IMF." World Trade Organization, "Members and Observers."

countries, including the UK and Canada, allocate aid using a version of the WB's Country Policy Institutional Assessment index, for instance.[141]

Finally, when necessary, parts of the global institutional system create formal mechanisms and councils that oversee and coordinate member institutions' actions. This helps ensure consistent international law and policy. The UN's chief executive committee reports bi-annually to the Economic and Social Council on collaboration between the UN and WTO, for instance.[142] The IMF and WB have a Joint Management Action Plan. "Under the plan, Fund and Bank country teams discuss their country-level work programs, which identify macro-critical sectoral issues, the division of labor, and the work needed from each institution in the coming year."[143] IMF and WB Governors meet once a year as part of the Development Committee. These organizations work together and with other parts of the global institutional system, like the UN Conference on Trade and Development and the UN Environment Program, "on trade and global environmental issues in addition to traditional development matters."[144]

In short, there is some reason to believe that the global institutional system has enough structure to qualify as a corporate agent. The analogy to the terrorist network above suggests that the global institutional system is much more than a conglomerate of independent institutions that have come to some agreements (e.g. not to violate each other's rules).[145] The global institutional system's key components were created at a single conference for a common purpose, its aims evolve over time, there is a division of labor amongst its parts, these parts create new agreements in pursuit of common aims, reaffirm their commitment to cooperation in subunits, set up independent committees to coordinate action when necessary, and use similar instruments to achieve and measure success in achieving shared aims.

The preceding argument at least shifts the burden of proof on to those who agree that the terrorist network can act and be held liable but think the global institutional system cannot. If the global institutional system

---

[141] Hassoun, "World Bank Rules for Aid Allocation."

[142] It has signed the "Arrangements for Effective Cooperation with other Intergovernmental Organizations-Relations Between the WTO and the United Nations," for instance. The UN's Chief Executive Board promotes coherence within the UN system and beyond. See: World Trade Organization, "Work With Other International Organizations."

[143] IMF, "Factsheet: The IMF and World Bank."

[144] Ibid.

[145] The global institutional system, like most corporations, sometimes violates its own rules.

satisfies all of the conditions above, critics must defend additional conditions for agency that only the terrorist network satisfies. This may be difficult as the global institutional system has more structure than the network. In any case, in the absence of this argument, it is plausible that the global institutional system is an agent of the relevant sort.

There are also a few other features of the global institutional system that the terrorist network may lack, that bolster the case for considering it a collective agent. First, the global institutional system is unified by shared norms. Second, it is deeply and extensively integrated. Consider each of these points in turn.

First, the global institutional system is unified by shared norms in H.L.A. Hart's sense. Parts of this system often take the rules of the system to provide reasons for their behavior.[146] They see these rules as providing norms that apply to them even when they have not explicitly agreed to work together. They do not see these rules as mere regularities; they take them as providing independent reasons for action.[147] "These normative attitudes … are expressed in their characteristic assertions when appealing to or enforcing the law, in their practices of blaming and criticizing, in the language and arguments of legislative proceedings and judicial decisions and so on."[148] The relevant norms are not, primarily, norms of convenience or self-interest. The reasons they provide are reasons for adherence even when adhering does not produce the outcome that parts of the global institutional system would prefer independently (e.g. as players in a non-cooperative game).[149] The relevant norms are based on shared aims and specify a division of labor for achieving these aims over time. They are shared governance norms that parts of the global institutional system see as *worth upholding*.[150]

---

[146] Hart, *The Concept of Law*. [147] Ibid.

[148] Cavellero, "Coercion, Inequality and the International Property Regime," 29. Parts of the global institutional system are like drivers who do not park their cars in the middle of the road because they do not want to provide an obstacle to others, not *just* because they want to keep their car intact.

[149] Cavellero, "Coercion, Inequality and the International Property Regime," 29. Cavellero does not seem to think that international law is like this. Arash Abizadeh argues convincingly, however, that coercion theorists cannot defend their view by denying this point. He says this would amount to hanging their argument on the claim that "'We not only coerce you, but we coerce you without subjecting our ongoing coercion to the constraints of a legal system and the rule of law, and therefore we have no responsibilities of comparative distributive justice to you.' The perversity of the argument is clear." Abizadeh, "Cooperation, Pervasive Impact, and Coercion," 351. Abizadeh focuses, however, on laws regulating immigration.

[150] Cavellero, "Coercion, Inequality and the International Property Regime," 29.

Primary amongst these norms is respect for the rules embodied in international treaties and customary law but also informal rules and processes. This is so for international judicial as well as political and economic institutions. Just as the Australian High Court takes the rulings of other Australian courts to have normative force (although Australia does not rely on a precedent system), international courts and appellate bodies take into consideration the rulings of other international courts and the body of international law. The Human Rights Committee in charge of monitoring the International Covenant on Civil and Political Rights will not even entertain individual complaints if another human rights court is examining them.[151]

Parts of the global institutional system also have competing norms and there may be points at which the relevant norms are simply undefined. Strong states often fail to follow international rules. States also interpret these rules in different ways or emphasize some rules more than others (it is interesting, for instance, to see how different states emphasize different human rights principles). Sometimes international rules are unclear or missing. There is also room for reasonable disagreement about the content of some such rules.

Still, I believe there are significant enough shared norms at the international level for it to make sense to talk about the shifting network of institutions abiding by these norms and their responsibilities. Even states like the USA, which sometimes claim to be exempt from international rules, often commit to acting in accordance with these rules in ways that cannot plausibly be construed as in their (pure) self-interest. These states also do a lot to uphold the general structure of international law. At least insofar as they do so, they are acting as part of this system.

The second (supplementary) reason to consider the global institutional system to be a collective agent is this: The global institutional system is deeply and extensively integrated. The Vienna Convention on the Law of Treaties is the foundation of most modern treaty law. It specifies that new treaties must be consistent with the existing body of treaty law. WTO rules must, for instance, take into account pre-existing treaty law including other trade agreements. The WTO must allow members of regional trade agreements, like NAFTA, to give each other special treatment. This is significant because, to do this, the WTO must amend one of its key

---

[151] See, for instance, the optional protocol signed by most states: Office of the United Nations High Commissioner for Human Rights, "Optional Protocol to the International Covenant on Civil and Political Rights."

principles – the most favored nation principle. Since regional agreements cover more than 50 percent of world trade, this requires the WTO to make a lot of exceptions to this principle.[152] Explicitly articulated agreements between parts of the global institutional system provide only part of the explanation for global integration. When states, like the USA, specify that international law is sovereign over state law, they deepen and extend integration within the global institutional system. (When they do so to insure coherence with international treaty law, they are also acting on shared norms.)

Some difficult questions remain, but this book will not continue with this dialectic. The aim of this section was only to make plausible the claim that there is a global institutional system that can qualify as an agent on some reasonable accounts. One need not be convinced by this section's argument to accept the Autonomy Argument's conclusion: Coercive international institutions have to ensure that their subjects secure what they need for sufficient autonomy.

2.7 CONCLUSION

Many people care about individual freedom. Some of those most concerned about this freedom (e.g. actual consent theorists) believe that rulers need not ensure that subjects secure sufficient autonomy because this requires some to sacrifice their freedom for others. Others deeply concerned about community (e.g. communitarians and statists) also reject the idea that all rulers have such significant obligations to their subjects.[153] They believe that few of our obligations extend beyond borders. Moreover, many people who do think there are obligations to the global poor believe these obligations are purely humanitarian. This chapter's argument addressed these people. The obligations of legitimacy it defended may entail, or provide an alternative to, obligations of justice like those Pogge and others defend. If this chapter's argument goes through, those who embrace its concern for liberal freedom should agree that coercive institutions have to do what they can to ensure that their subjects secure what they need for sufficient autonomy. To some, this chapter's argument may seem anemic because it does not appeal to the details of every competing position. But this argument is strong precisely because it only requires a

---

[152] World Trade Organization, "Regionalism: Friends or Rivals?"
[153] See: Blake, "Distributive Justice, State Coercion, and Autonomy." Also see: Richard Miller, "Cosmopolitan Respect and Patriotic Concern." Finally, see: Nagel, "The Problem of Global Justice."

very minimal commitment to individual freedom. Those who believe that rulers need not even protect individual's ability to reason and plan do not embrace the liberal commitment to freedom from which the Autonomy Argument starts; they may even be totalitarians.

The Autonomy Argument is also important because it shows that coercive institutions have some very significant obligations to the global poor. Our world is one in which many cannot secure sufficient autonomy because they lack access to minimally adequate food, water, shelter, medical care, and so forth. The second half of this book will argue that there are many things coercive international institutions can do to help these people. As Ghandi's Talisman suggests, there is reason to ensure that the poor can control their own lives and destinies, to secure "'swaraj' or self-rule for the hungry."[154]

---

[154] Pyarelal, *Mahatma Gandhi: The Last Phase*, 65.

CHAPTER 3

Libertarian obligations to the poor?

3.1 INTRODUCTION

The first chapter sketched an argument for an autonomy-based account of human rights on which people have a right to secure the food, water, shelter, education, health care, social support, and emotional goods they need for sufficient autonomy. The second chapter defended the Autonomy Argument for the conclusion that, to be legitimate, coercive institutions must do what they can to ensure that their subjects secure food, water, and whatever else they need for autonomy.[1] It derived the sub-conclusion that, to be legitimate, coercive institutions must ensure that their subjects secure sufficient autonomy from several different ways of understanding a basic commitment to individual freedom. Some, for instance (right-) libertarians and actual consent theorists, are likely to resist this conclusion.

This chapter takes libertarianism as the stalking horses for liberalism – providing the final philosophical lynchpin in this book's argument that liberals of many sorts should agree that there are significant obligations to the global poor. It does not do so primarily by arguing that libertarians must agree that coercive international institutions have such obligations. Nevertheless, this chapter argues that those who embrace even one of the most demanding and influential versions of libertarianism in the philosophical literature may be committed to some significant obligations to the global poor. This should be a striking conclusion as most libertarians notoriously reject positive social and economic rights. Those who already accept this conclusion, or do not think it is worth addressing libertarians, can simply skip this chapter. As noted in the Introduction to Part I, however, it is important to address skeptics about our obligations to the global

---

[1] As with autonomy, what is sufficient to ensure that people secure food, water, shelter, and so forth will vary, but the basic idea is that the only acceptable reason for a person not to actually secure what they need for sufficient autonomy is that they have chosen not to do so.

poor because doing so helps us get clearer on the proper scope of moral principles and their appropriate foundations.

Because this chapter presumes a commitment to some common (right-) libertarian propositions, it does not address every libertarian. The libertarians this chapter addresses (1) do not already accept its conclusions and (2) are not anarchists. They believe there should be some coercive institutions. They believe that there should be minimal states that exercise a monopoly on coercive force over their subjects and these states need not cede territory to any of those who cannot consent to the exercise of coercive force over them.[2] These libertarians (henceforth, simply, *libertarians*) also accept something like the following proposition: To be legitimate, an institution (or institutional system) can only exercise coercive force over rights-respecting individuals to protect the liberty of those individuals. This chapter provides reason to reject some formulations of this principle below. Since, however, this principle is only necessary to rule out versions of libertarianism on which it is more acceptable to coerce those who are only potentially capable of consent than it is to coerce others, there is no need to specify it precisely here.[3]

It is, of course, easy to imagine ways that this chapter's conclusion can conflict with other libertarian commitments. So, although it is framed as an argument for the conclusion that libertarians should endorse some significant obligations to the global poor, this chapter's import may really be to question the coherence of the libertarian view that denies this. Even if few libertarians, themselves, are convinced that their position is problematic, this chapter's argument should at least provide those who are not wedded to the view it confronts with good reasons for rejecting it.

In the past, others have questioned the coherence of libertarianism by arguing that libertarians have to endorse some significant obligations to the poor. James Sterba, for instance, claims that libertarians should

---

[2] This chapter will reserve the term *anarcho-capitalists* for anarchists who are only committed to libertarian rights in a state of nature. Unfortunately, I do not have the space to argue that libertarians should not be anarchists here. On this debate see: Long and Machan, *Anarchism/ Minarchism*.

[3] I deliberately leave this principle vague. I take it that most libertarians do not think it is acceptable to exercise coercive force over some individuals to protect others' liberty. Most libertarians accept a non-aggression principle on which each person should be free to do what they like as long as doing so is compatible with others having similar freedom. Some, however, might hold that we should just minimize rights violations. If what this chapter says below is correct, libertarians may have to accept something like the latter view. For now it is only important, however, to rule out the view that it is more acceptable to coerce those who are only potentially capable of consent for others' benefit than it is to coerce those who have sufficient autonomy for others' benefit.

accept this much.[4] He suggests that a minimal state, by enforcing property rights, prevents people from meeting their basic needs. Since individuals have a right to liberty, he says, there is a conflict of rights. The rich have a right to their property, the poor a right to take what they need from the rich. People must be able to do what morality requires (as the ought-implies-can principle directs). The rich can, but the poor cannot, refrain from exercising their rights. So, Sterba concludes, states must provide the poor with what they need if they are to be justified in protecting the property rights of the rich.[5] In *World Poverty and Human Rights* Pogge argues, similarly, that libertarians should embrace welfarism.[6] He suggests that those of us in the developed world are indirectly harming the poor, partly through our influence on international organizations like the WTO and IMF. He argues, for instance, that when they lend money to, and buy resources from, any individual or group that manages to gain control of a country, these institutions create incentives for coups and poor governance in developing countries.[7]

While there is almost certainly something to Sterba's and Pogge's conclusions, many reject their arguments. Many libertarians, following Machan, reject Sterba's claim that a minimal state, by enforcing property rights, prevents people from meeting their basic needs.[8] Other libertarians, following Douglas Rasmussen, seem to accept this point but reject Sterba's conclusion because they do not believe that a conflict of rights generates a duty on the part of the rich to aid the poor.[9] Furthermore, libertarians may deny that the poor have a right to take what they need from the rich. Similarly, Pogge's argument is controversial. Patten and Risse argue, for instance, that libertarians are likely to reject Pogge's baseline for harm. Patten and Risse suggest that, on the most plausible libertarian construals of this baseline, it is not at all clear that those of us in the developed world are harming the poor.[10]

This chapter avoids the problems with Sterba's and Pogge's arguments. It does not rely on there being a conflict of liberties or the ought-implies-can

[4] Sterba, *The Triumph of Practice Over Theory in Ethics*. Narveson and Sterba, *Are Liberty and Equality Compatible?*

[5] For Sterba's argument see: Sterba, *The Triumph of Practice Over Theory in Ethics*.

[6] Pogge, *World Poverty and Human Rights*.

[7] Also see: Pogge, "Eradicating Systemic Poverty," 59–77.

[8] Machan, "Sterba on Machan's 'Concession'," 241–3. Sterba, *The Triumph of Practice Over Theory in Ethics*.

[9] Sterba, "Progress in Reconciliation," 101–16. They might also reject the ought-implies-can principle. See, for instance: Kekes, "Ought Implies Can and Two Kinds of Morality," 459–67.

[10] Risse, "Do We Owe the Poor Assistance or Rectification?" 9–18. Patten, "Should We Stop Thinking about Poverty in Terms of Helping the Poor?" 19–27.

principle. Nor does it rely on the premise that those of us in the developed world are harming the global poor. Like the previous chapter, this chapter suggests that coercion alone generates an obligation to ensure that the coerced secure sufficient autonomy and hence food, water, shelter, and so forth. So, if this chapter's argument goes through, it may have some advantages over both Sterba's and Pogge's arguments.

More precisely, this chapter extends the previous chapter's argument to address libertarians, in particular. It suggests that there is a conditional remedial obligation to ensure that those subject to coercive rules secure sufficient autonomy. It derives this obligation from a plausible view about what free contracts require that even libertarians should accept. In doing so, it respects the distinction between autonomy, liberty, and freedom (it does not depend on libertarians embracing the value of autonomy). To distinguish this chapter's line of argument from the preceding chapter's, let us refer to it as the *Legitimacy Argument* in what follows. Again, it goes, roughly, like this:

(1) Coercive institutions must be legitimate.
(2) Roughly, for a coercive institution to be legitimate it must ensure that its subjects secure sufficient autonomy to autonomously consent to, or dissent from, its rules (henceforth *sufficient autonomy*).
(3) Everyone, to secure this autonomy, must secure some food and water, and most require some shelter, education, health care, social support, and emotional goods.
(4) There are many coercive international institutions.
(C) So, these institutions must (roughly) ensure that their subjects secure food, water, and whatever else they need for autonomy.

The second chapter defended the first and final premise of the Legitimacy Argument. It defended the first premise in a way intended to appeal to libertarians and many libertarians should also accept one strand of the second chapter's argument for the final premise of the Legitimacy Argument. So, although this chapter will say a bit more about why libertarians should accept the final premise of this argument at the end of Section 3.3, it will not belabor the point. After some preliminaries in Section 3.2, Section 3.3 lays the groundwork for the Legitimacy Argument by defending Simmons' claim that libertarians should be actual consent theorists. This chapter's main contribution comes in defense of the Legitimacy Argument's second premise. Section 3.4 defends this premise in two steps. First, it derives from actual consent theory the following claim: coercive institutions' rights-respecting subjects must secure sufficient autonomy to autonomously consent to their rules. In order to actually consent people must be able to do so. Next, it suggests that if rights-respecting subjects cannot secure sufficient autonomy on their own or with the help of friends or benefactors, the coercive institutions to which they are subject must ensure that they secure it. Given that these subjects must secure such autonomy, that is the only way these institutions can be legitimate. Because the first chapter defended the Legitimacy Argument's third premise, Section 3.5 concludes. In doing so, it considers some of the Legitimacy Argument's implications.

3.2 PRELIMINARIES

Like the previous chapter, this chapter will only assume that it is permissible for *legitimate* institutions to make coercive rules and give coercive commands. As Simmons suggests, many believe that if a coercive institution has a right to rule through force over its subjects, they are obligated to obey its dictates.[11] This chapter, like the previous one, will not require this much.

This chapter will work with a weak version of actual consent theory on which coercive institutions are legitimate *only if* they secure their *rights-respecting* subjects' autonomous consent. It will not assume that consent is a sufficient condition for legitimacy. More precisely, it will assume that coercive institutions must secure their rights-respecting subjects' autonomous consent if these subjects do not relinquish their right to consent and (at least with assistance) can secure the requisite autonomy. (On the most demanding account of actual consent theory, coercive institutions are legitimate if and only if they secure all of their subjects' autonomous consent.) Relying on the conditions for autonomy set out in previous chapters, it should be clear that autonomous consent requires some freedom and competence.[12]

A few of the qualifications implicit in this weak version of actual consent theory (henceforth simply *actual consent theory*) deserve comment. First, coercive institutions need only get the consent of individuals who respect others' rights. As noted in the preceding chapters, actual consent theorists may think that some acts are impermissible violations of individual liberty. Actual consent theorists may hold that such acts can be legitimately prevented by any person or institution even if prevention requires

[11] Simmons, "Consent Theory for Libertarians," 332. Also see: Beran, *The Consent Theory of Political Obligation*.
[12] Beran, *The Consent Theory of Political Obligation*, 6.

coercion. Perhaps, as John Simmons suggests, even "the Third Reich was justified in prohibiting rape and punishing rapists."[13]

Another qualification implicit in the weak version of actual consent theory is that coercive institutions need not secure the consent of people who could never secure the autonomy they need to consent under any implementable institution. Those in permanent comas, for instance, could never consent. Coercive institutions do not need to secure their consent. (Note: this is not because it is impossible to coerce such people. As the last chapter noted, *coercion* is being used to include the threat *or use* of force.)

Finally, legitimate coercive institutions may not need the consent of rights-respecting subjects, if they freely agree to relinquish their right to consent. It is not clear what, if any, obligations such institutions have to those who relinquish their right to consent. Whatever obligations coercive institutions have to these people, actual consent theorists need only agree to the following condition for legitimacy: coercive institutions require their rights-respecting subjects' consent until and unless these subjects freely relinquish their right to consent.

The basic intuition underlying actual consent theory is this: Just as the Sierra Club is justified in making people pay dues only if they have freely consented, coercive institutions are justified in exercising coercive force over their rights-respecting subjects only if their subjects have freely consented. Though there may be many answers to the following question, the intuition underlying actual consent theory gives it force: What gives any person or institution a right to coerce others without their consent?

Actual consent theory also has the advantage of being able to account for several key values in liberal theory including liberty and equality. As Allen Buchanan notes:

> The theory of consent flowered at a time when two key liberal notions were coming into their own: the idea that liberty is the proper condition of human beings and the idea of the fundamental moral equality of persons. If we are all equal, what can justify ... [a state] ... making, applying, and enforcing rules on us? How can the justified wielding of political power be squared with the fundamental equality of persons? And if liberty is our proper condition, how can the use of coercion ... be justified?[14]

One plausible answer to the first two questions about equality is that those who are coerced have freely consented to being coerced. The answer

---

[13] Simmons, "Justification and Legitimacy," 770.
[14] Buchanan, "Political Legitimacy and Democracy," 697–8.

to the last question about liberty is that "we best preserve our liberty by the free choice of consenting to a political power to enforce a regime of individual rights."[15] An institution is justified in exercising a coercive force over rights-respecting individuals, even for their own good, only if these individuals freely consent.

Perhaps, however, it is bad to rely on actual consent theory in trying to show that libertarians should accept some significant obligations to the global poor. Who cares, one might wonder, if libertarian actual consent theorists have to accept the Legitimacy Argument. Actual consent theories are implausible. Few who have considered consent theory have defended actual consent since John Locke. So why bother arguing, as this chapter does, that libertarian actual consent theorists must endorse some significant obligations to the global poor? Because this is a general objection to this chapter's argumentative strategy, it is worth considering it briefly here.

The most common objections to actual consent theory are these: If a coercive institution cannot secure the consent of its subjects because its subjects have irrational or nasty preferences, this does not undercut that institution's legitimacy. Alternately, if coercion is necessary to achieve a great good, it is justified.

These objections are compelling but libertarians should reject them. There is something plausible about the thought that a coercive institution can be legitimate if the only reason its subjects will not consent to its rule is that they have irrational or nasty preferences. Still, libertarians have reason to worry about this idea. It is not clear why, on a libertarian theory, coercive institutions should be able to coerce even the irrational, mean, or deluded as long as they are not violating others' rights. There is also something compelling about the idea that coercion is justified if it is necessary to achieve a great good. Nevertheless, few libertarians accept this premise, and the libertarians this chapter addresses deny that violating an individual's right to freedom can be justified whenever doing so achieves a greater good. They believe coercive institutions can only coerce rights-respecting people to protect their liberty. Furthermore, not only *are* some libertarians actual consent theorists but several authors have argued that libertarians of many stripes should be actual consent theorists.[16] Finally, this chapter's aim is not to defend actual consent theory. It just relies upon an argument to the effect that libertarians are committed

---

[15] Simmons, "Justification and Legitimacy," 770.
[16] Long and Machan, *Anarchism/Minarchism*.

to consent theory. So there is no immediate reason to reject this chapter's argumentative strategy.

The next section will argue that libertarians should be actual consent theorists. This chapter's main innovation and contribution comes in defense of the Legitimacy Argument's second premise (Section 3.4).

3.3 LAYING THE GROUNDWORK: WHY LIBERTARIANS SHOULD BE ACTUAL CONSENT THEORISTS

Several authors have argued that libertarians of many stripes should be actual consent theorists.[17] In his paper "Consent Theory for Libertarians," for instance, John Simmons gives a compelling version of this argument focusing on actual consent to states.[18] Simmons starts from the observation that libertarians generally do not discuss political legitimacy. He says that this is because doing so would expose a deep tension within libertarianism. Simmons suggests that there are two major strands in libertarian thought that lead naturally to two different, incompatible, accounts of legitimacy – consensualism and minimalism.[19] Because Simmons focuses on what could legitimate a state, in particular, this section will follow him in considering this question. It will then explain how accepting even these conditions for state legitimacy may be enough to establish obligations as extensive as those defended in the preceding chapters. Finally, it will consider how Simmons' argument might be extended. Simmons' argument entails that *all* coercive institutions must secure their rights-respecting subjects' consent. (At least his argument suggests consent is a requirement of legitimacy insofar as coercive institutions constrain rights-respecting individuals' ability to protect their rights.)

In their consensualist moments, libertarians advocate an almost unlimited right of contract. People, they insist, can freely agree to sell their labor and possessions or contract for protective services. Some libertarians even argue that people can legitimately contract into slavery.[20] Naturally, one would think, if people have an almost unlimited right of contract, they can autonomously consent to a state having a monopoly on the exercise of coercive force over them.[21] Further, since the contracts libertarians

---

[17] Ibid.
[18] He also argues that libertarians should agree that consent is necessary for justified authority.
[19] Simmons, "Consent Theory for Libertarians," 332.
[20] Nozick, *Anarchy, State, and Utopia*, 58; 283; 331.
[21] This can be weakened a bit to take into account the fact that states do not always succeed in exercising a monopoly on coercive force within their borders, but I set the relevant qualifications aside here. Presumably, coercive institutions must secure the consent of subjects in every generation.

defend are usually enforceable, if someone does autonomously consent to be ruled by a state, that state would usually be justified in forcing that individual to uphold his or her part of the contract. Subjects can legitimize almost any state by their free consent. In their minimalist moments, libertarians argue that only minimal states can be justified.[22] Minimal states only protect basic civil, political, and property rights.

The tension within libertarianism is this: If anything subjects freely consent to is legitimate, even non-minimal states can be legitimate. Subjects can legitimize non-minimal states by free consent. But if legitimate states must be minimal, non-minimal states cannot be legitimated even by free consent. To put the point another way, if libertarians embrace consensualism, people can legitimize almost anything by autonomously consenting to it. People can legitimize a non-minimal state by autonomously consenting to it (minimalism is false). But if libertarians embrace minimalism, they believe only minimal states can be legitimate. So people cannot legitimize a state that does more than (or fails to) protect basic civil, political, and property rights even by free consent (consensualism is false). Libertarians cannot embrace both consensualism and minimalism.

One might initially think that libertarians would want to deny consensualism rather than minimalism. After all, the paradigmatic libertarian Robert Nozick denies consensualism. He says independents can be forced to give up their right to self-defense without consent.

Simmons argues, however, that libertarians should accept consensualism and reject minimalism instead. He thinks Nozick is wrong to allow independents' rights to be abridged without consent. As Simmons puts it, "the 'principle of compensation' by which Nozick attempts to justify this final move is probably the *least* libertarian-looking component of … [Nozick's] … entire book (as well as one of the least independently plausible basic principles defended in Part I)."[23] At least if independents use safe methods of rights-enforcement their rights cannot be abridged without consent. After all, Nozick says that protective agencies of all sizes and unaffiliated individuals are "on a par in the nature of their rights to enforce other rights."[24] Simmons thinks Nozick really only defends the state's monopoly on the use of coercive force with a "very hesitant and enormously ad hoc speculation that perhaps the right to punish is 'the only [natural] right' that is possessed not individually, but jointly."[25] This

[22] Boaz, *Libertarianism: A Primer*, 127.
[23] Simmons, "Consent Theory for Libertarians," 335.
[24] Nozick, *Anarchy, State, and Utopia*, 134.
[25] Simmons, "Consent Theory for Libertarians," 338.

would mean that the state (because of its clients' free consent) would end up (by definition) having a bigger *part* of this collectively held right than its competitors. "Since Nozick himself can barely advance the argument with a straight face, we can ... safely disregard it."[26] Simmons concludes that libertarians should give up their minimalism. Libertarians should be actual consent theorists.

Perhaps libertarians could argue that only hypothetical consent is necessary for legitimacy as long as people have a formal right to exit from their states. At least when someone is unable to actually consent, their hypothetical consent may suffice to legitimize a state. If someone in a coma needs surgery it may be acceptable to operate as long as the person would consent, if able. Similarly, we do not ask children to consent to essential medical procedures. We think they would agree were they able.

These are dangerous counterfactuals that libertarians, because they are deeply committed to individual liberty, should be reluctant to accept. Just as Nozick says it does not matter how a distribution *could* have arisen, it matters how it *does* arise, libertarians should say it does not matter whether one *would* give up one's rights, it matters whether one *does* give them up. Libertarians should deny that merely maintaining for people a right to exit from a reasonable regime will do.[27] States must secure the consent of their rights-respecting subjects. (Again, states need not secure the consent of those who are incapable of securing basic capabilities because, for instance, they are too young or are in permanent comas.)

If this argument is right, it is easy to argue that libertarians should agree that *all* coercive institutions must secure their rights-respecting subjects' autonomous consent to be legitimate – that libertarians should be actual consent theorists. States' monopoly on coercive force must be justified via consent on a libertarian theory. That, however, is only because constraints on individuals' ability to protect their rights must be justified. Recall, however, that the previous chapter argued that coercion constrains individuals' natural right to freedom. So, there is a similar argument for the conclusion that all coercive institutions must secure their rights-respecting subjects' autonomous consent to be legitimate. This is particularly clear if coercion violates other rights as well. Even when coercion

---

[26] Ibid.

[27] Although libertarians may deny this, if the exit must be more than merely formal, people will probably have to secure sufficient autonomy to be free to leave.

does not violate other rights, however, libertarians should agree that it requires consent because it violates individuals' rights to liberty.

It is, however, an open question whether particular libertarians will think there are any coercive international institutions (that violate rights). Libertarians, like other liberals, may hold different accounts of coercion.

The previous chapter provided a few examples of how international institutions threaten to violate individuals' (if not countries') rights. Consider, here, a few more examples. On libertarian theories, individuals, if not countries, have a right to trade freely. Even if countries (like Singapore and Hong Kong) are not coerced into accepting trade agreements like "the Multi-Fibre Agreement, which regulates the international textile industry and prevents Singapore and Hong Kong and Taiwan from flooding the United States with their products,"[28] individuals in these countries are prohibited from selling their goods to willing buyers in the USA.

Countries' rights to punish are also violated by trade agreements. All existing trade agreements sanction some restrictions on trade. WTO member countries only have to reduce their tariffs to some set level – their "bound rate." So, the WTO prohibits other countries from punishing these countries for prohibiting free trade with tariffs at their bound rates.[29] Further, regional trade agreements allow countries to violate the WTO's most favored nation principle. So, they keep countries from having to liberalize. The WTO prohibits punishing these countries for violating individuals' rights to trade freely.

Some libertarians also accept less demanding accounts of coercion. Nozick, for instance, gave a two-pronged account of coercion. He held that some coercion is just backed by threats to make some less well off than they could otherwise (reasonably) expect to be.[30]

If coercion need only be backed by a threat to make some less well off than they could otherwise (reasonably) expect to be, there is a lot of international coercion. States are coerced into abiding by WTO rules, for example. Even if states are violating rules they agreed to, they are worse off than they can (reasonably) expect to be in the absence of the resulting

---

[28] Farer, "Political and Economic Coercion in Contemporary International Law," 406. US citizens' rights might also be violated (by their own government) if they are prohibited from trading with willing partners in Hong Kong and Taiwan except in prescribed ways. These prohibitions will all involve coercion of one kind or another.

[29] In doing so, it also violates the rights of people to have their countries protect their rights on some theories. When countries are prohibited from doing what their citizens have a right that they do, there is also a sense in which individuals are sanctioned.

[30] At least this is one way of interpreting Nozick's non-moralized baseline for coercive threats: Nozick, "Coercion."

[handwritten margin note: threatened w/ sanctions]

sanctions. Similarly, states are usually coerced into abiding by WB and IMF rules on this account. These states are threatened with sanctions – like bad credit reports and reduced access to funds in the future – if they do not follow these rules.

Some libertarians also appear sympathetic to an account of coercion on which coercion creates conditions under which the coerced have no good options but to abide by the coercer's rules.[31] It may be that individuals' property rights are undermined by the resource or borrowing privileges international institutions grant anyone who has de facto control over territory. These privileges have led terribly bad dictators to take power in poor countries – contributing to their dire situations.[32] If such policies must be justified by consent, the Legitimacy Argument should go through.

Whether or not libertarians agree that many international institutions are coercive, however, libertarians should agree that there are significant obligations to the poor. One way of arguing for this conclusion is to show that, whether or not many international institutions are coercive, they constrain rights-respecting people's ability to protect their rights and so require their rights-respecting subjects' autonomous consent.

It seems that libertarians must agree, for instance, that when international organizations control territory via the exercise of military force, they constrain rights-respecting individuals' ability to protect their own rights. The previous chapter suggested that international institutions like the UN, EU, and NATO constrain individuals' ability to protect their rights in this way.[33] There are many constraints on what people are permitted to do to protect their rights in safe zones, for instance. International organizations do not

---

[31] Cato Unbound. "Can the Resource Curse Be Lifted?" On this account of coercion, see: McGregor, "Bargaining Advantages and Coercion in the Market," 23–50; Virginia Held, "Coercion and Coercive Offers"; Van De Veer, "Coercion, Seduction, and Rights," 374–81.

[32] Pogge, *World Poverty and Human Rights. Wenor, Property Rights and the Resource Curse.*

[33] One might argue that other coercive institutions also constrain some individuals' ability to exercise their rights. Consider, for instance, WTO rules prohibiting tariffs. What libertarians should say about these rules depends on what kind of tariffs the WTO prohibits. Consider three kinds of tariffs. First, a tariff may (only) violate others' rights to do as they like with (e.g. trade) their justly acquired holdings. Second, a tariff may protect rights or compensate for rights violations without violating others' rights to do as they like with their justly acquired holdings. The tariff might, for instance, be an effective way to compensate those who have been unjustly deprived of their holdings. Finally, a tariff may fail to protect or compensate for rights violations without violating others' rights to do as they like with their justly acquired holdings. Prohibiting the second kind of tariff without consent is a rights violation (anyone including the most unjust coercive institution has a right to punish rights violations). Libertarians might also agree that prohibiting the last kind of tariff constrains individuals' ability to exercise their rights. For these prohibitions may violate states' rights to do as they like as long as they do not violate others' rights (which by hypothesis they are not doing). Only the first kind of tariff can be legitimately prohibited by the WTO. It is, of course, an empirical question how many of the

only prevent rights violations. They sometimes stop people from bringing weapons into safe zones to protect their own rights, for instance, even when they pose no unjustifiable risk to others. From a libertarian perspective, this matters even when it does not result in a massacre.[34] At least insofar as international institutions constrain rights-respecting people's ability to protect their rights in such ways, libertarians should agree that these institutions must secure these subjects' autonomous consent.

It is not even necessary, however, for libertarians to agree that international institutions must secure individuals' autonomous consent to conclude that they are committed to some significant obligations to the poor. Libertarians must agree that states must secure their rights-respecting subjects' autonomous consent to be legitimate. So, if the rest of this chapter's argument goes through, libertarians will have to agree that there are significant obligations to the poor. Almost everyone is subject to a state. The rest of this chapter will argue that securing subjects' autonomous consent requires ensuring that they secure sufficient autonomy.

3.4 THE LEGITIMACY ARGUMENT'S SECOND PREMISE

Assuming, then, that libertarians should accept actual consent theory, this section will defend the Legitimacy Argument's second premise: Roughly, to secure consent, coercive institutions must do what they can to ensure that their rights-respecting subjects secure sufficient autonomy. Previous chapters discussed many of this premise's components (see Chapter 1, Section 1.2 and Chapter 2, Section 2.3). People are *subject* to coercive institutions when the rules of these institutions apply to them. Even children and the severely mentally ill can be subject to institutions' rules, though the second premise does not say these institutions are obligated to ensure that all of these people secure basic capacities. Coercive institutions do not lose legitimacy if they do not ensure that their rights-respecting subjects secure sufficient autonomy if these subjects cannot secure sufficient autonomy under any implementable institution.[35] To *ensure* that

WTO's rules are legitimate, but there is reason to worry that many WTO rules violate some rights. Libertarians should agree that there is a lot of unjustly held property and some tariffs compensate those whose rights have been unjustly violated. I owe thanks to Peter Stone for discussion.

[34] United Nations, "Report of the Secretary-General Pursuant to General Assembly Resolution 53/35."

[35] Presumably some ways of securing autonomous consent (e.g. coercing third parties) will be ruled out by other conditions for legitimacy actual consent theorists endorse. Still, it follows from

someone secure sufficient autonomy, coercive institutions must do whatever is necessary for their rights-respecting subjects to become and remain autonomous until, and unless, they autonomously relinquish their ability to do so. What is necessary to ensure that subjects secure sufficient autonomy will vary with the case. Sometimes coercive institutions do not need to do anything to ensure that subjects secure sufficient autonomy. Sometimes, however, coercive institutions' rights-respecting subjects cannot secure autonomy without a lot of assistance from these institutions. In such cases, these institutions may have to do a lot. For it to be possible to ensure that rights-respecting subjects secure sufficient autonomy, there must be some implementable institutional set-up that could ensure that these people secure this autonomy. If there is, and the institutions to which these people are subject continue to coerce them, these institutions must do whatever is necessary to ensure that these people secure this autonomy.

The only component of the second premise that deserves further comment is what *sufficient autonomy* requires. Recall that subjects must secure whatever kind and amount of autonomy is sufficient for them to autonomously consent to their coercive institution(s).[36] Like other theorists, different actual consent theorists will have different views on what this requires. Fortunately, most should agree that subjects require the reasoning and planning abilities sketched in the first chapter.[37] Recall that the conception of autonomy cashed out in the first chapter is *minimal*. It is not Kantian. Nor is it a conception of autonomy on which people must be unique self-creators. People need not even live particularly unified lives to have this kind of autonomy. They can choose to become monks or ascetics or follow other hierarchical social orders.

---

actual consent theory and the nature of coercive institutions etc. that full legitimacy requires coercive institutions to do whatever they can to ensure that their subjects autonomously consent to their rule. See discussion that follows.

[36] Autonomy probably comes in degrees. One must secure whatever amount of reasoning and planning ability one needs to autonomously consent to a coercive institution. To make this idea precise, however, we might draw a threshold on the autonomy using the notion of competence. For some relevant work, see: Buchanan and Brock, *Deciding for Others*. Although one need not be perfectly rational to be competent, adaptive preferences might, for instance, undermine competency. See discussion in Chapter 1.

[37] Joseph Raz considers harder questions about what autonomy requires in *The Morality of Freedom*. He considers the case of a man trapped in a pit with enough food and water to survive. The man is precluded from doing anything besides choosing when to meet his basic needs. It would be reasonable to think that with such constrained options such a person is not autonomous, but even this much is not required for the Legitimacy Argument to succeed. See: Raz, *The Morality of Freedom*. See discussion in Chapter 1.

The conception of autonomy at issue does not even require that people have good options from which to choose. Some actual consent theorists will agree that contracts are not free unless the alternatives to contracting are decent.[38] Many libertarian actual consent theorists would probably deny this. Some libertarians hold that people can freely contract into slavery.[39] Even these people should agree, however, that individuals must have the minimal components of autonomy cashed out in the first chapter to enter into such contracts.

It should be enough for this chapter's purposes if libertarians agree that people must be able to do some instrumental reasoning and carry out some of their plans to have the relevant components of autonomy. They need only hold that those whose minds are so clouded that they are incompetent or incoherent, or who are enslaved or jailed, lack this kind of autonomy. (To consent to be subject to coercive institutions, people probably also require the ability to process at least some information.) Because the conception of autonomy at issue is so minimal, few should reject the idea that people need this much to autonomously agree to be subject to coercive institutions.

The first claim embodied in the above condition for legitimacy follows quickly. Insofar as possible, rights-respecting subjects must secure sufficient autonomy to consent to their coercive institution(s)' rule for their institution(s) to be legitimate. For recall that, on actual consent theory, coercive institutions are *legitimate* only if they secure their rights-respecting subjects' autonomous consent. The reason libertarian actual consent theorists have to accept the first claim embodied in the above condition for legitimacy is this.[40] *In order for someone to actually autonomously consent to a coercive institution that person must be able to do so.* Libertarian actual consent theorists believe that rights-respecting subjects must actually freely consent to their coercive institution(s) for their institution(s) to be legitimate. So, these libertarians should agree that, insofar as possible, these subjects must secure sufficient autonomy to consent to their coercive institution(s)' rule.

To put the point another way, this claim follows from the idea that legitimate coercive institutions must have their subjects' autonomous consent to be legitimate: For coercive institutions to be legitimate they must either (1) stop coercing people or (2) ensure that their rights-respecting

---

[38] Beran, *The Consent Theory of Political Obligation.*

[39] Nozick, *Anarchy, State, and Utopia.*

[40] Recall that saying coercive institutions should be as legitimate as possible is saying that they should be made to pass a threshold on legitimacy – the highest feasible threshold.

subjects secure sufficient autonomy (assuming no one else is doing so). Because coercive institutions are *coercive* institutions, they will not (1) stop coercing their subjects. So, (2) they must ensure that their rights-respecting subjects secure sufficient autonomy.

Libertarians might suggest that the preceding argument just points to a problem with the formulation of actual consent theory set out above. They might argue that it is okay to coerce the merely potentially autonomous in ways that do not protect their autonomy but that are respectful and advance the common good. These libertarians might maintain that this is legitimate since the potentially autonomous lack a natural right to freedom.

Recall, however, that the libertarians this chapter addresses hold something like the following principle: To be legitimate, coercive institutions can only exercise coercive force over rights-respecting individuals (autonomous or not) to protect the liberty of those individuals. Even if these libertarians do not want to say there is a positive duty to ensure that the merely potentially autonomous secure autonomy, they cannot say it is acceptable to coerce potentially autonomous people merely for others' benefit as long as these people respect others' rights. The view that coercive institutions can coerce the potentially autonomous just to benefit others is radically unintuitive. Such institutions do not have license to, for instance, coerce children just to benefit society.

Perhaps libertarians could posit the following counter-example to the claim that it is unacceptable to coerce the merely potentially autonomous except to protect their liberty. Suppose that a society contained only one potentially autonomous person. If everyone else in that society gave up their right to self-defense to a large security agency, this agency could legitimately protect everyone against this person.[41]

Anyone or institution, including a large security agency, can defend people against (even innocent) threats. Some potentially autonomous people – e.g. violent schizophrenics – pose a significant (if innocent) threat to others. Still, rights-respecting people, autonomous or not, retain their rights. Even if I am currently incapable of using my property, others are not justified in taking it away from me. Similarly, the fact that some potentially autonomous people cannot use their rights to protect themselves does not justify others in usurping or violating these rights. Further, it is important not to overlook the fact that some potentially autonomous people are rights-respecting and can protect themselves. So the fact that

---

[41] I owe thanks to David Boonin for suggesting this counter-example.

the dominant security agency could legitimately protect everyone against a potentially autonomous person violating others' rights does not show that this agency has a monopoly on coercive force. As long as potentially autonomous people respect others' rights and do not give up their right to protect their own rights, they retain these rights.[42]

At least, the Legitimacy Argument addresses those libertarians who accept the formulation of actual consent theory set out above; coercive institutions are legitimate only if they secure their rights-respecting subjects' autonomous consent. These libertarians should agree that legitimate coercive institutions' subjects must, insofar as possible, secure sufficient autonomy. This much is necessary for autonomous consent.

This chapter must say more to convince libertarians that coercive institutions must do what they can to ensure that their rights-respecting subjects secure sufficient autonomy. Consider an argument for this conclusion. When coercive institutions subject rights-respecting people who cannot secure sufficient autonomy to coercive rules and do not do whatever is possible to ensure that these people secure sufficient autonomy, they act wrongly. This is because such institutions are not justified in exercising coercive force over rights-respecting people who cannot secure sufficient autonomy. *If coercive institutions continue to exercise coercive force over rights-respecting people, legitimacy requires that they do whatever they can to ensure that these subjects secure sufficient autonomy.* Insofar as coercive institutions continue to coerce their rights-respecting subjects, they are obligated to do what they can to ensure that these people secure sufficient autonomy.

Libertarians might object that coercive institutions that subject rights-respecting people to coercive rules, even wrongly, do not thereby acquire an obligation to do what they can to ensure that these people secure sufficient autonomy. Recall the Alea analogy. The fact that Alea, who is not capable of autonomous consent, agrees to give me a large sum of money does not imply that I have a duty to do what I can to ensure that Alea secures sufficient autonomy. I merely fail to have a contract with her.

---

[42] There may be an argument that can convince even libertarians who think it is acceptable to coerce (rights-respecting) potentially autonomous people for others' benefit that coercive institutions are obligated to help some of these people secure autonomy. If these libertarians are very committed to having a state which literally operates a monopoly on coercive force over everyone, the state may have to help the temporarily non-autonomous who would attain autonomy at some time but would do so sooner with the state's assistance to attain autonomy as soon as they can. Otherwise, the state will illegitimately coerce these people at the moment when they attain autonomy naturally (i.e. without the state's help). This chapter will not explore this possibility, however. I owe thanks to Michael Otsuka for discussion of this point.

(I would act wrongly if I tried to enforce the agreement on Alea without securing her autonomous consent.) Similarly, libertarians might try to deny the legitimacy of actual coercive institutions but maintain that coercive institutions that only enforced the rights of those who actually autonomously consent could be legitimate. Such security agencies would not need to ensure that anyone consents. Perhaps the fact that legitimate coercive institutions must secure all of their rights-respecting subjects' autonomous consent just shows that they should not coerce anyone who does not consent. Rather, libertarians might point out, coercive institutions can enforce the rights of those who actually autonomously consent to their rule. They just cannot enforce the rights of those who do not autonomously consent.

This objection fails to appreciate one of two things. First, it may wrongly presuppose that the libertarians this chapter addresses can deny the legitimacy of all coercive institutions. They cannot. Recall that the libertarians this chapter addresses are not anarchists. They cannot say that, in fact, there should not be coercive institutions. Nor can they say coercive institutions are unjustifiable, in principle. They are at least committed to the idea that there should be (minimal) states.

Alternately, the objection may fail to appreciate the nature of coercive institutions in a different sense. These institutions do not acquire an obligation to do what they can to ensure that their rights-respecting subjects secure sufficient autonomy by subjecting them to coercive rules. Nevertheless, in the actual world, they are obligated to do what they can to ensure that these subjects secure sufficient autonomy. This is because coercive institutions continue to coerce people who have not consented to their rules. So, they can be legitimate *only if* they do what they can to ensure that their rights-respecting subjects secure sufficient autonomy. Insofar as these institutions continue to exercise coercive force, they must ensure that their rights-respecting subjects secure sufficient autonomy. The obligation for coercive institutions to do what they can to ensure that these subjects secure sufficient autonomy is a remedial obligation; there would be no such obligation were coercive institutions to cease exercising coercive force. Still, coercive institutions do continue to exercise coercive force. To be legitimate, they must, thus, do what they can to ensure that their rights-respecting subjects secure sufficient autonomy.

As the previous chapter notes, others may have primary responsibility for ensuring that people who cannot secure sufficient autonomy on their own secure this autonomy. Ensuring is like being a lender of last resort. Coercive institutions must step into the breach if help is required. It is only if they do this that all of their rights-respecting subjects will secure sufficient autonomy.

The second premise of the Legitimacy Argument implies that coercive institutions can be obligated to fix problems they did not create. A coercive institution may not be responsible for the fact that some people do not secure sufficient autonomy. Brain cancer, for instance, can undermine individuals' autonomy even if coercive institutions make their rights-respecting subjects more autonomous than they would otherwise be. Coercive institutions are not responsible for the fact that some of their rights-respecting subjects lack sufficient autonomy. Nevertheless, they are responsible for coercing these people. It is the fact that these institutions continue to coerce their rights-respecting subjects that generates the remedial obligation to ensure that these people secure the autonomy they need to consent.

Perhaps libertarians can object that the second premise of the Legitimacy Argument overlooks the distinction between autonomy and liberty. Libertarians only believe coercive institutions have an obligation to respect individuals' liberty. They do not believe these institutions must help their subjects secure any autonomy at all.

The second premise of the Legitimacy Argument follows from the claim that libertarians should be actual consent theorists, some observations about the nature of coercive institutions, and so forth. This chapter began with Simmons' argument that legitimate institutions must secure their rights-respecting subjects' autonomous consent. For people to consent they must be able to do so. If coercive institutions continue to coerce their rights-respecting subjects without securing their consent, they act illegitimately. Coercive institutions continue to coerce their rights-respecting subjects. If no one else is enabling these subjects to secure sufficient autonomy and these people cannot secure this autonomy on their own, these institutions must help them do so. That is the only way for these institutions to be legitimate. This may require coercive institutions to help these people secure this autonomy, not merely to refrain from interfering with their liberty. The argument so far is interesting for this reason; it entails that libertarians must agree that coercive institutions have positive obligations to their rights-respecting subjects. If it is correct, libertarians (surprisingly!) must agree that these institutions have to help rights-respecting subjects who would otherwise fail to secure sufficient autonomy.[43]

---

[43] Libertarians who grant that international institutions constrain individuals' ability to exercise their rights might argue that this is legitimate. They could suggest that, if states are legitimate, and international organizations have states' consent, these institutions are legitimate. If the above argument is right, however, it shows that most, if not all, states are illegitimate. Furthermore,

Libertarians might, instead, try to reject actual consent theory. They might argue that, if consent is necessary to avoid violating individuals' rights, actual consent theory cannot be qualified in the way this chapter suggested it should be. Every rights-respecting subject's actual consent is required, even if that person could not consent under any implementable institutional set-up. It is clearly impossible to secure this consent. Since ought-implies-can, libertarians might argue that we should reject actual consent theory.

I do not think this argument is consistent with libertarians' (foundational) commitment to basic rights. All coercive institutions have to fulfill the necessary condition for legitimacy this chapter has defended. Libertarians do not think it is acceptable to violate anyone's rights and they will violate each rights-respecting person's rights unless that person consents. So, even if they cannot secure the consent of some of the people they coerce, they must secure the remaining rights-respecting people's consent for it to be legitimate for them to coerce these people. Perhaps libertarians could argue that there is no obligation to ensure that a person has the autonomy to consent if that person would not do so. Nevertheless, they will have to grant that there are significant obligations to rights-respecting merely potentially autonomous people. We do not know who would consent were they able. So, if there are some legitimate ways of ensuring that *some* of these people secure the autonomy they need to consent, the coercive institutions to which they are subject must ensure that these people secure this autonomy. (This highlights the more general point that, at least on some liberal theories of legitimacy, the necessary conditions for legitimacy must be met even if full legitimacy is impossible.)

Some libertarians might prefer to accept anarchy than minimal obligations to the global poor.[44] While this chapter has offered some

---

it is not clear that even legitimate states could transfer their right to use coercive force to transnational organizations without their rights-respecting subjects' consent. Besides, if international institutions did secure all states' consent and all states were legitimate, every state would have ensured its rights-respecting subjects to secure food, water, and so forth. So, by the definition of ensuring, international institutions would have ensured that their rights-respecting subjects secured these things. See discussion in previous chapter.

[44] Libertarians might feel forced to accept anarchy if they think coercion without consent is unjustifiable and consent is impossible. They might try to argue that, even if states provide people with the conditions for autonomy they cannot secure their subjects' consent. Recall, however, that we are only considering obligations to those who could consent to some implementable institution. Simmons, "Justification and Legitimacy."

considerations that tell against anarchism, it has not provided definitive reason to reject the view. Most moderate libertarians, however, should accept some minimal obligations to the global poor rather than anarchy. This chapter merely tried to extend the consensus on these obligations.[45] Even if this chapter fails in its primary objective and convinces *all* libertarians to become anarchists, however, it will have eliminated one of the main philosophical positions in the literature on global justice.

3.5 CONCLUSION

This chapter has argued that libertarians should agree that coercive institutions have to do what they can to ensure that their rights-respecting subjects secure sufficient autonomy. The conclusion of the Legitimacy Argument follows. For the first chapter defended this argument's third premise. That chapter argued that, to secure sufficient autonomy, everyone must secure some food and water, and most require some shelter, education, health care, social support, and emotional goods. Libertarians should agree that coercive institutions have to do what they can to ensure that their subjects secure food, water, and whatever else they need for autonomy (as long as these people respect others' rights).

Perhaps libertarians can argue that this chapter's conclusion is of little practical significance. Nothing in this chapter requires any particular way of ensuring that people can secure food, water, shelter, and so forth (charity might suffice). If charitable donations, for instance, literally ensure that all rights-respecting people subject to coercive rules secure sufficient autonomy, this chapter's point might be merely theoretical. It would show that libertarians and actual consent theorists are committed to establishing welfare programs if necessary but, in fact, no such programs would be required.

Still, given some minimal empirical assumptions, the fact that libertarians and actual consent theorists should endorse any kind of obligations to the poor is as significant as it is shocking. After all, millions of people lose autonomy every year because they suffer from easily preventable

---

[45] Many libertarians would prefer to avoid anarchism as evidenced by their extensive arguments against the view: Long and Machan, *Anarchism/Minarchism*.

poverty-related illnesses.[46] Hundreds of thousands suffer but do not die from autonomy-undermining diseases like malaria.[47] Furthermore, the second half of this book will consider some empirical evidence that will support the claim that there are *some things* coercive institutions could do to ensure that more of their rights-respecting subjects secure this autonomy. Many people who do not live autonomous lives could do so if their coercive institutions helped them secure basic food, water, shelter, medical care and so forth.[48]

Before moving on, however, it is worth being very clear about what the Legitimacy Argument does and does not do. The obligations to the poor it suggests libertarians and actual consent theorists should accept will only be as robust as the conception of autonomy that they endorse. If they only accept the minimal conception of autonomy relied upon here, the obligations to the poor they should endorse will be very minimal indeed. Libertarians and actual consent theorists might only agree that coercive institutions have to ensure that their rights-respecting subjects *can* maintain autonomy. They might deny that coercive institutions must ensure that their rights-respecting subjects actually maintain their autonomy (for these subjects may give up their right to do so). Libertarians and actual consent theorists might even deny that coercive institutions must ensure that their rights-respecting subjects survive diseases that do not threaten subjects' autonomy. They might argue that coercive institutions can fulfill their obligations by leaving open to their subjects only one treacherous route to autonomy.

The obligations libertarians should accept will also be as radical as the non-aggression and actual consent principles libertarians adopt. If coercive institutions must literally avoid coercing all rights-respecting individuals without their consent, such institutions must literally do all they can to ensure that their rights-respecting subjects secure sufficient autonomy. Coercive institutions will have to provide extremely expensive health care for those who cannot otherwise secure this care but need it to secure

---

[46] World Health Organization, *World Health Report 2004*.

[47] World Health Organization, "Malaria is Alive and Well."

[48] Many who are not poor also suffer from autonomy-undermining disabilities. Although it is probably impossible for a coercive institution to be fully legitimate and ensure that all those who can secure sufficient autonomy do so, coercive institutions can be more or less legitimate. They may not, however, need to prevent people from participating in all risky activities. There may be other reasons to allow people to take on some risks (e.g. they have autonomously chosen to do so).

autonomy. They must, normally, ensure that even completely irresponsible free-riders secure sufficient autonomy unless and until these people freely consent or give up their right to do so. If rights-respecting free-riders never freely consent or relinquish their right to do so, their coercive institutions must ensure that they secure autonomy throughout their lives. Paradoxically, the libertarian commitments this chapter has relied upon may entail that coercive institutions have to violate rights to ensure that some of their rights-respecting subjects secure sufficient autonomy. It may just turn out, for instance, that the only way to secure the necessary resources is via illegitimate coercive taxation or, worse yet, terrible violence.

This last point exposes another potential problem for libertarians. If (1) ensuring that rights-respecting subjects can secure sufficient autonomy requires coercing others and (2) libertarians will not accept trade-offs between meeting different conditions for legitimacy, the libertarians' position may be incoherent. If ensuring that rights-respecting subjects can secure sufficient autonomy requires illegitimately coercing others, libertarians should at least reject some versions of the libertarian principle with which this chapter started. They cannot maintain that, to be legitimate, coercive institutions can only exercise coercive force over a rights-respecting individual to protect *that individual's* liberty. (Though they can accept something similar that allows coercive institutions to coerce some to protect others' liberty.) If ensuring that rights-respecting subjects can secure sufficient autonomy requires coercing others, libertarians must also decide how to resolve conflicts between mutually incompatible conditions for legitimacy. This may require them to abandon an absolute conception of rights and contend with Sterba's argument, for instance.

Assuming that there is some way to rescue libertarianism from incoherence, however, this chapter's conclusion follows: Libertarians, because they should be actual consent theorists, should endorse some obligations to the poor. This chapter suggested that, contrary to popular belief, libertarians should agree to the following claim: Coercive institutions must do what they can to ensure that their rights-respecting subjects secure sufficient autonomy. The first chapter argued that, to secure such autonomy, everyone needs some food and water and most require some shelter, education, health care, social support, and emotional goods. So, coercive institutions have to ensure that these people secure these things (as long as they respect others' rights and are subject to coercive rules). Hopefully another argument can show libertarians that they should accept more robust obligations to the poor. Still, this chapter's more modest conclusion is shocking in light of the fact that libertarians vehemently reject positive rights.[49] It is also an important conclusion in a world where libertarianism is gaining adherents and many cannot secure adequate food, water, shelter, and so forth.

---

[49] Narveson, *The Libertarian Idea*, Chapters 4 and 5. Lomasky, *Persons, Rights, and the Moral Community*, Chapter 5. Machan, "The Perils of Positive Rights." Nozick, *Anarchy, State, and Utopia*.

PART II

Introduction: Seeing the water for the sea

NECESSARY ASSUMPTIONS

The first part of this book contained three chapters. The first chapter argued that people have a human right to secure adequate food, water, shelter, and so forth. It considered objections to its conclusion that a new argument is necessary to address those who resist positive rights. The second chapter provided this argument. In doing so, it defended the claim that coercive institutions are responsible for enabling their subjects to secure food, water, shelter, and so forth. The third chapter suggested that some of those least likely to agree that the poor have a positive right to aid have reason to do so. It argued that libertarians and actual consent theorists, in particular, should agree that there are significant obligations to the global poor.

Since most of the global poor live in the developing world, Part II of this book examines some common development policies. Subsequent chapters consider whether or not there is reason to believe that aid or trade is likely to ameliorate autonomy-undermining poverty (henceforth simply poverty). They argue that the case for some aid and trade is strong but that free trade must be fair. These chapters consider how the obligations justified in Part I can be realized and developed into appropriate institutional policies.

For the second half of this book's arguments to be relevant for policy, however, one must accept something like the following assumption. Because there are significant obligations to the global poor, there is reason to take seriously policy proposals that can help these people secure things like food, water, and shelter.

Perhaps, for a coercive institution to be as legitimate as possible, it should not help some secure things like food, water, and shelter. Helping some may preclude helping a greater number of others that an institution is also obligated to help. Furthermore, there are many coercive institutions with overlapping constituencies. A theory of responsibility is necessary to decide which institutions or individuals, if any, are really responsible for helping different people.

There are certainly hard moral questions about how to distribute responsibility for making institutional changes that merit future research. The first half of this book did not defend any particular account of the responsibilities correlative to obligations to the global poor. The first chapter just sketched one possible account of these responsibilities. Individuals and states may have, at least, a secondary role to play in ensuring that international institutions fulfill their obligations. They might have to work to change these institutions' rules, or work around them, to find ways of ameliorating poverty. The second chapter noted some alternate ways of thinking about responsibility. One difficulty in assigning responsibility to institutions with overlapping constituencies is deciding how to coordinate institutional (never mind individual) action. Perhaps an adequate account of responsibility must be able to avoid large-scale coordination problems.[1] I have started to address some of these issues elsewhere but will not attempt to answer these questions here.[2] Subsequent chapters consider some of the main proposals for helping the poor that responsible institutions or persons might implement.[3]

In any case, the rest of this book will just assume that, if (1) an institution has an obligation to help some people, and (2) there is evidence that it can help these people, and (3) researchers have done their due diligence in looking for, but have failed to find, evidence that the requisite institutional changes will do more harm than good, (4) there is reason to implement these changes. Those of a more philosophical orientation need not accept this assumption. Philosophers can content themselves with learning a bit more about what is possible.

Because the second half of this book focuses on some of the main international development institutions' impacts in poor countries it is worth discussing a few of these institutions here. Though the development path each country takes is unique, most developing countries are subject to the rules of many international financial institutions (IFIs) and free trade agreements. These are some of the main international institutions and rules that have helped shape the current wave of globalization.

---

[1] I owe thanks to Teddy Seidenfeld for raising some of these questions.
[2] Hassoun, "Meeting Need," 250–75.
[3] See, however: Buchanan and Keohane "The Legitimacy of Global Governance Institutions." Also see: Hassoun, "Ideal Theory and Practice."

The IFIs and trade agreements have shaped the nature and terms of trade and development in poor countries.

In 1944, at the conclusion of World War II, a group of developed countries assembled the Bretton Woods conference for international discipline and exchange-rate stabilization. This conference created several of the most important IFIs including the IMF and the WB. It also created the first (nearly) global trade agreement – the General Agreement on Tariffs and Trade (GATT) – the predecessor to the WTO. Today these institutions help shape the fortunes of developing countries and their inhabitants. They are the engines of economic globalization.

The IMF and WB collaborate with the WTO to achieve "greater coherence in global economic policy-making."[4] Many of the IFIs' recommendations share with international free trade agreements a common objective – promoting free markets. The IFIs also help the poor, where necessary, with aid.

INTERNATIONAL FINANCIAL INSTITUTIONS

The IMF was created primarily to encourage macroeconomic stability. It promotes international monetary cooperation and encourages countries to liberalize their markets. It also lends money to member countries to prevent currency crises. Today, the IMF greatly influences developing countries' economic policies and provides emergency loans to struggling economies. In order to qualify for these loans, countries have to implement economic reforms the IMF believes will promote macroeconomic stability and growth. The conditions the IMF sets on its loans used to be called *Enhanced Structural Adjustment Facilities*. They are now called *Poverty Reduction Strategy Papers*.[5]

The WB was created to help finance post World War II reconstruction. It now tries to promote development by encouraging growth and poverty reduction. Like the IMF, the WB gives loans and policy advice to developing countries. Many of its loans have a large grant component and it also gives some pure grants to poor countries. Like the IMF and many other IFIs, the WB requires the countries it works with to adopt Poverty Reduction Strategy Papers.[6]

---

[4] Hoekman and Kostecki, *The Political Economy of the World Trading System*, cited in Hassoun, "Consumption."
[5] See, for instance: IMF, "Poverty Reduction Strategy Papers."
[6] See: African Development Bank Group, "Poverty Reduction Strategy Papers."

Poverty Reduction Strategy Papers often include requirements like these:

- Liberalizing trade to encourage outward-oriented growth (e.g. by reducing tariffs and other barriers to trade to make exports more competitive).
- Diminishing the role of the state in guiding the economy (e.g. by privatizing major sectors of the economy, decreasing government bureaucracy, and reducing spending – including spending on health, education, and welfare).
- Liberalizing financial markets (e.g. by allowing world markets to dictate exchange rates or devaluing the local currency against hard currencies such as the US dollar, in order to make exports more competitive).[7]

Through these measures the IFIs encourage liberalization, privatization, and deregulation.[8]

Because of worries about the timing, content, and success of IFI programs, they continue to evolve.[9] The WB, for example, is trying to target spending on education and health care to the poor. At least the International Development Association, the WB's branch that offers grants and loans to the world's poorest countries, aims to increase funding for poverty reduction programs and tries to help the poor benefit from economic growth.[10] The WB also hopes to increase transparency in its programs, encourage country ownership of its projects, and promote local control over fiscal expenditures.

Despite such changes, the IFIs remain committed to achieving poverty reduction through liberalization, privatization, and deregulation.[11] As IMF economist Vikram Haksar remarks, "in the past, structural adjustment programs that were detailed were untenable. We set the main goals on macro-economics broadly now – inflation is bad for poverty keep it

---

[7] Sachs, *The End of Poverty.* Reed, *Structural Adjustment.* Bello, "Structural Adjustment Programs."

[8] For further discussion of these conditions and their moral permissibility, see: Hassoun and Frank, "Are Debt-for-Nature Swaps Morally Permissible?"

[9] Stiglitz, *Globalization and Its Discontents.*

[10] Historically, the WB's commitment to poverty reduction has fluctuated. When Robert McNamara came to the WB in 1968 the commitment became more pronounced but in 1980s it was less pronounced. The WB's "attention to equity issues, from 1982 to the end of the decade, appears to have been somewhat token at least relative to its record in the 1970s." Stern and Ferreira, "The World Bank as 'intellectual actor'," 554) cited in: Hurrell, "Global Inequality and International Institutions," 34–57. The commitment to market liberalization, however, has been constant since at least the 1980s.

[11] World Bank, "Financing Instruments."

low – the rest is up to government and society."[12] Though some things are changing, the basic reforms are still the same.[13]

GLOBAL TRADE AGREEMENTS

Like IFIs, there are many free trade agreements (e.g. the North American Free Trade Agreement or the Southern African Development Community). Most free trade agreements are regional. Some free trade agreements are (nearly) global. These agreements are embodied in the WTO.

As noted above, the WTO is the successor and extension of the GATT created after World War II. Like the GATT, the agreements making up the WTO were arrived at by consensus. One of the main differences between the WTO and the GATT is that the WTO has an improved dispute settlement process.

While the rules of GATT are still primary in governing trade in goods under the WTO, the WTO has established new rules for service industries, intellectual property rights, dispute settlement, and trade policy. In 1997, for instance, WTO member countries agreed to liberalize telecommunications, financial services, and technological industries. In 2000, further talks on the agricultural and service industries began. The last round of talks, which began in 2001 in Doha, have yet to be completed. They are supposed to be focused on issues brought up by developing countries.[14]

Today there are approximately 30,000 pages of agreements and WTO rules in effect. Over 150 countries are members of the WTO. About 97 percent of trade occurs under its auspices.[15]

While Poverty Reduction Strategy Papers often require countries to liberalize trade, this is the explicit aim of trade agreements. The main provisions of the WTO (which remain from the GATT) can be summarized as follows, for instance:

---

[12] Hassoun, Nicole, unpublished interview with Vikram Haksar, Manila, Philippines, 2004.
[13] Some might object that this is no longer the case. See, for instance: Rodrik, "Is There a New Washington Consensus?" Looking at the World Bank's Poverty Reduction Strategy Papers guidebook for countries, however, it seems privatization, liberalization, and freer trade are encouraged. World Bank, "PRSP Sourcebook: Chapter and Annexes." Attending to the content of the particular programs implemented in developing countries after the supposed end of structural adjustment also allows us to see how similar the new requirements are to the old requirements. IMF, "Tanzania Poverty Reduction Strategy Paper Progress Report," 33. Compare to: IMF, "Zambia." Also see: Craig and Porter, "Poverty Reduction Strategy Papers."
[14] World Trade Organization, "The World Trade Organization in Brief."
[15] Ibid.

- Member countries should only protect their domestic production using tariffs, and they should try to liberalize trade policies whenever possible. In most cases, countries should not use quantitative restrictions on trade. An important exception is that countries with balance-of-payments difficulties are allowed to restrict imports in order to safeguard their external financial position.
- Member countries should work to reduce and eliminate tariffs and other trade barriers through multilateral negotiations. Each country has a tariff-line basis that sets "bound rates" (or limits) for tariffs. Countries should not increase tariffs above these limits.
- Member countries should not impose taxes on imported products higher than those levied on products produced in their domestic markets. This is known as "the national treatment" rule.[16]
- Member countries should not discriminate against countries from which they import and to which they export goods (this is embodied in the "most favored nation" principle).[17] Some preferential treatment is allowed at the regional level, through regional trade agreements, however.

In short, discrimination between member countries is prohibited, reciprocity is required, market access should be extended, and competition encouraged.[18] These same principles govern many bilateral and regional free trade agreements too.[19]

MOVING ON TO AID AND TRADE

Subsequent chapters consider the case for aid and trade. The next chapter argues that the case for aid is stronger than many people presume. There is, thus, reason to consider aid in trying to effectively reduce poverty. Subsequent chapters consider the case for different kinds of trade. The fifth chapter suggests that the main argument for free trade in no way guarantees poverty reduction. So it is worth considering ways of altering the rules of trade or working around them to better enable people to secure adequate food, water, shelter, education, health care, social support, and emotional goods. Trade-related adjustment assistance programs,

---

[16] World Trade Organization, "The General Agreement on Tariffs and Trade," Article III (Sections 1, 2, and 4).

[17] Ibid., Article 1 (Section 1).

[18] The fact that most countries are required to liberalize access to their markets in order to gain admission to the WTO may be justified by the reciprocity condition. Non-trade policy requests, however, are more questionable (e.g. Russia was pressured to sign the Kyoto agreement in order to get European backing to join the WTO). P. Baker, "Russia Backs Kyoto," A15. See, however: Hassoun, "Free Trade and the Environment," 51–66.

[19] Moellendorf, "World Trade Organization and Egalitarian Justice," 145–62.

linkage, trade barriers, and consumer movements – like the Fair Trade movement – may be necessary and desirable. So, the sixth chapter makes a preliminary case for one kind of Fair Trade in particular.

If the arguments in these chapters go through, they will allow us to reach the following conclusions. There is good evidence that aid can bring significant benefits to the global poor. Free trade probably has mixed effects. There are many ways to capture some of the benefits of free trade for the poor while avoiding some of the costs.

Do not despair that the positive proposals this book canvasses will not completely eliminate poverty. They provide hope, if we look closely enough. There is no simple solution to the poverty problem. There is not a single problem to solve. It is possible to do a lot to address some of the problems poor people face. That can make all the difference in the world for some people. We must learn to avoid futility thinking – to appreciate the good in whatever good we can do. We must reflect on the fact that even saving one life is, after all, saving a life.

CHAPTER 4

Empirical evidence and the case for aid

4.1 INTRODUCTION

There are many ways we might try to address world poverty. Perhaps the most obvious solution is aid. Recall Tamil's story from the Introduction to Part 1. Her family got emergency medical care and vitamins from The Philippine Community and Christian Funds. The Asian Development Bank and other NGOs also offer aid to the people of Smokey Mountain. If international organizations had continued to fund agricultural extension offices in the Philippines her family might never have had to move to the dump. There are many other aid programs that could help people like Tamil secure things they need. Perhaps we can replicate or scale up these efforts?

Recently, however, critics have questioned whether aid can help prevent the worst forms of (e.g. autonomy-undermining) poverty.[1] These critics argue that aid is either ineffective or counter-productive.[2] Some doubt that we can have good evidence that aid is effective.[3] This chapter

---

This chapter is a revised version of the following paper: Hassoun, "Making the Case for Foreign Aid," 1–20. I would like to thank *Public Affairs Quarterly* for the permission to reprint it here.

[1] There are, of course, other philosophers who advocate aid. See, for instance: Pogge, *World Poverty and Human Rights*; Aiken and La Follette (eds.), *World Hunger and Moral Obligation*; Brock and Moellendorf, *Current Debates in Global Justice*; Chatterjee (ed.), *The Ethics of Assistance*. Also see: Hassoun, "World Poverty and Individual Freedom," 191–8.

[2] David Schmidtz, for instance, says aid in Africa is often counter-productive and implies that we would do better just to try not to harm people. Dale Jamieson suggests making it easier for poor people to meet their needs by reducing trade barriers against developing countries instead of giving aid. Andrew Kuper argues that it may be better to purchase goods the poor make and vacation in poor countries. See: Schmidtz, "Islands in a Sea of Obligation," 685; Jamieson, "Duties to the Distant," 151–70; Kuper, "More Than Charity," 107–20. Though Jamieson points out that Singer also makes general claims about aid's efficacy, he says "that providing development assistance is ... 'usually the better long-term investment'." Jamieson, "Duties to the Distant," 158. This claim likewise requires more evidence.

[3] See, for instance: Wenar, "Poverty is No Pond." Wenar argues that potential donors cannot be confident that their donation, in particular, will help and will not harm. This chapter suggests

is not concerned to address the details of particular critics' arguments (the critics appeal to a mixture of fundamental principles and empirical considerations).[4] Rather, this chapter examines the kind of empirical justification necessary to arrive at sound conclusions regarding aid's efficacy.[5] Using the best available data, this chapter then makes a strong case for at least some aid programs. It also suggests that some kinds of aid may generally be good for the poor.

This chapter's methodological lessons are, moreover, quite general. It considers what types of data are necessary for establishing the kinds of empirical claims often relied upon in the political philosophy and

that potential donors can have good evidence that the programs to which they want to donate are effective. Implicitly, it suggests that if potential donors lack evidence that their donation will harm and they have good evidence that the programs to which they want to donate are effective, they have reason to give some aid. At least this seems plausible when evaluators have looked for but failed to find evidence that the aid program harms some people. Also see: Wenar, "The Basic Structure as Object," 253–78.

[4] If this chapter is correct, however, it should be clear to those familiar with the critics' arguments that many of them rely in part on anecdotes and/or statistical evidence that does not support the requisite causal inferences. Consider, for instance, one of the anecdotes Schmidtz provides in questioning the empirical premise of Singer's argument. Schmidtz says "When I recently crossed the border from Zimbabwe into Zambia, a large sign warned that bringing second-hand clothing into Zimbabwe from Zambia is prohibited. Puzzled, I wondered whether second-hand clothing might carry some disease. When I passed through the town of Livingstone, just north of the border, I asked what the sign was about, and I was told by three different sources (two white men, one black woman, all local residents) that Livingstone had until recently been the hub of Zambia's textile industry. Cotton was grown, processed, and woven into cloth there. However, a few years ago, in the wake of a severe and highly publicized drought, international relief agencies decided that what Zambia needed was planeloads of second-hand clothing. Livingstone manufacturers could not compete with free clothing, though. Today, the unemployment rate in Livingstone is ninety percent." Schmidtz, "Islands in a Sea of Obligation," 685. The story Schmidtz relates is probably true, in fact this kind of story has probably been repeated in many places around the world. This chapter will argue, however, that even this fact would do little to undercut Singer's argument. Anecdotal evidence cannot establish the conclusion that aid generally does more harm than good.

[5] Schmidtz is not alone in appealing to the wrong sort of evidence to make his points. Kuper also defends his claim that we should embrace a structural approach to dealing with poverty instead of giving aid, with anecdotes (implying that aid is generally harmful or at least that we cannot know that aid will do any good). He says: "Consider, most starkly, the perpetuation and intensification of the Rwandan conflict and the human misery aggravated by aid agencies that sustained refugee camps. In spite of the camps becoming bases for militiamen and incubators for cholera, the prospect of international NGO aid encouraged people not to return to their homes even when it was safer to do so, thus intensifying and prolonging the conflict. Consider also the 'food relief' of the 1970s that so damaged the situation of developing world farmers and their dependents." Kuper, "More Than Charity," 113–14. Kuper suggests that the ways our actions impact the poor are complex and multifaceted and that the best way to relieve poverty is not obvious. He is probably right, but this chapter will argue that the anecdotal evidence Kuper provides in questioning Singer's empirical premise cannot establish this. This chapter will argue that statistical data is necessary to make a general case for or against aid. That is

public policy literature. This is important as such empirical claims under-lie debates about everything from free trade, to immigration policy, and taxation to population control. Many of the same problems that beset crit-ics of aid also undermine arguments in these other areas.[6] Furthermore, subsequent chapters will rely on empirical evidence considering the mer-its of different kinds of trade.

This chapter also has something to say to those working on the empir-ics of aid, though its methodological lessons will probably not interest economists and other social scientists. Most of the empirical work on aid looks at aid's impact on growth at the country level.[7] This chapter sug-gests that this emphasis is a mistake. Further, most aid is given to coun-tries.[8] This chapter (implicitly) questions the assumption that most aid should be going to countries at all. It may be better to fund smaller-scale anti-poverty programs or to give to NGOs. Finally, this chapter raises some foundational questions about the nature of poverty and how best to measure it.

---

not to say that all statistical evidence is equally good. For the chapter's argument should also make it clear that sometimes Singer's critics also cite inappropriate statistical data for mak-ing their points. In support of the claim that development assistance is *usually* ineffective, for instance, Jamieson says "[T]here is little empirical evidence that [development assistance] … has substantially improved the welfare of the poor. A recent report from the Commonwealth Secretariat claims that although more than US$1.2 trillion was spent on official development assistance between 1950 and 2000, the gap between the incomes of people in developed and developing countries has widened." Jamieson, "Duties to the Distant," 160. He cites similar data from the UN. But inequality may have widened for many reasons and inequality can get worse even as poverty declines if the rich gain more than the poor gain. This chapter will argue that the kind of statistical evidence Jamieson provides (even in conjunction with the examples he gives) provides little support for the conclusion that any kind of aid generally does more harm than good.

6 Gillian Brock, *Global Justice*. Pogge, *World Poverty and Human Rights*. Hassoun, "Free Trade, Poverty, and Inequality," 5–44. Risse, "On the Morality of Immigration," 25–33.

7 Clemens et al. argue that aid can increase growth. Clemens, Radelet, et al., "Counting Chickens when they Hatch." Collier and Dollar argue that aid increases growth in "good" policy envir-onments (e.g. when countries have a fiscal surplus, low inflation, and are open to trade). Burnside and Dollar, "Aid, Policies and Growth," 847–68. Collier and Dollar, "Development Effectiveness," F244–71. Hansen et al. counter that, if aid has diminishing returns, these results may not hold. Hansen and Tarp, "Aid and Growth Regressions," 547–70. Dalgaard, Hansen and Tarp argue that climatic conditions actually explain the relationship between aid and growth better than policy environment. Dalgaard, Hansen, and Tarp, "On the Empirics of Foreign Aid and Growth," F191–216. The list goes on.

8 The Development Co-operative Directorate (DCD-DAC) of the Organisation for Economic Co-operation and Development (OECD) even defines Official Development Assistance (ODA) as aid to developing countries or multilateral institutions. ODA is often used as the aid variable in empirical studies. A quick look at the DCD-DAC database reveals that most ODA goes to countries. See: OECD, "Aid Statistics, Recipient Aid Charts."

Before making the case for some aid programs, the next section will consider the different kinds of – micro- and macro-level – empirical data available.[9] Macro-level data tells us how aid affects (or types of aid affect) all countries (or at least large regions). Micro-level data tells us how particular aid projects or small subsets of projects are doing. So the best data to use if one wants to conclude that aid is generally good or bad is macro-level data. Micro-level data is better if one wants to know whether a particular aid program is good or bad.

4.2 THE MACRO-LEVEL DATA

There have been, roughly, three waves of macro-level work on aid's efficacy.[10] Studies in all three look, primarily, at aid's impact on growth.[11] Over time these studies have become more sophisticated, testing more complicated models of how different kinds of aid impact growth.[12] Some surveys of the literature, such as those of C. Michalopoulos &

[9] This chapter does not tell us what to do in the absence of good evidence. Even if one could show that aid does not work, we might have other obligations to the poor. Hassoun, "World Poverty and Individual Freedom," 191–8. Hassoun, "Free Trade, Poverty, and the Environment," 353–80. Hassoun, "Coercion, Legitimacy, and Global Justice." For discussion of how we might go about fulfilling these obligations in theory, see: Hassoun, "Meeting Need," 250–75.

[10] Leif Wenar is one of the few philosophers who has looked at the empirical data on the impact of aid. Wenar concludes that we do not have the requisite data to come to firm conclusions about these matters. While I agree that the macro evidence is certainly not conclusive, we can learn a lot by considering it. See: Wenar, "Accountability in International Development Aid"; Wenar, "Poverty is No Pond."

[11] Clemens et al. argue that aid can increase growth. Clemens, Radelet, et al., "Counting Chickens when they Hatch." Mosley et al. failed to find a positive relationship between aid and growth. Mosley, Hudson, and Horrell, "Aid, the Public Sector and the Market in Less Developed Countries," 616–41. Collier and Dollar argue that aid increases growth in "good" policy environments (e.g. when countries have a fiscal surplus, low inflation, and are open to trade). Burnside and Dollar, "Aid, Policies and Growth," 847–68. Collier and Dollar, "Development Effectiveness," F244–71. Hansen and Tarp counter that, if aid has diminishing returns, these results may not hold. Hansen and Tarp, "Aid and Growth Regressions," 547–70. Easterly worries that the definitions of "aid," "good policy," and "growth" have not been sufficiently well justified. Easterly, "Can Foreign Aid Buy Growth?" 23–48. Dalgaard et al. argue that climatic conditions actually explain the relationship between aid and growth better than policy environment. Dalgaard et al., "On the Empirics of Foreign Aid and Growth," F191–F216. For an accessible review of this debate, see: Tarp, "Aid and Development," 9–61.

[12] Problems with defining aid infect the macro-level data. Many researchers use an overly expansive definition of "aid" that captures almost everything besides normal business transactions and loans. See, for instance: Clemens, Radelet, et al., "Counting Chickens when they Hatch." Even Official Development Assistance includes things many probably do not think of as aid like concessional loans. Different studies also look at aid's impact on different populations etc. Some studies look at "program" versus "project" aid. Mavrotas, "Assessing Aid Effectiveness in Uganda." Cordella and Dell-Ariccia, "Budget Support versus Project Aid." Others consider grants and official development assistance excluding things like technical cooperation and food

V. Sukhatme and of H. White, suggest that the evidence is ambiguous.[13] H. Hansen and Finn Tarp present one of the most sensitive reviews. They suggest that "aid works, even in countries hampered by an unfavorable policy environment."[14] They question the robustness and appropriateness of models underlying many of the studies which deny this conclusion.[15]

Unfortunately, the evidence about aid's impact on growth cannot tell us what impact aid has on the global poor.[16] Even if aid increases growth, it may not reduce poverty. Growth can increase even if the poor become poorer as long as the rich or middle class gain more than the poor lose. Furthermore, different causes of growth affect the poor differently.[17] The growth impact of aid alone does not tell anything about how aid impacts poverty.[18]

Fortunately, there are some studies that may plausibly tell us something about aid's impact on autonomy-undermining poverty (though different

aid. Gomanee, Girma, and Morrissey, "Aid and Growth in Sub-Saharan Africa." Some look at development versus humanitarian aid. Owens and Hoddinott, "Investing in Development or Investing in Relief." Others create their own categorization, e.g. "aid that could plausibly stimulate growth in four years." Clemens, Radelet, et al., "Counting Chickens when they Hatch." It is not clear that one can conclude that aid increases or decreases growth based on a survey of studies looking at all of these different things. Furthermore, it is important to pay attention to the specific data sources each study uses as even those who say they are talking about the same kind of aid (e.g. program aid) may mean different things by these terms.

[13] Michalopoulos and Sukhatme, "The Impact of Development Assistance," 111–24. White, "The Macroeconomic Impact of Development Aid," 163–240.

[14] Hansen and Tarp, "The Effectiveness of Foreign Aid."

[15] There are some theoretical reasons to question the model underlying this work as well, though this chapter will not take on this task.

[16] Different authors give different accounts of when aid is morally permissible or required. For views that contrast with Singer's see, for instance: Rieff, *A Bed for the Night: Humanitarianism in Crisis*; Jamieson, "Duties to the Distant," 151–70.

[17] Zhuang, et al., "Financial Sector Development, Economic Growth, and Poverty Reduction." Loayza and Raddatz, "The Composition of Growth Matters for Poverty Alleviation." Bigsten and Levin, "Growth, Income Distribution, and Poverty," Ch. 12. Rajan and Subramanian, "Aid and Growth." Heltberg, "The Growth Elasticity of Poverty." Hansen and Tarp, "Aid Effectiveness Disputed." World Bank, *World Development Indicators 2002*.

[18] Furthermore, even the available macroeconomic studies of aid's impact on the poor have significant problems. Some of these problems stem from the fact that the most common measures of poverty are inadequate. On most poverty measures, changes in the number of rich people in a population alone can reduce poverty. For discussion see: Hassoun, "Another Mere Addition Paradox." Also see: Hassoun and Subramanian, "Variable Population Poverty Comparison." Further, the World Bank's method of measuring poverty changed in the 1990s and different poverty lines are incommensurable. The survey data underlying the purchasing power parity (PPP) exchange rates that are used in calculating poverty internationally is not representative. In all, the PPP exchange rates may overestimate the purchasing power of the poor. See discussion in text. Reddy and Pogge, "How Not to Count the Poor." Also see: Hassoun, "Free Trade, Poverty, and Inequality," 5–44. Hassoun, "Global Poverty."

ways of measuring aid's impact on poverty yield different results).[19] Peter Boone, for instance, shows that non-military aid did not reduce infant mortality, increase life expectancy, or increase primary schooling in the 1970s and 1980s.[20] More recently, however, Paul Mosley, John Hudson, and Arjan Verschoor find that aid positively impacts pro-poor spending in low-income countries. They find that such aid usually reduces income poverty and infant mortality.[21] Finally, Mosley et al. argue that aid has an especially large positive impact on poverty when there is not too much inequality or corruption. Boone's study does not consider aid's impact on infant mortality *in low-income countries* in the 1970s and 1980s. So, even if Boone is right, Mosley et al.'s study gives us reason to think aid generally reduced infant mortality in low-income countries in the 1970s and 1980s. When inequality and corruption are low, there is also reason to think aid has a positive impact on income poverty in these countries.[22] Others replicate some of these results, finding even greater impacts of aid from European NGOs on infant mortality than Official Bilateral Aid which affects public sector spending.[23] A study by Karuna Gomanee and Oliver Morrissey looks at aid's impact on public expenditure, infant mortality, and the Human Development Index (HDI). Looking at a panel of countries from 1980 to 1998 Gomanee and Morrissey find that aid increases public expenditures and decreases mortality rates (increasing the HDI).[24] Though there may not be enough macro-level data to conclude that aid generally reduces poverty, there is evidence in favor of some kinds of aid.[25]

Nevertheless, trying to make a general case for aid may be like trying to make a general case for investment.[26] What we really need to

---

[19] This should become obvious below, but this chapter will say more about different measures of poverty in subsequent sections.

[20] See: Boone, "Politics and the Effectiveness of Foreign Aid," 289–329. Statistics on life expectancy and infant mortality rates, like GDP, are aggregate statistics.

[21] See: Mosley et al., "Aid, Poverty Reduction and the 'New Conditionality'," F217–43. Mosley et al. construct an index for how spending impacts the poor.

[22] Because both Boone and Mosley et al.'s analyses are complicated this is all a bit imprecise. Boone, for instance, excludes Israel and those countries with high aid to GNP ratios from his analysis because he is interested in testing the impact of political structure on aid's distribution. Readers interested in the full story should refer to the relevant articles. There are also some worries about interaction variables that might apply to Boone's analysis (though I know of no papers analyzing Boone's paper's use of such variables). See: Pattillo, Polak, and Roy, "Measuring the Effect of Foreign Aid on Growth and Poverty Reduction."

[23] Masud and Yontcheva, "Does Foreign Aid Reduce Poverty?"

[24] Gomanee and Morrissey, "Evaluating Aid Effectiveness Against a Poverty Reduction Criterion."

[25] Wenar, "The Basic Structure as Object."

[26] I would like to thank Clark Glymour for the analogy.

know may just be what investments to make and what aid to give.[27] So, the next section will turn to the micro-level data to get more information.[28]

4.3 THE MICRO-LEVEL DATA

Micro-level data can be *experimental*, *quasi-experimental*, or *non-experimental* (so can macro-level data, though most of it is quasi- or non-experimental). Most micro-level data is non-experimental. Non-experimental evidence can include, for instance, historical records, observational studies, and anecdotal evidence. Both quasi-experimental and experimental evaluations help test the causal efficacy of aid programs; they help insure a study's *internal validity*. A study has high *internal validity* when it captures the causal relationships between the particular program, policy, or process being evaluated and the particular outcome observed (no matter how unique the circumstances of the study). In *experimental* studies people (or other units of analysis) are assigned randomly to treatment groups (e.g. those receiving aid) and comparison groups (e.g. those not receiving aid).[29] This helps isolate a program's impact on participants. *Quasi-experimental* studies do not use random assignment to insure internal validity. Instead, researchers try to minimize *selection bias* in other ways. *Selection bias* results from differences between the treatment and the comparison groups.

Experimental data is often best for insuring internal validity.[30] Random assignment to treatment and comparison groups ensures that, on average, there will be no relevant differences between participants and non-participants. With a quasi-experimental design participants are more likely to differ from those in the comparison group in important ways.

[27] This is the point made in: Sachs, *The End of Poverty*. For discussion that seems to miss this point, see: Easterly, *The White Man's Burden*. For equally famous but not particularly sophisticated work by social scientists on aid, see: Moyo, *Dead Aid*. For classic work of this kind, see: Bauer, *Dissent on Development*; Bauer, "N. H. Stern on Substance and Method in Development Economics," 387–405; Easterly, "Can Foreign Aid Buy Growth?" 23–48; Hayter, *Aid as Imperialism*; Hayter and Watson, *Aid: Rhetoric or Reality?* For more recent work, see: Black and White (eds.), *Critical Perspectives on the Millennium Development Goals*.

[28] For an interesting simulation showing that, theoretically, redistribution can reduce poverty see: Dagdeviren, van der Hoeven, and Weeks, "Redistribution Does Matter."

[29] I know of no analogue to a placebo in tests of foreign aid, though it might be possible to develop an analogue in some cases.

[30] Sometimes randomization is not the best way to achieve independence between the criteria for allocation to treatment and control groups and the hypothesized effect of aid. This chapter cannot consider the conditions under which an alternative is better here, however.

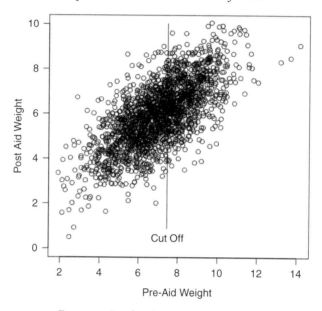

Figure 4.1 Results when aid is unsuccessful.

(Figures 4.1 and 4.2 from Hassoun, Nicole, "Empirical Evidence and the Case for
Foreign Aid," *Public Affairs Quarterly*, 24 (2010), 4.)

An example will help illustrate the advantages and limitations of experimental and quasi-experimental studies. Suppose we want to evaluate an
aid program to reduce malnutrition in a particular village. If villagers or
researchers decide who gets to participate, there may be a selection bias.
Many participants, for example, may be well nourished. Even if participants do better than non-participants, researchers will not know if the
program was successful.

Using a quasi-experimental method may help. Consider, for example,
one such method – *regression discontinuity design*. With regression discontinuity design, researchers use explicit selection criteria to select participants to receive aid. Aid might, for example, only be offered to people
who are underweight for their age. The comparison group would then be
made up of those who are just over the weight limit. Next, researchers see
if there is a discontinuity in how people fare just above and just below the
cut-off point for inclusion in the program.

Consider a graphical illustration of the results.[31] The *o*'s on the left side of the dividing line indicate those who start out underweight and so receive aid; the *o*'s on the right side of the dividing line indicate those who start out overweight. In Figure 4.1 aid has no effect. In Figure 4.2 aid has a good effect. On average, those receiving aid do better than those not receiving aid at the cut-off point (notice the discontinuity).

Unfortunately, there can be differences between those just above and below the cut-off point that cause problems for regression discontinuity studies. Those just above the cut-off point might, for example, participate in another aid program. If so, creating a comparison group made up of people right above the cut-off point will introduce selection bias. Contrasting the treatment with the comparison group will not tell us whether the aid program is successful; we will not know how the malnourished would have fared without aid.

True experiments better prevent selection bias; randomization gives us reason to think the treatment group is relevantly similar to the control group. It will not matter if those above the weight limit can participate in another aid program. With proper randomization, the comparison group will be made up of people who, like those receiving aid, are below the limit. So, it should be easier to conclude that a perceived effect is due to aid.[32]

Experimental evaluations can help us determine the efficacy of processes and policies as well as particular programs. Many evaluations of microfinance test processes like particular loan or savings products, for instance.[33] Other evaluations test the efficacy of different policies regarding, for example, the distribution of things like bed nets.[34] It is possible to use experimental micro-level studies to predict responses to macro-level policies (though larger samples are necessary to do this sort of research). Researchers have recently evaluated how young women in Kenya respond to an AIDS awareness campaign, for instance. The campaign encourages young women to choose partners in their age cohort.[35] Older partners are more likely to have acquired HIV. The researchers predict that the program will reduce HIV transmission rates amongst teenage girls in Kenya.

---

[31] Hassoun, "Empirical Evidence and the Case for Foreign Aid," 4.
[32] Researchers have developed ways of addressing this possibility.
[33] Karlan and Goldberg, "Impact Evaluation for Microfinance."
[34] Cohen and Dupas, "Free Distribution or Cost-Sharing?" For criticism that suggests the need for replication in multiple locations, see: Rodrik, "The New Development Economics."
[35] Dupas, "Relative Risks and the Market for Sex."

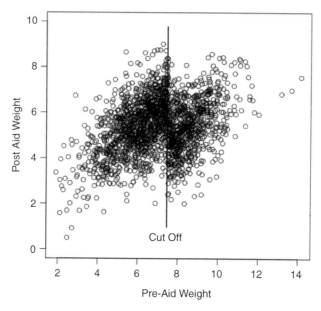

Figure 4.2 Results when aid is successful.

(They are probably justified in doing so for the 328 primary schools in which test programs were randomly implemented.)

It is important, however, to be careful not to generalize beyond what the data warrants. A good program can fail because the staff, beneficiaries, culture, or environment change. Test projects can be more exciting and, so, more successful than normal programs just because they are test projects; this is called the Hawthorne effect. Fortunately, there are ways to deal with such problems like the Hawthorne effect. Increasing the time span and scale of the evaluation reduces this effect, for example. Testing programs in multiple locations at a large scale strengthens the case for replication or scaling up.

Often, however, experiments are hard to perform. Participants can drop out of treatment. Those in the control group can sometimes gain access to treatment illicitly. Suppose, for instance, the program to combat malnutrition was offered at randomly selected schools. Parents might move their children to schools offering the program (or away from such schools). This may bias results. Similarly, researchers may select a biased sample. Suppose, for instance, researchers randomly select people to participate in a study from a non-representative subgroup of a population (say, students participating in an after-school program). They may inadvertently end up with results that will not generalize well to the other segments of the population.

There are ways of dealing with some of these problems. Double-blinding is a traditional solution to minimizing selection problems. If neither researchers nor participants know who is receiving treatment that will prevent much intentional manipulation. It may be hard to find an appropriate "placebo" in the context of an aid program. Parents and students usually know what kinds of programs are being carried out in local schools, for instance. Worse, inadvertent selection biases can be just as problematic as intentional selection effects. People may move out of a study area for reasons other than their desire to remain in or leave the program. Furthermore, the above example illustrates how researchers may select biased samples precisely because they do not recognize potential problems.

Worse, even truly randomly selected groups may exhibit some potentially biasing regularity. One group may, for instance, include more boys than the other group. Randomization only guarantees that there are no differences between the treatment and control groups if researchers select from an infinite sample. Obviously, in the real world, samples are not infinite. So, simply due to chance, the two groups may differ in significant ways.

There are ways of dealing with potentially problematic differences between treatment and control groups due to chance. Participants may be matched along potentially distorting dimensions (e.g. their sex) before being randomized. One person from each stratified matched pair would receive treatment. The other would become part of the control group. Alternately, there are ways of taking into account potentially relevant factors econometrically. In effect, however, using these methods or stratified matching makes the resulting evidence quasi-experimental rather than fully experimental. (One must assume that there are no other factors that explain observed differences that have not been taken into account.)[36] Nevertheless, randomization is an

---

[36] A final point worth mentioning is that to generalize to a larger population (to show that experimental results are significant), researchers must make some assumptions about the way the treatment affects the group that are not experimentally verifiable. Similar assumptions are necessary for non- and quasi-experimental designs; which require the most faith depends on the particular design. For more on this point and the importance of theory to development economics, see: Deaton, "Instruments for Development." For a thoughtful consideration of criticism of experimental methodology, see: Banerjee and Duflo, "The Experimental Approach to Development Economics."

important tool (amongst others) that helps us take into consideration potential differences between these groups. So, this chapter will consider experimental as well as quasi-experimental micro-level evidence regarding aid's efficacy below. This evidence will let us conclude that there are lots of good aid programs that can probably be successfully replicated and scaled up.

4.4 MAKING THE CASE FOR SOME AID

Few advocates or critics of aid explicitly consider how we should measure aid's impact on poverty (never mind autonomy-undermining poverty). So before arguing that there are lots of good aid programs, this chapter will consider what a *good* program looks like.

There are many ways to measure extreme poverty. We might, for instance, use an assortment of indicators such as education and caloric intake. Alternately, we might use a unitary measure of poverty. Unitary measures either specify a single formula for combining many disparate indicators of poverty or specify a single indicator (like income or gross domestic product [GDP]).

In discussing the macro-level data, this chapter suggested that, if we care about how aid impacts the poor, growth in aggregate GDP is not a good (unitary) indicator of aid's success. It cited studies that used a mixture of indicators. Better unitary measures are the Human Development Index (HDI) and the World Bank's poverty lines. The HDI includes information about income, education, and life expectancy in a single indicator. It combines (the logarithm of) GDP per capita at purchasing power parity (PPP), literacy and primary, secondary and tertiary enrollment rates, and life expectancy at birth.[37] The World Bank uses PPP income-based measures of poverty.[38]

The HDI includes more than income. This is a mark in its favor. Unfortunately, it has some problems. Poverty may be correlated with income, education, and life expectancy. Still, it is not clear that the HDI is a better measure of poverty than the alternatives. Education, income, and life expectancy may each be correlated with poverty in different ways. One of these may, alone, provide a better proxy for poverty than the

---

[37] This section draws on Hassoun, "Free Trade, Poverty, and Inequality," 5–44.
[38] There is also a Human Poverty Index (HPI) but I know of no empirical work measuring the general impact of aid on the HPI perhaps because it is a relatively new index. Ibid.

combination.[39] Researchers should justify a measure of poverty in light of a philosophical account of poverty to show that the measure is capturing the right thing. Neither the United Nations Development Program nor Amartya Sen who helped develop the measure has specified what set of basic functionings people need to avoid poverty.[40] The point is not just, as Sen recognized, that the HDI conceals important dimensions of poverty.[41] The point is that some philosophical justification is necessary to establish that the HDI is even a reasonably good indicator.

This book has assumed that those who are unable to secure basic food, water, shelter, and so forth are characteristically poor. (It also suggested that these things are necessary for most people to secure sufficient autonomy.) It is not clear, however, that the HDI measures this kind of poverty or even provides a good proxy for it.

Another problem for using the HDI as a measure of poverty (never mind autonomy-undermining poverty) is that it relies on average income levels.[42] So, a country where half of the population is well off, and half very poorly off, may have the same HDI as a country where everyone is doing equally, and moderately, well.[43] Germany, for instance, has the 14th most equal income distribution, while Hong Kong is 84th.[44] Germany's HDI (0.930) is very close to Hong Kong's (0.916).[45] This last problem is so severe, it basically renders the HDI useless for our purposes.[46]

Because the World Bank's poverty lines avoid this problem, we might use one of these indicators instead. Unfortunately, the World Bank's

---

[39] Income is discounted at all levels but at an increasing rate. Rich countries appear less developed than they would if this scaling was not done. As the average income level rises, poverty appears to be less and less affected by increases in average income. Because the HDI does not take into account distribution within countries, it is not clear that the HDI can tell us whether or not this is really the case in any given country. Ibid.

[40] Although Sen has written a lot about capabilities and uses examples throughout his work, he refuses to provide a comprehensive list of basic capabilities.

[41] One might also worry about whether the weight given to each of the HDI's components is appropriate (implicit weights are given to components when they are normalized though each is supposed to account for one-third of the indicator). See: Sen, "Human Development Index," 256–9.

[42] Although, as Sen points out, there is some attempt to account for distribution in giving income declining marginal utility, the examples below provide reason to worry about whether the weighting is adequate. See ibid.

[43] Due to changes in the methodology, HDI figures cannot be compared between years – though this is also the case for the World Bank's poverty lines.

[44] Sen, "Human Development Index," 256–9.

[45] United Nations Development Program, *Human Development Report*.

[46] For discussion of other problems with the HDI, see: Raworth and Stewart, "Critiques of the HDI."

poverty lines share another problem with the HDI that stems from the PPP exchange rates they rely upon.

PPP exchange rates make incomes comparable between countries and individuals in different countries. Consider a simple example of how to calculate such an exchange rate between two countries for a single good. Suppose it costs one dollar to get a bag of corn in the USA. Suppose it costs two pesos to do so in Mexico. The PPP exchange rate for corn would be 2:1 (0.5 pesos to a dollar or 2 dollars to a peso). PPP exchange rates are calculated for many countries to find relative prices for many of the goods and services that make up GDP. They usually express the result in terms of US$ equivalents.[47]

There are several problems with relying on PPP exchange rates in measuring poverty. First, the data these measures rely upon is questionable. PPP measures are based on the Penn World Tables (PWT) and the International Comparison Project (ICP) surveys. These surveys are of variable quality. They often measure different things (e.g. income vs. consumption). They are adjusted significantly for consistency.[48] Furthermore, these surveys do not have adequate coverage.[49] In 2005 China was included for the first time; India was included for the first time since 1985.[50] The surveys may not provide good estimates of poor countries' or individuals' incomes.

Furthermore, the most common methods of comparing purchasing power make it seem like the poor are doing better than they are. The Geary–Khamis method, for instance, basically averages international price differentials for all commodities weighting "each commodity in proportion to its share in international consumption expenditure."[51] Essentially it considers how much it costs in each country to purchase the average "basket" of goods consumed in all countries. The problem is that this "basket" includes many things (e.g. services), for instance, that the poor do not buy. Services are relatively cheap in developing countries.[52] This makes it seem like the poor in these countries are doing better than they are. While food is relatively cheap in developing countries,

---

[47] International Comparison Program, "Global Purchasing Power."

[48] Deaton, "Counting the World's Poor."

[49] Wade, "Is Globalization Reducing Poverty and Inequality?" 572.

[50] International Comparison Program, "Global Purchasing Power." Urban regions were over-represented in both countries' surveys.

[51] Reddy and Pogge, "How Not to Count the Poor."

[52] International Comparison Program, "Global Purchasing Power."

it is not as cheap as PPP estimates suggest.[53] Services have also come to make up a larger proportion of the international consumption "basket" over time. This makes it seem that the poor are doing better simply because of a change in the rich's consumption patterns.

Fortunately, there may be some ways of ameliorating the problems with PPP measures. For calculating the World Bank's poverty lines, it might help to compare purchasing power over a representative basket of goods the poor consume, for instance.[54]

Even if such changes were made, however, it is not clear that the World Bank's poverty lines would accurately capture the amount of poverty in a situation. More than money can reduce poverty. Different people need different amounts of money to avoid poverty. Subsistence farmers whose states provide health care and education, for instance, may not need much money. If aid harms the poor financially but provides them with these benefits, it may decrease poverty. Alternately, aid may bring small financial benefits to the poor but harm the poor greatly in other ways. So aid may increase poverty. Income is just one indicator of poverty. It may not be the best indicator. Having more than one indicator may be best.

This chapter will consider what micro-level studies tell us about how aid impacts individuals' access to things like education, health care, food, water, and shelter directly. Different indicators of poverty, like health and education levels, can exhibit opposite trajectories. Without a unitary measure, we may not be able to tell whether an aid program is making things better or worse overall. It may also be impossible to tell how much things are getting better or worse. We might, for instance, find that an aid program helps some people go to school but makes it less likely that others will get sufficient food. Sometimes, more than one thing may also be necessary to decrease poverty. Some medicines, for instance, may not work without food. Still, if there is evidence that a program helps people get basic water, food, shelter, health care, or education, and there is no evidence that the program makes it harder for people to access these things, that is evidence that the program reduces poverty. After all, helping people secure some of these things may help them secure others. If, for instance, children are well-nourished, they may learn more in school. At least I hope most of the advocates and critics of aid can agree on this

---

[53] Looking at some of the poorest countries included in the 1985 ICP survey, for instance, the prices for basic foodstuffs "Breads and Cereals" averaged 111 percent higher than consumer prices generally. International Comparison Program, "Global Purchasing Power."

[54] International Comparison Program, "Global Purchasing Power."

much. So, on this assumption, this chapter will look at programs funded by many sources – governmental and non-governmental.

About one-quarter of the world's population is infected with worms like schistosomiasis and hookworm.[55] These infections can cause protein deficiency, anemia, and other kinds of malnutrition, which can interfere with children's schooling. In parts of Kenya, more than 90 percent of school children are infected with worms.[56] Internationaal Christelijk Steunfonds Africa, a Dutch NGO, along with the District Ministry of Health started de-worming children in Kenyan schools. Researchers wanted to carry out an experimental evaluation of the program in Kenya's Busia school district. Unfortunately, administrators would not allow randomization to determine which schools would get the medication and which would not. So the researchers used a heuristic for randomness based on the alphabet.[57] They found that the program decreased absenteeism by 25 percent or more. Because the program lowered illness transmission rates, absenteeism even decreased in nearby schools.[58] The program was replicated in India. It was extended to provide iron supplements since lots of the Indian children were anemic. One year later, "researchers found a nearly 50% reduction in moderate to severe anemia, large weight gains, and a 7% reduction in absenteeism among 4–6 year olds."[59]

Globally only five out of six boys and four out of five girls are in elementary school.[60] The Inter-American Development Bank, along with the Mexican government, created a conditional cash transfer project called Progresa/Oportunidades to help the poorest educate and get medical care for their children.[61] Mothers of participating children had to attend nutrition and health programs (e.g. prenatal care, nutrition monitoring, well-baby care, immunization, supplementation, and preventive

---

[55] Kremer, "The Role of Randomized Evaluations."

[56] Ibid.

[57] Administrators might have used the same heuristic to determine which schools received other sorts of benefits biasing the results. Still, the quasi-experimental design provided some evidence in favor of the program. Deaton, "Instruments for Development."

[58] All programs I discuss were funded at least in part by either private or public foreign aid. I do not distinguish between private and public funded programs here although one might fruitfully compare the efficacy of programs distinguished in this way. Miguel and Kremer, "Worms," cited in: Duflo and Kremer, "Use of Randomization in the Evaluation of Development Effectiveness."

[59] Bobonis, Miguel, and Sharma, *"Iron Supplementation and Early Childhood Development,"* cited in: Duflo and Kremer, "Use of Randomization in the Evaluation of Development Effectiveness."

[60] United Nations *The Millennium Development Goals Report.*

[61] Skoufias et al., "Is PROGRESA Working?"

care programs).[62] Their children received scholarships to go to school –
with larger scholarships going to girls than boys. When the government
wanted to expand the program half of the 506 eligible communities were
randomly selected to participate. Comparing educational and health
outcomes in these communities to those in the comparison group, outside experts at the University of California Berkeley showed that children who stayed in the program for two years were about 40 percent less
likely to fall ill than children who did not participate.[63] They were also
about 25 percent less likely to be anemic, grew quicker, and returned to
school more frequently after emergencies.[64] On average, the percentage of
children enrolled in first through eighth grades increased 3.4 percent in
participating communities.[65] The percentage of girls who completed sixth
grade rose 14.8 percent.[66] Even adults benefited. Parents took 19 percent
fewer sick days, on average.[67] Progresa/Oportunidades was so successful
that it was extended to urban schools throughout Mexico. Similar evaluations show that conditional cash transfer programs are successful around
the world.[68]

In India only 35 percent of females and 61 percent of males were lit-
erate in 1990.[69] In 1994, Pratham, an Indian NGO, created a remedial
education program. Pratham got support from a handful of aid agencies,
including Oxfam, Novib, and the Al-Imdaad Foundation. It hired local
women to tutor children who were not doing well in elementary school.
An experimental evaluation of the program randomly assigned tutors to
one half of the 98 eligible schools within the city of Vadodara. A similar experiment was performed in the L-ward of the Mumbai schools.
The evaluation showed that the program "increased student test scores

---

[62] Ibid.
[63] This program was funded in part by the International American Development Bank. Similar
programs include Argentina's Plan Familias, Brazil's Bolsa Família, Chile's Chile Solidario,
Colombia's Familias en Acción, Costa Rica's Superémonos, the Dominican Republic's
Solidaridad, Ecuador's Bono de Desarrollo Humano, El Salvador's Red Solidaria, Honduras's
RAF, Jamaica's PATH, Nicaragua's Red de Protección Social, and Peru's Juntos. Inter-American
Development Bank, "Programs of Conditional Cash Transfers."
[64] Inter-American Development Bank, "Programs of Conditional Cash Transfers."
[65] Shultz, "School Subsidies for the Poor," cited in: Duflo and Kremer, "Use of Randomization in
the Evaluation of Development Effectiveness."
[66] Ibid.
[67] Gertler and Boyce, "An Experiment in Incentive-Based Welfare," cited in: Duflo and Kremer,
"Use of Randomization in the Evaluation of Development Effectiveness."
[68] World Bank, *Assessing Aid*. World Bank, "The Impact of Conditional Cash Transfer Programs."
Rawlings and Rubio, "Evaluating the Impact of Conditional Cash Transfer Programs,"
29–56.
[69] United Nations Educational, Scientific and Cultural Organization, "Education in India."

by .39 standard deviations."[70] Moreover, the improvements were "largest for children at the bottom of the distribution."[71] The program resulted in gains, per dollar, ten times greater than hiring new teachers. Its returns improved over time.[72] Pratham now runs similar programs in twenty cities for 161,000 children.[73]

There may be reason to evaluate many other programs. Has the Asian Development Bank's program to improve the lives of people living on Smokey Mountain done any good?[74] Is The Philippine Christian Foundation's training center for residents (funded by the Australian Embassy's Direct Aid Program) helping the people secure better jobs or better manage their finances? Is their school working?[75] Will WE International Philippines' project to help the people collect rainwater work?[76]

Further evidence might also be necessary to support some programs that already have high-quality evaluations. Consider, for instance, a Dutch NGO International Child Support's seed and fertilizer program. International Child Support decided to provide fertilizer to the (primarily) sustenance farmers in the rural Busia District of Western Kenya to increase agricultural yields and, thus, food supply. Parents of students in the local school were randomly selected to participate in the program for six years. The farmers were given calcium ammonium nitrate fertilizer to apply to a random plot of their land and hybrid maize to plant. They received diammonium phosphate fertilizer for another randomly selected plot. A comparison plot was randomly selected for traditional seed and fertilizer. The NGO also provided help in the first applications and tracked farmers' progress.

---

[70] The authors of the Pratham study probably generalize beyond what their data justifies; they suggest that the Pratham program can be replicated widely in India. Banerjee, Cole, Duflo, and Linden, "Improving the Quality of Education in India," cited in: Duflo and Kremer, "Use of Randomization in the Evaluation of Development Effectiveness." We can conclude, however, that the program can be replicated or scaled up within the city of Vadodara and the L-ward of the Mumbai schools.

[71] "Children in the bottom third gained 0.6 standard deviations after two years." Banerjee et al., "Improving the Quality of Education in India," cited in: Duflo and Kremer, "Use of Randomization in the Evaluation of Development Effectiveness."

[72] Ibid., cited in: Duflo and Kremer, "Use of Randomization in the Evaluation of Development Effectiveness."

[73] Ibid., cited in: Duflo and Kremer, "Use of Randomization in the Evaluation of Development Effectiveness."

[74] On this program see: Asian Development Bank, "Smokey Mountain Remediation and Development Project."

[75] For information about the Philippine Christian Foundation Programs, see: The Philippine Christian Foundation, "What We Do."

[76] For information about WE International Inc. Philippines see: WE International Inc., "Programs."

It helped harvest and weigh the crops. The quantities of fertilizer provided varied between growing seasons. Researchers found that the right amount of fertilizer and seeds could increase yields by over 90 percent.[77] Further, the evidence suggested that well-timed price reductions induce some farmers to purchase and apply fertilizers themselves.[78] It is important to consider, however, the large-scale, long-term impacts of fertilizer use. Fertilizers may degrade soil quality or have other harmful environmental effects.[79]

That said, some of the studies discussed above do consider and find primarily positive large-scale, long-term impacts (as do some of the quasi-experimental studies of Fair Trade discussed in the next chapter). There are many other successful programs that help people – from microfinance to school voucher programs.[80] Many of these programs have been success-fully replicated and scaled up.[81] Aid does do *some* good.

4.5 CONCLUSION

Several philosophers have questioned the common assumption that aid can ameliorate poverty. Many of aid's critics fail to provide the requis-ite kind of data to make their case.[82] So, this chapter has canvassed the strengths and weaknesses of different kinds of empirical evidence for establishing different conclusions about aid's efficacy. In doing so, it addressed the more general methodological question: What types of data are necessary for establishing normative conclusions in debates in political philosophy and public policy? It defended one answer to this question. It suggested that macro-level empirical data is necessary to establish general claims about the efficacy of different policies. It argued that micro-level experimental data may suffice for establishing claims about the efficacy

---

[77] Duflo, Kremer, and Robinson, "Nudging Farmers to Use Fertilizer."

[78] Ibid.

[79] I would like to thank Elizabeth O'Neill for making this point. I also owe special thanks to Clark Glymour, Richard Scheines, and Alex London for their help with this chapter.

[80] Ashraf, Karlan, and Yin, "Female Empowerment." Cassen, *Does Aid Work?* Isbam, Narayan, and Pritchett, "Does Participation Improve Project Performance." World Bank, *World Development Indicators 2002.* Kehler, "Humanitarian Exchange." Oxfam, "Food Aid or Hidden Dumping?" Duflo, Glennerster, and Kremer, "Using Randomization in Development Economics Research."

[81] Duflo and Kremer, "Use of Randomization in the Evaluation of Development Effectiveness." Zaman, "Poverty and BRAC's Microcredit Programme." Morduch, "Does Microfinance Really Help the Poor?" Pitt, "Reply to Jonathan Morduch." BRAC, *BRAC at a Glance.* Center for Global Development, "Making It Pay to Stay in School."

[82] Kuper, "More Than Charity," 107–20. Schmidtz, "Islands in a Sea of Obligation," 683–705. Jamieson, "Duties to the Distant," 151–70.

of particular programs. It, thus, provides some important guidance for resolving debates about everything from free trade and immigration to taxation and population control policy.[83]

With regard to the debate about aid, in particular, this chapter argued that macro-level data is necessary to make a strong case regarding aid's impact on the poor in general. Unfortunately, most macro-level studies of aid do not address the question of whether aid generally reduces poverty. Nevertheless, this chapter canvassed some relevant macro-level studies suggesting that certain kinds of aid reduce poverty. Furthermore, it argued that there are many good micro-level studies. These studies suggest that at least some aid programs are successful and can probably be replicated and scaled up.

In making this case, this chapter questioned the widespread assumption amongst economists and policy makers that we should primarily be concerned with aid's impact on growth at the country level. Further, it implicitly questioned the assumption that most aid should be going to countries at all. It may be better to fund smaller-scale anti-poverty programs, or to give to NGOs. Finally this chapter raised some foundational questions about the nature of poverty and how it is best to measure it.

There are many questions for further research. It would be great to know, for instance, what factors contribute to successful aid programs, policies, and processes and how aid is distorted differently by different factors.[84] The practical importance of that knowledge may, however, be limited. This chapter has done enough to establish the empirical claim that aid can ameliorate poverty. Even if aid is generally a bad idea, we should not neglect the good we can do for some, even if we cannot completely ameliorate poverty. We need not only see the forest for the trees, we must not neglect the water for the seas.

[83] Gillian Brock, *Cosmopolitan Justice and Patriotic Concern*. Pogge, *World Poverty and Human Rights*. Hassoun, "Free Trade, Poverty, and Inequality," 5–44. Risse and Blake, "Immigration and Original Ownership of the Earth," 133–67.

[84] This chapter gives us reason to be skeptical of others' claims to have isolated the factors underlying good programs. Recall that the majority of macro-level evidence looks at aid's impact on growth. See previous notes.

CHAPTER 5

Free trade and poverty

5.1 INTRODUCTION

The previous chapter argued that there is good evidence that aid can bring significant benefits to the global poor. Some claim, however, that the solution to world poverty lies in trade, not aid. Proponents of free trade argue that the moral case for free trade is strong in light of the fact that it is the quickest way to reduce poverty. Most people are familiar with *The Economist*'s, World Bank's, and International Monetary Fund's claims to this effect.[1] Some philosophers and lawyers also argue that the case for free trade is strong because it will reduce poverty. Some provide purely empirical support for this conclusion, citing correlations between liberalization and falling poverty rates, for instance. Others use purely theoretical arguments to suggest that free trade is morally required because it will ameliorate poverty. Teson and Klick, for instance, follow many economists in suggesting that the Argument from Comparative Advantage largely vindicates this conclusion.[2] If they are right, this conclusion may justify some international rules of trade and development embodied in institutions like the World Trade Organization (WTO). But are they right?

This chapter considers the case for free trade on the assumption that there are some significant obligations to the global poor. Recall that the first part of this book defended the conclusion that there are such obligations. It argued that coercive institutions must do what they can to ensure that their subjects secure food, water, shelter, and so forth. After

This chapter draws greatly on: Hassoun, "Free Trade, Poverty, and the Environment," 353–80. Interested readers should also see: Hassoun, "Free Trade and the Environment," 51–66. The material regarding Fair Trade's impact was adapted from: Hassoun, "Making Free Trade Fair." It also appears in: Hassoun, "Fair Trade."

[1] See, for instance: World Bank, *Globalization, Growth, and Poverty.*
[2] Teson, "On Trade and Justice," 192. Teson and Klick, "Global Justice and Trade."

critiquing the simplest version of the Argument from Comparative Advantage and suggesting that free trade may have mixed effects on the poor, it canvasses and defends a class of proposals that capture some of the benefits, while avoiding some of the costs, of free trade for the poor. Trade-related adjustment assistance programs, linkage, trade barriers, and consumer movements, like the Fair Trade movement, may be necessary and desirable. At least, this chapter concludes, these alternatives merit consideration if they are efficient means of helping the poor and appropriate institutional safeguards are put in place to prevent abuse. The WTO's proscription of some of these alternatives may be unjustifiable.[3]

The next section reviews the normative conclusion defended in the first part of this book. It explains that this chapter will consider the case for free trade in light of the obligation to ameliorate autonomy-undermining poverty (henceforth *poverty*). The third section articulates and critiques the simplest version of one of the main arguments for free trade – the Argument from Comparative Advantage. The fourth section considers free trade's impact in practice. It suggests that free trade has mixed impacts on the poor. It probably benefits some of the poor and harms others. The fifth section suggests a few ways trade policies might be changed to capture some of the benefits of free trade for the poor while avoiding some of the costs. Finally, the sixth section responds to objections to using trade policy to meet ethical objectives.

5.2 NORMATIVE FRAMEWORK

Poverty causes a lot of death and suffering. Millions die every year from easily preventable poverty-related illnesses.[4] About a billion people are undernourished, cannot secure safe water, essential drugs, basic sanitation, or adequate shelter.[5]

The first half of this book offered a new argument for the conclusion that there are some extensive obligations to the global poor. It argued that coercive institutions are obligated to do what they can to ensure that their subjects avoid poverty. As with the last chapter, one need not accept this

---

[3] Linkage, for instance, violates WTO rules as do many trade barriers. For more information, see: World Trade Organization, "The General Agreement on Tariffs and Trade."

[4] World Health Organization, World Health Report 2004, Annex Table 2.

[5] Food and Agriculture Organization, "The State of Food Insecurity in the World."

much to endorse the arguments below. One only needs to agree that *there is an obligation to ameliorate poverty.*[6]

Many people believe that there are more extensive obligations to their subjects than those this book has defended. Authors like Gillian Brock and Simon Caney argue, for instance, that everyone should be able to live good human lives[7] or have equal opportunities.[8] Others follow Charles Beitz in suggesting that the global distribution of primary goods must be to the maximal advantage of the least well off.[9] Perhaps this book's new argument can support a conclusion along these lines as authors like Michael Blake, Thomas Nagel, and Richard Miller suggest that coercion generates such extensive obligations.[10]

There are also many other ways that one could support the obligation to ameliorate poverty. Some do not accept this book's novel argument. Some deny all of the more extensive accounts of our obligations. Still these people might agree that there is an obligation to help the poor. They might, for instance, accept the human rights argument discussed in the first chapter.

This chapter's inquiry is limited; it only considers what to say about free trade in light of the minimal obligation to ameliorate poverty. More extensive obligations may provide reasons to view the impacts of free trade differently. One must, however, provide a way of deciding between any competing considerations before one can decide what to say about free trade all things considered. What follows may be just the first step on a long journey.

5.3 THE CASE FOR FREE TRADE

5.3.1 *The Argument from Comparative Advantage*

There are a few reasons to consider the simplest version of the main theoretical argument for free trade: the Argument from Comparative

---

[6] One need not be a cosmopolitan to accept this much. See, for instance: David Miller, *On Nationality*. Also see: Rawls, *A Theory of Justice*.

[7] Gillian Brock, "Egalitarianism, Ideals, and Cosmopolitan Justice," 1–30.

[8] Caney, "Cosmopolitan Justice and Equalizing Opportunities," 113–34.

[9] Beitz, *Political Theory and International Relations*. Also see: Pogge, *Realizing Rawls*.

[10] Blake, "Distributive Justice State Coercion and Autonomy," 257–96; Nagel, "The Problem of Global Justice," 113–47; Richard Miller, "Cosmopolitan Respect and Patriotic Concern," 202–24.

Advantage. There are many versions of this argument, and other purely theoretical arguments, for free trade. Nevertheless, free trade's advocates often rest their case for free trade's helping the poor on some version of this argument.[11] Furthermore, many of the other arguments for free trade share at least some of the problems this chapter will canvass for the simplest version of the Argument from Comparative Advantage.

The idea of comparative advantage underlies the Argument from Comparative Advantage. A country has a comparative advantage in a commodity if the opportunity costs to that country of producing that commodity are less than the opportunity costs to another country of producing the same commodity. The opportunity costs of producing a good in a country are the costs to that country in terms of the most valuable opportunity forgone. The concept of comparative advantage is different from that of absolute advantage. If a country has an absolute advantage in the production of a good, that country can make that good at a lower cost than another country. A country can have a comparative advantage in the production for a good, even if it costs the country more to produce everything than another country.

The Argument from Comparative Advantage shows that if a country specializes in the production of those commodities in which it has a comparative advantage, it can gain from trade. A country can gain from trade *even if it does not have an absolute advantage in the production of any good.* So, the Argument from Comparative Advantage shows that poor countries can gain from trade even if they are not more efficient than rich countries at producing anything at all.

Further, it is easy to conclude from the Argument from Comparative Advantage that poor individuals will gain from trade. Assuming that workers are paid for their productivity, wages will rise as productivity rises on the model underlying this argument. Under the standard neoclassical assumptions, trade will continue until an Arrow–Debreu competitive equilibrium is reached. Such competitive equilibria are Pareto optimal. This is what the first theorem of welfare economics says. That is, if countries are allowed to trade freely, markets will reach a state such that no one can be made better off without making someone else worse off.[12] The poor will gain in the process. (Those who are not familiar with the

---

[11] Teson, "On Trade and Justice," 192. Teson and Klick, "Global Justice and Trade."

[12] When the relevant assumptions are relaxed to account for things like the fact of unemployment, the best that can be proven is constrained Pareto optimality. Efficiency wage theories,

Argument from Comparative Advantage may want to review Appendix A, at the end of this chapter, for a textbook explication of the argument.)

5.3.2 Critique of the Argument from Comparative Advantage

If the Argument from Comparative Advantage is correct, how much poor countries will benefit from free trade depends on the terms of trade (see Appendix B). They may not benefit much at all.

Further, many of the assumptions required by the Argument from Comparative Advantage are important and unrealistic.[13] The most straightforward version of the argument assumes, for instance, that there are zero transaction costs, full employment, and homogeneous labor markets within each country.[14] This version of the Argument from Comparative Advantage also assumes that the goods produced in each country are identical and that consumers and firms strive to maximize utility and profit, respectively. Furthermore, it assumes that labor cannot move between countries but that it costs nothing for laborers to switch industries. Many of these assumptions are false in the real world.

Without the assumptions sketched above, the Argument from Comparative Advantage will not hold and free trade may even hurt the poor.[15] If, for instance, there is not full employment after trade, the argument does not say anything about the distribution of benefits to individuals that will result from free trade. Poor people may not benefit from any resulting growth at all. They may even suffer. Poor people may lose their jobs as production shifts to commodities made by people who are not poor, for instance.

The case for free trade, thus, depends on whether the model of free trade's impact sketched above can be modified so that it will hold in the real world.[16] Free trade may only result in Kaldor–Hicks Pareto optimality

---

for example, allow us to take into account the information problems that drive unemployment. They explain how markets can reach equilibrium with unemployment. Unfortunately, the equilibria that are guaranteed are not Pareto optimal.

[13] There are many endogenous growth models that predict that openness will be correlated with growth that start with different assumptions from the model we have discussed. Some of these models point to the potential benefits of technology transfer, availability of inputs, technical assistance, and reduced networking costs from free trade. See: McCulloch, Winters, and Cirera, *Trade Liberalization and Poverty*.

[14] Although economists have succeeded in weakening some of these assumptions, many controversial assumptions remain. For pioneering work in the area, see: Devarajan and Rodrik, "Trade Liberalization in Developing Countries," 283–7.

[15] Ibid.

[16] Buchanan, *Ethics, Efficiency, and the Market*.

in the real world. On the Kaldor–Hicks criterion, a change from one state of affairs to another is optimal if the benefits of the change exceed the costs of the change. The benefits could go to the rich and the costs to the poor. At least on this interpretation of the Paretian criterion, "Pareto Optimality can, like 'Caesar's spirit', 'come hot from hell'."[17]

In sum, the simplest version of the Argument from Comparative Advantage provides no reason to believe that free trade will benefit the poor, never mind completely eliminate poverty. It does not say anything about the size of the benefits from free trade to poor countries or individuals. Nor does it say anything about the distribution of benefits from free trade within poor countries. It is possible that free trade will bring great gains to the poor or completely eliminate poverty. The simple version of the Argument from Comparative Advantage *alone* provides no reason to believe this, however. It does not even provide reason to conclude that the poor are more likely than not to benefit from free trade. Poor people may not benefit at all. Free trade may even make it less likely that some will avoid poverty in the real world. The simplest version of the Argument from Comparative Advantage does not allow us to conclude anything about what free trade's impact on the poor will be.

There are many ways of making the Argument from Comparative Advantage more realistic, as well as other theoretical arguments for free trade, but the alternatives suffer from similar problems. Many more sophisticated versions of the Argument from Comparative Advantage weaken the assumptions in the argument. Other theoretical arguments for free trade also permit things like externalities and economies of scale.[18] Nevertheless, these models retain many unrealistic assumptions and sometimes add new simplifying assumptions that undermine attempts to draw any straightforward conclusions about how free trade impacts poverty from the model.[19] Rather than making this case here, however, the next section will start by considering the empirical evidence about free trade's actual impact on poverty. It will then use some of the results of the most sophisticated theoretical models of free trade's impact to suggest that, on the best estimates, free trade will have mixed impacts on the poor.

---

[17] Sen, *On Ethics and Economics*. It does not, in general, suffice if the initial conditions just approximate those of a perfect market: Lipsey and Lancaster, "The General Theory of Second Best," 11–32.

[18] Externalities are positive and negative impacts of trade on outsiders. Economies of scale allow that doubling the input to production may more than double the output.

[19] For an accessible introduction to new growth theory, as well as traditional models, see the initial sections of this paper: Mayer, "Implications of New Trade and Endogenous Growth Theories." Also see: Cockburn and Giordano (eds.), *Trade and Poverty in the Developing World*.

5.4 FREE TRADE AND POVERTY IN THE REAL WORLD

Social scientists disagree about whether, on average, free trade reforms are good or bad for the poor.[20] There is a fairly broad consensus amongst development economists that free trade increases growth and growth reduces poverty.[21] Nevertheless, some economists question the conclusion that *free trade-related growth* reduces poverty.[22] Others worry that estimates of growth's impact on poverty, in general, often hinge on unjustified assumptions about how growth impacts inequality and poverty.[23] Free trade can also affect poverty through many channels besides growth if, for instance, it changes prices.[24] Other social scientists are generally less sanguine than many economists about concluding that free trade is, on average, good for the poor.[25] Some argue, for instance, that problems with the common measures of free trade and poverty may be so severe that they undermine attempts to determine whether free trade reduces poverty in general. The previous chapter reviewed a few of these problems.[26] Others suggest that many studies fail to rule out alternative explanations of any observed correlations between free trade and poverty they report.[27]

[20] Wade, "Is Globalization Reducing Poverty and Inequality?" 567–89. Milanovic, "The Two Faces of Globalization," 667–83. World Bank, *Globalization, Growth, and Poverty.*

[21] World Bank, *Globalization, Growth, and Poverty.* Dollar, "Outward Oriented Developing Countries Really Do Grow More Rapidly," 523–44. Frankel and Romer, "Does Trade Cause Growth?" 379–99. M. Wolf, *Why Globalization Works,* 168. Adams Jr., "Economic Growth, Inequality, and Poverty," 1989–2014. Dollar and Kraay, "Growth is Good for the Poor," 195–225. Chen and Ravallion, "How Have the World's Poorest Fared since the Early 1980s?" 141–69. Sala-i-Martin, "The World Distribution of Income," 375.

[22] Milanovic, "The Two Faces of Globalization," 667–83. Rodriguez and Rodrik, "Trade Policy and Economic Growth." Harrison and Hanson, "Who Gains from Trade Reform?" 125–54. M. Wolf, *Why Globalization Works,* 168.

[23] For an informal review of theoretical and empirical arguments regarding trade's impact on poverty, see: Cockburn and Giordano, *Trade and Poverty in the Developing World.* This point is alluded to on page 93 of Gauci and Karingi, "Trade and Poverty: the Little We Know of the Effect in Africa and Possibly Why," 87–108. Also see: Hassoun, "Free Trade, Poverty, and Inequality," 5–44. For discussion of the poverty-elasticity of growth, see: Heltberg, "The Poverty Elasticity of Growth."

[24] Winters, McCulloch, and McKay, "Trade Liberalization and Poverty," 72–115.

[25] Teson and Klick, "Global Justice and Trade." Wade, "Is Globalization Reducing Poverty and Inequality?" 567–89. Hassoun, "Free Trade, Poverty, and Inequality," 5–44.

[26] Reddy and Pogge, "How Not to Count the Poor," 25. Pogge and Reddy, "Unknown," 1. Deaton, "Counting the World's Poor." International Comparison Project, "Global Purchasing Power." Temple, "The New Growth Evidence," 112–56. Harrison and Hanson, "Who Gains from Trade Reform?" 125–54. Hassoun, "Another Mere Addition Paradox." Hassoun and Subramanian, "An Aspect of Variable Population Poverty Comparisons."

[27] For references see: Hassoun, "Free Trade, Poverty, and Inequality," 5–44. This paper critiques some of the main arguments for the conclusion that free trade reduces poverty in general. It suggests, for instance, that one of the most common arguments for this conclusion relies on an

Yet others argue that there are more technical problems with the main studies supporting the conclusion that *free trade-related growth* reduces poverty.[28] This chapter does not need to resolve this dispute, however, if free trade reforms have mixed effects on the poor. This chapter can come to some significant normative conclusions as long as different free trade reforms may impact the poor in different ways. All other things being equal, the obligation to reduce world poverty provides reason to support free trade reforms only insofar as they help the poor.

So, the next subsection argues that, in practice, free trade reforms may have mixed effects on the poor. It suggests that some free trade reforms may benefit the poor, while some may hurt the poor. Other free trade reforms may have some good and some bad effects on the poor.[29] Sections 5.5 and 5.6 suggest and defend ways of capturing the benefits, while avoiding the costs, of free trade for the poor. If these arguments go through, current international trade law, embodied in institutions like the WTO, may be unjustifiable.

5.4.1 Differential impacts

There are several ways of estimating trade's impact on the poor, but no matter which method is used, they all suggest that the impact is mixed. The methods for estimating trade's impact range from historical observation to regression techniques and models utilizing household data and information about pricing.[30] The main approach is to use a partial or general equilibrium model.[31] There are problems with some of the assumptions underlying each of the methods, so perhaps we should not be very

---

invalid inference – that growth with falling or stable inequality will reduce poverty. At least on the main index of inequality (the Gini), growth can be inequality neutral if it only increases the income of the middle class. If, for instance, there are an equal number of rich and poor people, the increasing inequality between the middle class and the poor may be offset by the decrease in inequality between the middle class and the rich.

[28] Harrison and Hanson, "Who Gains from Trade Reform?" 125–54. Wade, "Is Globalization Reducing Poverty and Inequality?" 567–89.

[29] Cashin, Mauro, Pattillo, and Sahay, "Macroeconomic Policies and Poverty Reduction."

[30] For country-level studies, see: Besley and Cord, *Delivering on the Promise of Pro-Poor Growth: Insight and Lessons from Country Experiences*; World Bank, *Pro-Poor Growth in the 1990s: Lessons and Insights from 14 Countries*; Ravallion and Datt, "Why has Economic Growth been More Pro-Poor in Some States of India than Others?" 381–400; Ravallion and Chen, "Measuring Pro-Poor Growth," 93–9; Ravallion and Lokshin, "Gainers and Losers from Trade Reform in Morocco"; Arbache et al., "Trade Liberalization and Wages in Developing Countries," 73–96.

[31] Some computable general equilibrium models (CGEs) are dynamic but most dynamic models are "rudimentary" not even incorporating all of the insights from new trade theory. "Typically, a recursive framework is used to drive 'dynamics' in the form of updating stock variables,

confident about the exact numbers we get using them.[32] Fortunately, however, we do not need to figure out which is the best. They all suggest that trade's impact on the poor is mixed.[33]

especially of capital and labour. The LINKAGE, GTAP and IFPRI frameworks often additionally assume that total factor productivity growth is endogenous, as a response to trade openness. The latter assumption is admittedly ad hoc and not uncontested empirically … Also, and perhaps even more importantly, these CGE frameworks deal poorly with imperfect competition, as much as they are unable to handle activities shifting towards product differentiation or the introduction of entirely new activities, which may well be part of dynamic and diversification responses to trade integration. In general, while the insights from new trade theory are gradually being incorporated in some CGE applications, the more widely used model frameworks and especially those most influential in the policy debate are still quite far from fully incorporating such insights." Vos, "What We Do and Don't Know About Trade Liberalization," 52–4.

[32] Partial equilibrium models are not as comprehensive as general equilibrium models. So they are less likely to account for all of the important ways that trade can impact poverty. The main general equilibrium models are extremely sensitive to assumptions about, for instance, the rate of substitutability between domestic products and foreign ones and this leads to widely divergent estimates of trade's impact. Another important unrealistic assumption is about whether as "in much of the World Bank's global trade analyses, wages are uniform across sectors and labour is perfectly mobile and fully employed." Vos, "What We Do and Don't Know About Trade Liberalization," 49. Under alternative specifications developing countries may not fare as well and the gains to different countries and sectors, e.g. agriculture, may also be different. "Some studies predict, for instance, that agricultural liberalization in the context of the Doha Round will lead to average income gains for Sub-Saharan Africa, while others will show losses." Vos, "What We Do and Don't Know About Trade Liberalization," 45. "The World Bank's LINKAGE model, for instance, uses higher [trade substitution] elasticities than those generated by the Global Trade Analysis Project (GTAP) network, consequently yielding expected benefits from multilateral trade liberalization that are 33 percent higher." Under "standard assumptions" it also suggests that Doha will lead to "terms-of-trade losses for developing countries, especially those in Sub-Saharan Africa." Vos, "What We Do and Don't Know About Trade Liberalization," 45–8. One must also make some other important decisions in specifying these models: "one can either assume that the trade balance is fixed and the real exchange rate adjusts to equilibrate aggregate exports and imports, or that the real exchange rate is fixed and the trade balance is endogenous." Vos, "What We Do and Don't Know About Trade Liberalization," 51. An alternative methodology is the micro-level approach combining household surveys data with general or partial equilibrium estimates. This method uses predicted impacts and actual data to estimate freer trade's historical and future impact. Using this method Martin Ravallion says, for instance, that when China joined the WTO that had "a small poverty-reducing effect in the aggregate." Ravallion, "Looking Beyond Averages in the Trade and Poverty Debate," 23–4. He predicts that liberalizing cereal markets in Morocco will have a small negative impact on poverty in general. "However, in both China and Morocco, a micro empirical lens points to considerable heterogeneity in impacts underlying the aggregates … In both countries, rural families tend to lose; urban households tend to gain … The most vulnerable households tend to be rural, dependent on agriculture, with relatively few workers, and with weak economic links to the outside economy though migration." Ravallion, "Looking Beyond Averages in the Trade and Poverty Debate," 23–4. Also see Bourguignon, de Melo and Suwa-Eisenmann, "Distributional Effects of Adjustment Policies," 339–66. Ganuza, Paes de Barros, and Vos, "Labour Market Adjustment, Poverty and Inequality during Liberalisation," 54–88. There are some ways of dealing with potential problems with this method, but it is relatively new and these problems require further consideration. For discussion see: Vos, "What We Do and Don't Know About Trade Liberalization," 55–7.

[33] Using both partial and general equilibrium methods, Ravallion and Michael Lokshin argue that in Morocco, for instance, there is "a small negative impact on mean household consumption

Consider free trade in agriculture to see how free trade may have mixed impacts on the poor. On some estimates, US$142 billion of US$248 billion in fixed productivity gains will go to low-income countries.[34] There is a wide consensus that agricultural tariffs have primarily negative impacts on the fortunes of developing countries.[35] Nevertheless, some studies find that agricultural trade barriers protect important developing country markets.[36] Even the WTO admits that free trade in some commodities could be devastating for net food importers.[37] Some poor countries may be hurt by free trade in agriculture.[38]

Furthermore, even in those regions that would gain from free trade in agriculture, many argue that some countries will do worse.[39] Studies suggest that how countries and regions within them will fare depends on what kinds of liberalization occur and what kinds of preferential agreements are made.[40] In the South Asia Free Trade Area, for instance, how countries fare may depend on how much these countries liberalize. Some countries will probably do better than others. Under some scenarios, small countries in the region are expected to do worse, even if these countries would generally gain from free trade.[41]

I know of no one who maintains that the poor, even within countries that will gain from trade, will always benefit. Even staunch defenders of free trade suggest that "the impact of trade liberalization, particularly

and a small increase in inequality ... Rural families tend to lose; urban households tend to gain ... There are clearly sizeable welfare losses amongst the poor in ... specific regions." Ravallion and Lokshin, "Gainers and Losers from Trade Reform in Morocco," 23. Some also argue that when there are economies of scale and imperfect competition, trade liberalization can have a negative impact on welfare. Devarajan and Rodrik, "Trade Liberalization in Developing Countries?" 283–7. Rodrik, "Imperfect Competition, Scale Economies, and Trade Policy in Developing Countries," 109–44. For a non-technical introduction to the empirical evidence, see: Cicoweiz and Conconi, "Linking Trade and Pro-poor Growth," 7–30. Looking at household survey data for employed adults of working age, Arbache, Dickerson, and Green suggest that liberalization reduced wages for the poorest in Brazil and returns to education below university level. Arbache et al., "Trade Liberalization and Wages in Developing Countries," 73–96.

[34] Ingco and Nash, "What's at Stake?" 1–22. European Commission, "The EU and Eastern Caribbean Bananas." Bourne, "Poverty and Its Alleviation in the Caribbean."

[35] Ibid.   [36] Ibid.

[37] World Trade Organization, "Committee Settles Three Implementation Issues."

[38] Sachs, *The End of Poverty*.

[39] Wade, "Is Globalization Reducing Poverty and Inequality?" 567–89.

[40] This is the finding in the following paper: Bandara and Yu, "How Desirable is the South Asian Free Trade Area?" 1293–323. This paper notes, however, that even though many disagree about the impacts of particular reforms, authors using very different models find that different ways of liberalizing will carry with them different costs and benefits.

[41] Bandara and Yu, "How Desirable is the South Asian Free Trade Area?" 1293–323.

on poverty, will depend on the environment in which it is carried out, including the policies that accompany it … it depends on the country context."[42] World Bank and IMF researchers concur.[43] Liberalizing trade in cereals will probably have mixed impacts on the poor within Morocco, for instance.[44]

We need not work out all of the ways that different reforms will impact the poor to arrive at an important moral conclusion: There is reason to try to capture the benefits, while avoiding the costs, of free trade for the poor. Some free trade reforms will probably reduce poverty in general. Some will probably worsen poverty in general. Many reforms probably have mixed impacts. As long as different free trade reforms impact the poor in different ways, there is reason to try to capture the benefits, while avoiding the costs, of free trade for the poor.

5.5 RESTRUCTURING THE RULES OF TRADE

An obligation to ameliorate poverty does not, alone, provide reason to support unfettered free trade or isolationism. Some authors, like Mathias Risse, deny that protectionism can be justified. Nonetheless, there is reason to support those policies, protectionist or not, that ensure that people avoid poverty.[45] Whether or not one should ultimately support a particular policy will depend on many things. It will depend, for instance, on what other options there are and whether or not there are competing moral obligations.

The rest of this chapter sets out a few trade policies that might help people avoid poverty. The seemingly innocuous proposition that there is reason to consider embracing those policies, protectionist or not, that ensure that people avoid poverty directly contravenes current international law embodied in the WTO.[46] So, this section considers how it is possible to restructure the rules of trade embodied in the WTO or work around

---

[42] Winters, et al., "Trade Liberalization and Poverty," 107.

[43] Bannister and Thugge, "International Trade and Poverty Alleviation." Kym Anderson, "Agricultural Trade Reform and Poverty Reduction in Developing Countries."

[44] See preceding notes for evidence and: Ravallion and Lokshin, "Gainers and Losers from Trade Reform in Morocco," 23. For a non-technical introduction to the empirical evidence, see: Cicoweiz and Conconi, "Linking Trade and Pro-poor Growth," 7–30.

[45] Risse, "Fairness in Trade."

[46] The WTO does make some provisions for the poor. Provisions embodied in Article xx of the GATT/WTO agreement, for instance, suspend the most favored nation and national treatment rules to protect the poor. These provisions are not as broad as those this chapter is considering, however. The WTO explicitly prohibits many trade barriers, for instance. For more information, see: World Trade Organization, "The General Agreement on Tariffs and Trade."

them to better reduce poverty. The next section concludes by considering objections to the claim that there is reason to consider using trade policy to reduce poverty. This will help isolate some of the conditions under which using trade policy to reduce poverty may be acceptable. If there are defensible ways to restructure the rules of trade so that they help the poor more, current WTO rules are unjustified.

There are many ways WTO rules might be altered to better capture the benefits, while avoiding the costs, of free trade for the poor. One possibility is to use some of the gains from trade to *compensate* the poorest when they are hurt by free trade. Consider an example of trade-related compensation. Paragraph 4 of the Marrakech NFIDC Decision of the WTO says that agreements on agriculture have to make appropriate provision for the needs of net food-importing developing and least-developed countries.[47] The rationale is that net food-importing countries are the ones most likely to be hurt by rising prices of agricultural commodities with free trade. Though the Marrakech decision has yet to be appropriately implemented, a similar, more sustainable program may be possible.[48]

The WTO might, in conjunction with other international institutions, also create programs to compensate poor *individuals* who lose from free trade or require countries to implement such programs. Such compensation should take a long-term perspective on helping beneficiaries. It should allow them to adapt and maintain employment as economic conditions change. One possibility is to create trade-related adjustment assistance programs. There are many examples of such programs. The US trade-related adjustment assistance program "provides trade-displaced workers with extended unemployment benefits, relocation expenses and (compulsory) training as a bridge to a new job with similar levels of income and benefits."[49] It also compensates the workers for free trade's harms. There are similar programs in place in other countries. Together the WTO and other international institutions might create a global trade-related adjustment assistance program to help the poor.[50]

---

[47] World Trade Organization, "Committee Settles Three Implementation Issues."

[48] The provisions suggested by the committee set up to consider the matter included increased levels of food aid, financing facilities, and financial and technical assistance for increasing agricultural productivity for net food-importing developing countries and least developed countries. For more information, see: World Trade Organization, "Committee Settles Three Implementation Issues." Also see: World Trade Organization, "Committee on Agriculture."

[49] McCulloch et al., *Trade Liberalization and Poverty*, 152.

[50] Another alternative is to come up with feasible ways of redistributing property rights that underlie free trade to ensure that all people can meet their needs. Thomas Pogge argues, for instance, for an alternative to the trade-related intellectual property rights provisions of the WTO that might be better for the poor. See: Pogge, "Human Rights and Global Health," 182–209.

In trying to help poor individuals, it may be important to integrate poverty diagnostics with trade policies. This may help policy makers isolate ways of ensuring trade benefits, and does not harm, the poor. Poverty mapping may assist policy makers in figuring out where the poor live and what segments of society to focus on assisting (e.g. women, wage earners, or the unemployed). Poverty mapping can also help determine how people are affected by trade reforms. Gathering data may be essential for "devising trade reforms that benefit the poor. Poverty decomposition along sectoral lines also provides an analytical tool to evaluate who benefits from trade liberalization and helps to devise intervention strategies to mitigate the welfare losses."[51] This data should form the basis for devising other kinds of appropriate programs.

There are also many other ways of restructuring the rules of global trade so that they *proactively* reduce poverty. Christian Barry and Sanjay Reddy argue that free trade agreements and agreements to improve labor standards and wages in developing countries should be linked.[52] At least, they argue, doing so may be a good idea if linkage "arises from a fair process of negotiation between states, is transparent and rule-based, is applied in a manner that reflects the level of development of a country, incorporates adequate international burden-sharing, and takes appropriate account of viewpoints within each country."[53] Their arguments are cogent and compelling.

Similarly, the WTO might be altered so that it allows countries to use trade policy to unilaterally improve the position of the poor. Consider a simple example of how imposing a trade barrier may help the poor. Suppose that Destitute is a very large country and raises a tariff against marsupials from any other country. This will reduce demand for foreign marsupials in Destitute. Producers in Destitute who sell their goods domestically will benefit since they will be able to sell marsupials at higher prices. Consumers in Destitute will lose out because they will have to pay these higher prices. Any producers in Destitute selling overseas will make less since more marsupials will be sold overseas at lower cost. Still, the money captured from the foreign marsupials that are sold in Destitute, plus the extra revenue the producers make in Destitute, may leave Destitute as a whole better off. Suppose the following conditions hold as well: The poorest in Destitute do not buy marsupials but produce them for domestic sale and the poorest in foreign countries do not produce

---

[51] Gauci and Karingi, "Trade and Poverty: The Little We Know of the Effect in Africa and Possibly Why," 102.
[52] Barry and Reddy, *Just Linkage.*   [53] Ibid., 1.

marsupials but consume them. In this case, the impact of this tariff could be good for all poor people in present generations. Suppose, further, that marsupial production produces a lot of greenhouse gas. Since the tariff would decrease overall production of marsupials, it might even help poor people in future generations. Although this is a hypothetical example, similar tariffs might bring great gains to the poor. If WTO rules allowed countries to use such trade barriers, trade policy could provide a useful tool for reducing poverty.[54]

Finally, even individuals can promote free trade that does not increase poverty.[55] They might, for instance, buy Fair Trade certified goods.[56] Goods sold as Fair Trade certified must meet certain standards.[57] At a minimum, they must be produced by people paid a living wage.[58]

Using the example of the Fair Trade movement it is easy to make the case that there are some ways of restructuring or working around the rules of trade that can help the poor.[59] There is a lot of evidence that suggests Fair Trade programs often help the poor in developing countries.[60] Impact assessments of Fair Trade projects suggest that they benefit the poor by raising prices for Fair Trade goods.[61] In "One Cup at a Time: Poverty Alleviation and Fair Trade Coffee in Latin America," Douglas Murray et al. report that participation in Fair Trade networks helps farmers throughout Latin America secure better prices, credit, training, and meet their basic needs for things like education and food.[62] In "Assessing the Potential of Fair Trade for Poverty Reduction and Conflict Prevention: A Case Study of Bolivian Coffee Producers," Sandra Imhof and Andrew

---

[54] The WTO might also allow barriers which bring net benefits to the poor with appropriate compensation.

[55] On Fair Trade certification, see: Risse, "Fairness in Trade."

[56] There are many Fair Trade certification schemes. Some are better than others. For an example, see: Fairtrade Foundation, "What is Fairtrade?"

[57] Often, Fair Trade certification organizations provide producers with credit services and access to training.

[58] Fair Trade certified coffee is usually shade grown, for instance. Coffee produced in this way is grown under the rainforest's canopy rather than in clearings usually created by burning down rainforests.

[59] The rest of this subsection is adapted from: Hassoun, "Free Trade, Poverty, and Inequality," 5–44.

[60] There is also some evidence that Fair Trade can increase gender inequality and encourage specialization that can leave individual farmers vulnerable to changing economic conditions. Ruben, *The Impact of Fair Trade*. Raynolds, "Poverty Alleviation Through Participation in Fair Trade Coffee Networks." Bacon, "Confronting the Coffee Crisis," 497–511.

[61] McMahon, "'Cause Coffees' Produce a Cup with an Agenda," A1–2.

[62] Murray, Raynolds, and Taylor, "One Cup at a Time."

Lee use quantitative and qualitative data to argue that Fair Trade coffee producers make more than their competitors.[63]

Yet other researchers argue that farmers participating in Fair Trade cooperatives develop important skills.[64] Their studies suggest that Fair Trade organizations enhance the capacity of participating cooperatives to market their goods[65] and have other positive effects on producers.[66] In "Coffee, Co-operatives and Competition: The Impact of Fair Trade," for instance, Anna Milford uses a theoretical model and case study evidence to argue that the Fair Trade premium helps cooperatives maintain cohesion and use collective bargaining power to destabilize cartels and secure higher prices for farmers' products.[67]

The higher prices they can secure with Fair Trade can help the poor in many ways. Often they simply help farmers make ends meet. Higher prices can also help farmers secure food, water, shelter, and so forth. In "Confronting the Coffee Crisis: Can Fair Trade, Organic, and Specialty Coffees Reduce Small-Scale Farmer Vulnerability in Northern Nicaragua?" not only did Christopher Bacon find that coffee farmers in Nicaragua received higher, less variable prices, credit, and training, but he says this helped them reduce their vulnerability to the coffee crisis.[68] His surveys suggest that the Fair Trade farmers are four times less likely to lose their land than traditional farmers.[69] In "Revaluing Peasant Coffee Production: Organic and Fair Trade Markets in Mexico," Muriel Calo and Timothy Wise use theoretical models along with survey data to argue that the Fair Trade farmers they studied end up better off than those who turn to organic production alone.[70] In "One Cup at a Time: Poverty Alleviation and Fair Trade Coffee in Latin America," Douglas Murray,

---

[63] Imhof and Lee, "Assessing the Potential of Fair Trade for Poverty Reduction and Conflict Prevention."

[64] International Institute for Environment & Development, "Fair Trade: Overview, Impact, Challenges."

[65] See Hopkins, "Impact Assessment Study," cited in: Raynolds, "Poverty Alleviation Through Participation in Fair Trade Coffee Networks."

[66] Calo and Wise, "Revaluing Peasant Coffee Production." Milford, "Coffee, Co-operatives and Competition." Ronchi, "Fair Trade in Costa Rica." Bacon, "Confronting the Coffee Crisis," 497–511. Peter Leigh Taylor, "Poverty Alleviation Through Participation in Fair Trade Coffee Networks." Imhof and Lee, "Assessing the Potential of Fair Trade for Poverty Reduction and Conflict Prevention."

[67] Milford suggests that these cooperatives not only improve welfare by providing education and credit services but give farmers essential information and lobbying power. Milford, "Coffee, Co-operatives and Competition."

[68] Bacon, "Confronting the Coffee Crisis," 497–511.

[69] Bacon, "Confronting the Coffee Crisis," 506.

[70] Calo and Wise. "Revaluing Peasant Coffee Production." Milford, "Coffee, Co-operatives and Competition." Ronchi, "Fair Trade in Costa Rica." Bacon, "Confronting the Coffee Crisis,"

Laura Raynolds, and Peter Taylor suggest that those who participate in Fair Trade programs are often better able to educate their children and meet their basic needs for things like food, water, and housing.[71]

The studies of Fair Trade's impact discussed above are, of course, open to criticism. In "Introduction: Impact Evaluation in Official Development Agencies," Howard White and Michael Bamberger argue, for instance, that such evaluations may fail to isolate the cause of (e.g.) Fair Trade farmers' success.[72] Some use only survey data and many do not try to control for other factors that may explain their data. Studies of Fair Trade's efficacy vary in quality and breadth of coverage.

Nevertheless, Fair Trade impact evaluations are becoming more sophisticated all of the time. Some of the best are quasi-experimental.[73] A recent study commissioned by the Center for International Development Issues in the Netherlands is particularly comprehensive, containing eight case studies looking at Fair Trade in different commodities in different places.[74] It is a quasi-experimental study that tries to establish causation by comparing participants in Fair Trade programs to similar non-participants (using a sophisticated form of propensity score matching).[75] The authors argue that the Fair Trade programs they study generally increase participants' food consumption. Many participants also invest more in housing, land, and education than those in the non-Fair Trade comparison group.[76]

The suggestion is not that purchasing Fair Trade certified goods will completely solve the problems free trade can cause for the poor, but it might do a lot of good if it leads to rising production standards.[77] The collective impact of individual choices can be large. Altering some trade policies may help the Fair Trade certification movement. The WTO might require countries to label goods produced in sustainable ways as Fair Trade certified. Even unassisted consumer action is powerful. Boycotts

---

497–511. Peter Leigh Taylor, "Poverty Alleviation Through Participation in Fair Trade Coffee Networks." Imhof and Lee, "Assessing the Potential of Fair Trade for Poverty Reduction and Conflict Prevention." There is some evidence, however, that organic Fair Trade markets can be particularly lucrative. Ruben, *The Impact of Fair Trade*.

[71] Murray et al., "One Cup at a Time."

[72] White and Bamberger, "Introduction," 1–11.

[73] For discussion of different kinds of empirical evidence, See Chapter 6 and also see: Hassoun, "Free Trade, Poverty, and Inequality," 5–44.

[74] Ruben, *The Impact of Fair Trade*.

[75] White and Bamberger, "Introduction," 1–11.

[76] Some of the studies tested for regional effects of Fair Trade, finding general increases in market prices and wages once Fair Trade made up a significant portion of the market.

[77] For further discussion of Fair Trade's moral status, see: Hassoun, "Making Free Trade Fair."

of tuna not caught in dolphin safe nets changed the tuna-fishing industry when the WTO failed to do so.[78] Purchasing Fair Trade certified goods may help those whose lives individuals' consumption choices most directly impact. The next chapter will consider how a new Fair Trade proposal might help the poor secure adequate medical care, for instance.

5.6 CONSIDERING OBJECTIONS

Consider a few objections to altering or circumventing the rules of trade. This is important because doing so may require changing international trade law embodied in the WTO, and good intentions do not always produce good results.

5.6.1 Using trade policy to reduce poverty is inefficient

Consider, first, an objection to using trade barriers to reduce poverty. Trade barriers like tariffs, quotas, and export taxes may be the most contentious trade policies. Proponents of unfettered free trade often argue that trade barriers are an inefficient way to help the poor.[79] They believe that such barriers are unjustifiable independent of which country raises what kind of barrier. The worry is that there is usually a net loss in using such barriers to reduce poverty. One might, thus, conclude that taxation (or another kind of market reform) is better for ameliorating poverty than trade barriers.

There is something right about this argument. If world poverty provides a reason to consider using trade barriers to help the poor, it also provides a reason to consider other market reforms.[80] There are, for instance, many interesting proposals for global taxes to fund development assistance to the poor.[81] Taxes are not always more efficient than trade barriers in ameliorating poverty.

In theory, trade barriers can be just as efficient as other market reforms. Consider how some barriers compare to some taxes. Some trade barriers, namely tariffs, just are taxes. They are taxes on imports or exports.

Proponents of free trade might qualify the argument above. They might suggest that, although taxes and other market reforms intended

---

[78] World Trade Organization, "Mexico etc. vs. US: 'Tuna Dolphin'."
[79] Teson, "Global Justice, Socioeconomic Rights, and Trade."
[80] This book has mentioned some options above.
[81] See for instance: Pogge, *World Poverty and Human Rights*.

to help the poor result in some deadweight loss, trade barriers are less efficient than some alternative market reforms. Proponents of free trade may suggest that quotas, in particular, are generally less efficient than tariffs and taxes. Furthermore, proponents of free trade may contend, taxes (including tariffs) result in less deadweight loss the broader their base.[82] Because tariffs usually do not have a very broad base, they are unjustifiable.

It is not clear that even this refined objection goes through, however. Which taxes or market reforms are best depends on a variety of factors. Some argue, for instance, that which kind of reform is best depends on how easily employers can substitute one kind of labor (e.g. high skill) for another (e.g. low skill) in the production process.[83] In theory, trade barriers can be just as good and efficient as taxation (or other market reforms) in ameliorating poverty, they can even result in a net gain.[84]

As Edward Buffie and Manoj Atolia put it: "The perception that free trade is first-best has acted as a formidable barrier to … serious, meaningful debate about the merits of activist trade policy … exhortations to liberalize as much and as fast as possible have taken its place."[85] They build a dynamic general equilibrium model and find that "the results consistently recommend policy packages that combine an escalated structure of protection with an escalated structure of export promotion. There is no support for the view that free trade or a low uniform tariff is approximately optimal."[86] Applying their model to Zambia they find the following:

Protection and export promotion should be moderate and that tariffs should be higher on intermediates than on capital goods. In the Zambian case, trade policy is both pro-poor and pro-development when a 30% export subsidy + tariff on agricultural products and manufactured consumer goods combines with a 20% tariff on intermediates and a 10% tariff on machinery and equipment. Across steady states, this policy package increases real wage for unskilled labor 17%, aggregate consumption 10%, and the aggregate capital stock 14%.[87]

Trade barriers may be essential for reducing poverty.

---

[82] Saez, "Direct or Indirect Tax Instruments for Redistribution," 503–18. Also see: James Anderson, "The Relative Inefficiency of Quotas," 65–81.
[83] Ibid.   [84] Ibid.
[85] Buffie and Atolia, "Trade Policy, Poverty, and Development in a Dynamic General Equilibrium Model for Zambia," 2–3.
[86] Ibid., 3.   [87] Ibid., 3.

Even if trade barriers are rarely one of the best ways to ensure that people avoid poverty in theory, the world is not perfect. There may be reasons of political economy to use such barriers rather than taxes or other market reforms to reduce poverty. It may be easier to get developed countries, or corporate producers, to reduce poverty through discriminatory tariffs than through taxes or other market reforms. There may even be some cases where the only realistic way to reduce poverty is to levy tariffs against countries decimating their populations or ignoring the poverty of their citizens. The threat of trade barriers may be essential in getting some countries to agree to international development treaties, for instance.[88] There may be few other ways to punish those failing to live up to their obligations to ameliorate poverty.

5.6.2 Using trade policy to reduce poverty is paternalistic

A second argument against using trade policy to reduce poverty goes roughly as follows: People in different countries have different preferences, resources, and needs. Because this is so, each country should get to decide on its own what it wants to do about poverty. Preventing countries from fulfilling these preferences is paternalistic.[89] Those who are concerned about poverty should, thus, do something about it within the borders of their own country. Using trade policy to alter countries' choices is unjust.[90] Such behavior should be illegal under the WTO, and countries should not use such policies.[91]

The first reason why the Paternalism Argument does not tell against using trade policy to reduce poverty is this: there are many reasons why a country with the ability to ensure that its citizens avoid poverty may not do so. There are many despotic countries that do not show much concern for their citizens' welfare, for instance. Even democratic countries may, in effect, be ruled by wealthy individuals who do not care

---

[88] For discussion of the conditions under which sanctions tend to work, see: Ang and Peksen, "When Do Economic Sanctions Work?" 135–45. Note, however, that the threat of sanctions may suffice to ensure policy change in some cases.

[89] European Union, "Economic Partnership Agreements and Free Trade."

[90] It is not clear that the Paternalism Argument tells against countries using trade policy to reduce poverty within their own borders. If Destitute can prevent its own citizens from selling necessary goods abroad it may lower prices for these goods domestically. This may help poor people in Destitute avoid poverty.

[91] For an analogue of this argument against those who want to use trade to encourage countries to adopt sustainable environmental policies, see: van Beers, "International Trade, Environment, and Sustainable Development."

about the poor.[92] It is not clearly paternalistic to help the poor in countries that refuse to do so because they are despotic or have tyrannical majorities. Poor people in these countries may very well *want* to avoid poverty.

Another reason why the Paternalism Argument does not tell against using trade policy to reduce poverty is this: Some countries simply do not have the resources to ensure that all of their people avoid poverty. These countries do not ensure that their citizens avoid poverty because they prefer, in any morally significant sense, to use their money for other purposes. It does not follow from the fact that countries cannot afford to ensure that their citizens avoid poverty that it is illegitimate to use trade policy to help them do so. Specifying that countries *prefer* whatever they will pay for is not the same as arguing that countries should only get what they will pay for. To put this another way, saying that countries do not want to reduce poverty because they do not have the money to do so is either false or, if made true by definition, irrelevant to the question of whether it is okay to help them do so.[93]

Finally, even if interfering with the wishes of any sovereign country is paternalistic, it is not clear that such paternalism is unacceptable. Further argument is necessary to show that it is illegitimate to interfere with a country's, or even a poor person's, desire not to receive aid, especially since the first part of this book suggests that interference may even be required.

5.6.3 The information necessary to use trade policy to reduce poverty does not exist

A third argument tells against using any trade policy to reduce poverty that restrains free trade. It goes roughly as follows: It is hard to figure out what the impact of a particular restraint on free trade on the poor will be. Perhaps economists can only figure out that the aggregate benefits of free trade for the poor will be large. It is not, therefore, acceptable to use a policy that restrains free trade to try to reduce poverty. Instead, trade should be as free as possible.

There are two main problems with this argument. The first is that its premises are not clearly correct. There is disagreement even about the

---

[92] For further discussion, see: Pogge, *World Poverty and Human Rights*.
[93] After all, most poor people do not choose to be poor; many are children. For further discussion, see: Pogge, "Severe Poverty as a Human Rights Violation," 11–54.

claim that free trade will bring great aggregate benefits to the poor just as there is disagreement about how some particular restraints on free trade will impact individuals' ability to avoid poverty. Nevertheless, previous sections canvassed some of the methods for estimating free trade's impact on the poor. It is possible to rigorously examine how particular countries are likely to fare when they implement different kinds of reforms.[94] Empirical evidence can provide reason to liberalize and restrain trade in some ways rather than others. At least there is reason to seriously consider whether some restraints on trade may be beneficial. After all, similar protective measures may have benefited the Asian Tigers, China and India until their growth rates increased sufficiently.[95] Some compensation for the poor who lose from free trade may also be possible.[96] The second problem with this argument is that its premise does not clearly imply its conclusion. Economists may be much less certain about how a particular restriction on free trade will impact individuals' ability to meet their needs than that the aggregate impact of free trade on the poor will be large. Still, if there is some reason to think that free trade will increase poverty in a particular case without reducing the benefits of free trade too much, it seems reasonable to consider the restriction. The restriction may even be required. In any case, the objection does not go through without further defense.

5.6.4 Using trade policy to reduce poverty opens the door to harmful protectionism

A final reason against using trade policy to reduce poverty is this: People may disingenuously cite poverty alleviation as the reason for protectionist measures. Producers or consumers seeking protection from competition

---

[94] For discussion of some methods for isolating this impact, see: Cheong, "Methods for Ex Ante Economic Evaluation of Free Trade Agreements." The following papers use some of these methods to examine some of the likely impacts of different free trade agreements: Corong, Reyes, and Taningco, "Poverty Impacts of Preferential and Multilateral Trade Liberalization on the Philippines"; Cororaton, Cockburn, and Corong, "Doha Scenarios, Trade Reforms, and Poverty in the Philippines," Ch. 13; Hertel, Hummels, Ivanic, and Keeney, "How Confident Can We Be in CGE-Based Assessments of Free Trade Agreements?"; Busse, Borrmann, and Großmann, "The Impact of ACP/EU Economic Partnership Agreements on ECOWAS Countries"; Bandara and Yu, "How Desirable is the South Asian Free Trade Area?" 1293–323. The paper by Bandara and Yu notes, however, that even though many disagree about the impacts of particular reforms, authors using very different models find that different ways of liberalizing will carry with them different costs and benefits.

[95] See: Wade, "Is Globalization Reducing Poverty and Inequality?" 567–89. Also see: Rodrik, "Globalization, Growth and Poverty."

[96] World Trade Organization, "Committee Settles Three Implementation Issues."

may take advantage of well-intentioned concern about poverty to lobby for unfair economic benefits. Ethanol producers, for instance, might disingenuously cite worries about the food security of net food-importing countries as a reason for subsidizing US corn production.

This is probably the strongest argument against using trade policy to reduce poverty. Self-interested producers that gain from protectionism *may* use the poor as an excuse for protection that harms the poor. Nevertheless, some collusion between self-interested producers or consumers and those who genuinely care about world poverty may not be bad. Suppose it is possible to build coalitions of those who care about the poor and those seeking protection. These groups are not mutually exclusive. It may then be possible to adopt appropriate trade policy more quickly. Suppose the poor will benefit from keeping corn prices low. Suppose further that ethanol producers will not undermine the interests of the poor when they gain as well. Then, corn subsidies may be acceptable.

Still, it is clear that there may be a problem. Concern for the poor may function as a cover for protectionism that does not benefit, or even harms, the poor. Lower prices may not help the poor, even in aggregate, if other policies increase the demand for corn. Alternately, subsidized corn may primarily be used for fuel and land diverted away from food production.[97] Though some poor people who produce corn for fuel may benefit from subsidies, this may harm the poor in the aggregate. Advocates of poverty relief may even be fooled into supporting such protectionism.

Fortunately, there are a few ways to address this problem. One is through the dispute resolution panels of international trade agreements like the WTO. These panels may develop standards for judging whether a protectionist measure will actually reduce poverty.[98] If proposed measures to benefit the poor do not do so then, unless there is another reason to implement such measures, they should not be allowed.[99] Educating those who care about the poor so that they will not be fooled into supporting inappropriate trade policies may also help prevent such exploitation. Allowing tariffs and other trade barriers is risky since they can be used to

---

[97] For discussion of how ethanol policies actually influenced the 2008 food crisis, see: Christiaensen, "Revisiting the Global Food Architecture."

[98] The analysis will be more difficult since we are only assuming that there is an obligation to help the poor who cannot secure autonomy in any other way. Economists will probably have to use an imperfect (e.g. income) proxy to get at how policies are likely to affect these people.

[99] Perhaps such panels could also decide whether a trade policy that does help the poor can be justified in light of competing considerations.

the detriment of the poor. Still, the fact that protectionism can hurt the poor does not tell against using protectionism to benefit the poor when it is possible to do so.

5.7 CONCLUSION

Proponents of free trade argue that trade, not aid, is the quickest way to lift the world's poorest from poverty. Unfortunately, one cannot rely on the simplest version of the Argument from Comparative Advantage to arrive at this conclusion. The potential benefits of free trade for ameliorating world poverty are large. In practice, however, there is reason to be skeptical of the claim that free trade is always the best way to reduce poverty. Trade-related adjustment assistance programs, linkage, trade barriers, and consumer movements may be necessary or desirable. There is reason to restructure the rules of trade or work around them to ameliorate poverty. At least, these alternatives merit consideration if they are efficient means of helping the poor and appropriate institutional safeguards are put in place to prevent abuse. The WTO's proscription of many of these alternatives may be unjustifiable.

Appendix A

Consider a textbook illustration of the Argument from Comparative Advantage using a simple two-country two-good model. Doing so will illustrate how it is possible for a country to gain from trade, even if that country does not have an absolute advantage in anything. Similar critiques can be made of many of the more complicated models (e.g. a mixed Ricardian/Heckscher–Ohlin model). Suppose that there are only two goods (marsupials and xylophones) and two countries (*Wealthy* and *Destitute*). Suppose that Wealthy has an absolute advantage in producing both goods. It costs Wealthy less to produce xylophones than it costs Destitute to produce xylophones. It also costs Wealthy less to produce marsupials than it costs Destitute to produce marsupials. Suppose that the production costs in terms of labor for both goods in each country are as follows (where L is the total amount of labor available for production in each country and x and m indicate the quantity of xylophones and marsupials produced):[100]

---

[100] Let us assume here that we are in a pure exchange economy where labor is the only input relevant for producing marsupials and xylophones.

Table 5.1

Wealthy	$x = 1$	$m = 2$	$L = 24$
Destitute	$x = 6$	$m = 3$	$L = 24$

Each country has 24 labor hours available for production. It costs Wealthy one labor hour to produce a xylophone and two labor hours to produce a marsupial. It costs Destitute six labor hours to produce a xylophone and three labor hours to produce a marsupial.

The opportunity cost of producing a xylophone is the number of marsupials that a country could produce instead of the xylophone. Wealthy has to give up ½ a marsupial to produce a xylophone. Destitute has to give up two marsupials to produce a xylophone. So Wealthy has a comparative advantage in producing xylophones. Destitute, however, has a comparative advantage in producing marsupials. Destitute only has to give up ½ a xylophone to produce a marsupial. Wealthy has to give up two xylophones to produce a marsupial. Depending on demand for these commodities, it may be possible for both countries to gain from trade. To maximize profit, each country needs to focus on producing only one commodity. Then each can exchange their surplus production for the other commodity. Because Wealthy has a comparative advantage in xylophones and Destitute has a comparative advantage in marsupials, Wealthy should concentrate production on xylophones and Destitute should concentrate on marsupials.

Consider how each country may fare with and without trade. Assume that this is the situation before trade:

Table 5.2

Production without specialization		
	Xylophones	Marsupials
Wealthy	16	4
Destitute	3	2
World total	19	6

Wealthy spends 16 hours producing xylophones and so produces 16 xylophones. Destitute spends hours producing marsupials and produces two marsupials. And so forth. If each country specializes in the commodity in which it has a comparative advantage, this situation will result:

Table 5.3

Production with specialization		
	Xylophones	Marsupials
Wealthy	24	0
Destitute	0	8
World total	24	8

There are a total of five extra xylophones and two extra marsupials produced than in the situation without specialization. It is clear that there is room to gain from trade (but since consumers demand some marsupials and some xylophones in both countries, the gains are only possible through trade). If the going price is five marsupials for every four xylophones, each country will do better in both commodities than they did before trade. This situation may result:

Table 5.4

Production with specialization		
	Xylophones	Marsupials
Wealthy	20	5
Destitute	4	3
World Total	24	8

In sum, the Argument from Comparative Advantage shows that poor countries can gain from trade even if they are not more efficient than rich countries at producing anything at all.

Appendix B

Recall that, in the example in Appendix A, five extra xylophones and two extra marsupials were produced by specialization than were produced without specialization. The going price was five marsupials in exchange for four xylophones. So, each country did better in both commodities than they did before trade. If, however, it cost six marsupials to get four xylophones this situation may result:

Table 5.5

Production with specialization		
	Xylophones	Marsupials
Rich	20	6
Poor	4	2
World total	24	8

In this situation, Rich ends up with 20 xylophones rather than 16 and six marsupials rather than four. Poor ends up with four rather than three xylophones but only two marsupials. Poor does not do as well when the terms of trade are not in Poor's favor. The Argument from Comparative Advantage does not say much about the size of the benefits to poor countries or individuals that will benefit from trade.

CHAPTER 6

Making free trade fair

6.1 INTRODUCTION

The fourth chapter argued that there is good evidence that foreign aid can bring significant benefits to the global poor. The last chapter suggested that trade may also bring significant benefits to the global poor. It argued, however, that there may be reason to re-work, or work around, some of the rules of trade to capture the benefits of trade for the poor while avoiding the costs. This chapter focuses on one specific proposal for working around some of the rules of trade embodied in the WTO's Agreement on Trade Related Aspects of Intellectual Property Rights (TRIPS) agreement. If successful, this proposal will address some of the poor's health problems, in particular. This chapter does not suggest that coming up with ways of modifying or working around the international intellectual property regime is particularly important for achieving global justice, though that may be so. Rather, like the preceding chapters, this one tries to combat futility thinking. It is intended to illustrate that there are ways of making incremental progress, but progress nonetheless, towards reducing world poverty. Just as there is no single cause of poverty, there is no single solution. We need to think creatively about different ways of helping the poor that might have some impact.

Every year 9 million people are diagnosed with tuberculosis, every day more than 13,400 people are infected with HIV, every 30 seconds malaria kills a child.[1] About a third of all deaths are poverty-related.[2] Most of the world's health problems afflict poor countries and their poorest inhabitants.[3] There are many reasons why so many people die of poverty-related

This chapter is adapted from and extends the argument in Hassoun, "Global Health Impact: A Basis for Labeling and Licensing Campaigns?"

[1] Centers for Disease Control and Prevention, "World TB Day, March 24th 2005." UNICEF, "Millennium Development Goals." UNAIDS, "World AIDS Day 2004."
[2] World Health Organization, *World Health Report 2004*, Annex Table 2.
[3] World Health Organization, *World Health Report 2004*.

causes. One reason is that the poor cannot access many of the existing drugs and technologies they need. Another is that little of the research and development done on new drugs and technologies benefits the poor. In light of these facts, a few have suggested ways of restructuring the incentives biotechnology and pharmaceutical (henceforth: Bio) companies face to encourage them to target their technologies to the poor.[4] Still, the problem remains – the poor are suffering and dying from lack of access to essential medicines. So, on the assumption that there is reason to consider such alternative incentive structures, this chapter suggests a new way of bringing about the requisite change. Namely, it presents a new package of Fair Trade proposals. The next section motivates this inquiry.

6.2 MOTIVATING THE PROPOSAL

There are many reasons the poor bear the brunt of the global burden of disease (GBD). Recall Tamil's story related in the Introduction to Part I. Her family suffered from some easily preventable poverty-related illnesses due to poor living conditions, poor nutrition, and lack of access to clean water and basic preventative health care. Tamil's family, like many poor families, also lacks the resources to secure the existing drugs and technologies that they so desperately need. In 2002, the top ten causes of death in low-income countries were lower respiratory infections, HIV/AIDS, perinatal conditions, stroke and other cerebrovascular diseases, diarrheal diseases, coronary heart disease, malaria, traffic accidents, tuberculosis, and chronic obstructive pulmonary disease.[5] Reliable treatments exist for many of these conditions but few poor people can afford the treatments.

Inadequate health-related infrastructure can make it hard for the poor to secure essential drugs and technologies even if they are cheap or free. In many countries, there are too few clinics and many of the existing clinics are hard to access.[6] Some clinics lack staff, equipment, resources, and personnel.[7] Others lack basic services like the consistent electricity necessary for refrigerating vaccines and other medicines.[8] When Tamil lived in the provinces, the nearest clinic was very far away. She would have to spend

---

[4] Pogge, "Intellectual Property Rights and Access to Essential Medicines."
[5] World Health Organization, "The Top 10 Causes of Death."
[6] Global Health Watch, *Global Health Watch 2005–2006.*
[7] The fact that many health workers are poorly paid and sick also makes it hard for the poor to get the drugs and technologies they need. Developing country health workers often migrate to developed countries for better pay. Barnard, "In the High Court of South Africa," 159–74.
[8] Barnard, "In the High Court of South Africa," 159–74.

Table 6.1. *R&D and GBD*

Condition	GDP (million DALYs)	% of total GBD	R&D funding (US$ millions)	R&D funding (US$ per DALY)
All GBD	1,470	100	105,900	72
HIV/AIDS + tuberculosis + Malaria	167	11.4	1,400	8.4
Cardiovascular disease	148.19	9.9	9,402	63.45
Diabetes	16.19	1.1	1,653	102.07
HIV/AIDS	84.46	5.7	2,049	24.26
Malaria	46.49	3.1	288	6.2
Tuberculosis	34.74	2.3	378	10.88

Modified from: Global Forum for Health Research, "Monitoring Financial Flows for Health Research 2006," 90.

most of the day traveling and walk for several miles to get to the clinic. Then, she might have to wait for a day or two until a doctor arrived.

Even if it were possible to circumvent these problems, however, poor people also face a different problem. Few existing drugs and technologies address the most prevalent diseases in poor countries.[9] "Malaria, pneumonia, diarrhoea, and tuberculosis, which together account for 21 percent of the GBD, receive 0.31 percent of all public and private funds devoted to health research."[10] Between 1975 and 1999, only 13 of 1,393 new drugs were indicated for tropical diseases and five resulted from veterinary research.[11]

Furthermore, since the TRIPS Agreement, new medicines may become even harder to secure. The TRIPS Agreement extends patent protection on new medicines internationally. Poor countries do not do much research and development on new drugs and technologies and the Philippines

[9] Part of the problem is that, from a Bio company's perspective, the ideal drug is one that treats chronic diseases or disorders that do not kill affluent patients. So, "vastly more money and human ingenuity are invested toward finding remedies for hair loss, pimples, and erectile dysfunction than toward developing effective medicines for diseases that are decimating the world's poor." Pogge, "Intellectual Property Rights and Access to Essential Medicines." Healthy patients do not need medication and poor patients do not pay.

[10] Pogge, "Intellectual Property Rights and Access to Essential Medicines."

[11] Ibid. Trouiller et al., "Drugs for Neglected Diseases," 945–51. Most of the newly approved drugs are not new molecular entities (NMEs). "In 2002, only seventeen of the seventy-eight newly approved drugs were NMEs." Angell, *The Truth About the Drug Companies*, 43.

may not be able to import drugs from countries like India which reverse engineer new products.

This chapter suggests a way of restructuring the incentives Bio companies face so that they can extend access to essential drugs and medications to the poor.[12] This chapter articulates a concrete, specific, proposal that has the potential to bring significant benefits to these people. Finally, it argues that this proposal has some advantages over and, can be used in conjunction with, its main competitors. Even those who reject the argument in the first half of this book might embrace this proposal. The critics need only agree that it is a good thing if there is a feasible way of restructuring the incentives Bio companies face so that they can extend access to essential drugs and technologies to the poor.

6.3 FAIR TRADE BIO

6.3.1 Fair Trade Bio labeling

One way to encourage Bio companies to do more for the poor is to develop a Fair Trade Bio label. The idea is to rate Bio companies based on how their policies impact poor peoples' access to essential drugs and technologies. The best companies, in a given year, will be Fair Trade Bio certified and would be allowed to use a Fair Trade Bio label on their products.[13] These companies will then have an incentive to (voluntarily) use the label to garner a larger share of the market.[14] If Pfizer was highly rated, Pfizer could use the Fair Trade Bio label on Advil (ibuprofen). Pfizer would have an incentive to do so because consumers and doctors might, in some cases, prefer to purchase and prescribe Fair Trade Bio Advil over the alternative analgesics and insurance companies may give preference to highly rated companies in creating their formularies. If even a small percentage of consumers, doctors, or insurance companies prefer Fair Trade Bio products, the incentive to use this label for analgesics alone could be significant in this approximately two billion

---

[12] Flory and Kitcher, "Global Health and the Scientific Research Agenda," 36–65.

[13] It might be good if the agency only certified companies in the top few percentiles of the ranking. Then standards for receiving Fair Trade certification will keep rising over time as companies compete to be amongst the highest rated. The system might be designed so that standards would rise quickly at least until the GBD is greatly reduced. Economic analysis considering how companies respond to a particular certification system may be necessary to design the ideal system.

[14] Companies might be charged a modest licensing fee to offset the costs of maintaining the rating system and to market the label.

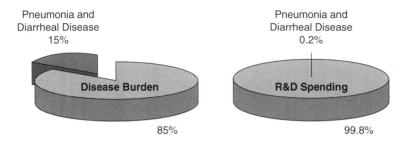

Figure 6.1 Large mismatch: R&D spending and disease burden (DALYs) for the largest killers in 1990 – pneumonia and diarrheal disease. (From World Health Organization, "Investing in Health Research and Development," Figure S.2.)

dollar a year market.[15] (Note: The top ten analgesic pills seem to capture between 2 and 14 percent of the market each and they are all available over the counter from Walgreens and other pharmacies.)[16]

The possibility of any Fair Trade depends on developing a good rating system to indicate what kinds of trade and investments are "Fair." One possibility is to use parts of the recently released Access to Medicine Index (Figure 6.2) publicized by the *New York Times*.[17] This chapter will consider how to create a more objective index below.

It is worth exploring the possibility of Fair Trade Bio since it is similar in some ways to other very successful Fair Trade proposals. In 2000, European countries sold 27 million pounds of coffee worth more than US$300 million.[18] Fair Trade coffee was sold in more than 35,000 supermarkets, as well as many universities and government offices. Sales amounted to about 1.2 percent of the European market.[19] In the USA the Fair Trade coffee market grew by 79 percent in 2000–2001 and experts predict it will be the largest Fair Trade coffee market.[20] Ninety-seven percent of roasters including Starbucks, Peets, and Green Mountain Coffee sell Fair Trade certified coffee; even Exxon Mobil

[15] In 1986, the market for pain relievers was US$1.7 billion. Ibuprofen pain relievers only captured 9 percent of the market. *New York Times*, "Analgesic Makers in a Battle."
[16] Chain Drug Review, "Internal Analgesic Tablets." Walgreens, "Search Results."
[17] Access to Medicine Foundation, "Access to Medicine Index."
[18] TransFair USA, "TransFair USA," and Max Havelaar Belgium, "Cafe," both cited in: Raynolds, "Poverty Alleviation Through Participation in Fair Trade Coffee Networks."
[19] EFTA, *Fair Trade in Europe*, cited in: Raynolds, "Poverty Alleviation Through Participation in Fair Trade Coffee Networks."
[20] McMahon, "'Cause Coffees' Produce a Cup with an Agenda."

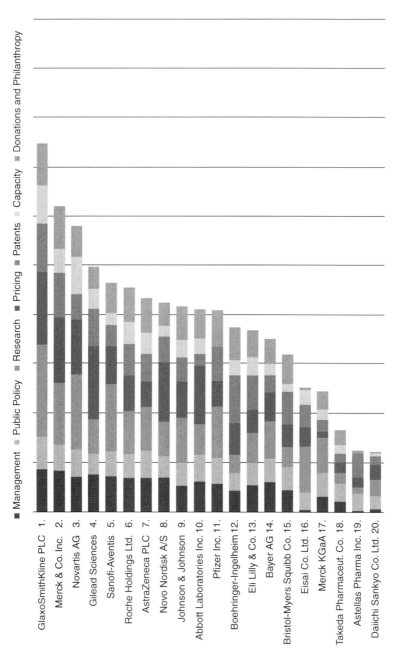

Figure 6.2 Select Access to Medicine Index ratings.

sells the stuff.[21] And it is not just coffee. In 2000, there were 400 million dollars worth of sales in Fair Trade labeled products and the Fair Trade market was growing at 30 percent per year.[22] By 2007, Fair Trade certified sales were approximately €2.3 billion.[23]

The way this chapter conceives of Fair Trade is new. Traditionally, Fair Trade programs have focused on improving the lives of poor producers or workers. Fair Trade coffee, for instance, must be picked by harvesters who are paid a living wage. One can imagine a Fair Trade proposal along these lines that would reward Bio companies that are doing a good job of producing drugs in developing countries, e.g. treating their employees well in the process. That, however, is not the idea here. Note, however, that some Fair Trade certification schemas are different from standard Fair Trade certification schemas. Some try to prevent companies from employing certain kinds of workers. Like RugMark (now known as GoodWeave International), "Respect: Fair Trade Sports," for example, focuses on eliminating child labor.[24]

This chapter's way of thinking about Fair Trade might allow us to extend the idea far beyond Bio firms. This chapter extends the idea of Fair Trade beyond production processes. This way of looking at Fair Trade takes into account how producers impact even those poor people they do not employ. This allows Fair Trade standards to apply to all producers – even large transnational corporations that employ no poor people at all. The practices of competing energy or extractive resource firms might also be rated and the best of these companies given Fair Trade certification. Energy companies that develop and help poor people secure access to renewable energy sources might, for instance, be Fair Trade certified.

Although this kind of Fair Trade is different from traditional Fair Trade in some ways, it is similar in many others. Traditional Fair Trade programs promote social justice by shaping the terms of trade to benefit the poor.[25] This chapter's Fair Trade proposal aims to shape the terms of trade and direct investment in ways that encourage Bio companies to extend access to essential drugs and technologies to the poor.

The difference between this chapter's Fair Trade Bio proposal and traditional Fair Trade campaigns does not automatically undercut the support

---

[21] Conroy, "Can Advocacy-Led Certification Systems Transform Global Corporate Practices?"and TransFair USA, "TransFair USA," both cited in: Raynolds, "Poverty Alleviation Through Participation in Fair Trade Coffee Networks."

[22] Fairtrade Foundation, "What is Fairtrade?"

[23] Fairtrade Labelling Organizations International, "Facts and Figures."

[24] Respect Fair Trade Sports, "Gear Shop."

[25] International Fair Trade Association, "What is Fair Trade?"

that the success of traditional campaigns provides for considering this new alternative. Ethical consumption is generally on the rise. In the UK, for instance, combined ethical purchasing in energy, housing, household goods, personal items, transportation, personal items, and subscriptions rose from about 1.3 to 1.6 percent from 1999 to 2000, much faster than the general growth in these markets.[26]

The proposal is also similar to other successful labeling campaigns. Such campaigns include Buy Red and Buy Pink – for companies willing to donate a portion of the sale of a product to the Millennium Development Corporation and breast cancer awareness. Red has provided US$150 million to the Global Fund and is one of its largest contributors.[27] The proposal also resembles the US Department of Agriculture (USDA) Organic label, Leeds certification for green buildings, and Forest Stewardship Council (FSC) and Smart Wood Certified Forestry sustainable forestry labeling.

This proposal fits more easily into the "Fair Trade" than many other categories, like the "green" and "organic" movements, as it focuses primarily on improving the lives of the poor. So, this chapter will continue to talk about the proposal as "Fair Trade Bio," though other names are possible. If one wants to reserve the label "Fair Trade" for companies with decent production processes, one might just create a new label for this proposal.

There is, in any case, reason to think that a Fair Trade Bio label could create large incentives for positive change.[28] One percent of the market in analgesics alone – less than the percentage of the European market in coffee captured by Fair Trade coffee – is twice the size of the revenue of some Bio companies as 1 percent of the US$2 billion market is US$20 million.[29] Markets for other pharmaceutical products are much larger. The US market for prescription allergy medicines, in 2001 alone, generated revenues

[26] Doane, "Taking Flight."

[27] The Global Fund to Fight AIDS, Tuberculosis and Malaria, "REDTM Generates Landmark."

[28] The biggest pharmaceutical company, Pfizer, has revenues of about US$48 billion per year. Pfizer, "Pfizer Reports." But a quick web search suggests that several of the 23 companies producing the 26 orphan drugs with the most potential to benefit the poor only have revenues or sales of US$1–10 million a year. This list was selected by a panel of three experts in international health at the University of Pittsburgh Medical Center. Contact the author for further information. Revenue estimates were found here: Jigsaw, "Hoechst Marion Roussel Company Information." Jigsaw, "Romark Laboratories Lc Company Information." Jigsaw, "Braintree Laboratories Inc. Company Information." Many of these companies make products for developed country markets or merge with other small companies that do so. See, for instance: Braintree Laboratories, "Products."

[29] In 1986, the market for pain relievers was US$1.7 billion. Ibuprofen pain relievers only captured 9 percent of the market. *New York Times*, February 18, 1986, "Analgesic Makers in a Battle." For statistics on Fair Trade coffee, see: EFTA, *Fair Trade in Europe*, cited in: Raynolds, "Poverty Alleviation Through Participation in Fair Trade Coffee Networks."

of more than US$6.45 billion (US$1.7 billion came from over-the-counter allergy and asthma products *before* Claritin, Allegra, and Zyrtec were off prescription).[30]

Patients, doctors, and insurance companies will not always prefer Fair Trade Bio drugs and technologies. Sometimes there will be one medicine that is best for a particular condition. In that case, its Fair Trade Bio status may not matter. In many cases it would not even be a good idea for patients, doctors, or insurance companies to choose Fair Trade Bio products. They may not be the best choice for a given illness.

Many drugs have equally good competitors, however. In 2006, 63 percent of all prescriptions were for generic drugs. When there is an equally good competitor for drugs under patents, patients and doctors might take companies' ratings into account.[31] Furthermore, many over-the-counter medications have equally good competitors. The market for over-the-counter medicines in 2004, alone, was US$16 billion.[32] This market includes many drugs made by major Bio companies including Nicorette, Monistat, and Claritin that have reasonable competitors.

If generic companies were also rated, e.g. on the basis of their drug donation programs and charitable contributions, the potential impact of Fair Trade Bio labeling would be even larger. The retail market for generics was estimated to be over US$20 billion in 2003,[33] and consumers are often indifferent, or nearly indifferent, between generics and other medicines.[34] So the fact that pharmacies usually do not carry more than one generic of the same molecule should provide no objection to this proposal. People might prefer a Fair Trade Bio certified generic medication to its patented competitors.

Both over-the-counter and generic markets are much larger than the market captured by almost all Fair Trade products, including coffee.[35] So there is reason to believe Fair Trade Bio could have some impact. If

[30] See: BBC Research, "The U.S. Market for Prescription Allergy Treatment and Management." Also see: Kalorama Information, "The U.S. Market for Over-the-Counter Allergy and Asthma Products."

[31] Frank, "The Ongoing Regulation of Generic Drugs," cited in: Kesselheim, "Think Globally, Prescribe Locally," 125–39.

[32] Mahecha, "Outlook: Rx-to-OTC Switches," 380–6.

[33] For statistics see: Mullins, Palumbo, and Stuart, "Projections of Drug Approvals, Patent Expirations, and Generic Entry." Also see: *The Economist*, "Fair Enough," 33.

[34] Sometimes companies may not want to use a label on generic products if they would prefer their customers buy their higher priced brand name drugs. They can choose to use the label only on their brand name products, if that is the case.

[35] For statistics see: Mullins et al., "Projections of Drug Approvals, Patent Expirations, and Generic Entry." Also see: *The Economist*, "Fair Enough," 33.

consumption of Fair Trade Bio goods reached 1 percent of the market in over-the-counter and generic medications – which, as we saw, is less than the proportion of the market captured by Fair Trade coffee – that would yield at least US$360 million worth of incentive for Bio companies to become Fair Trade Bio certified.[36] This number looks big enough to incentivize even Pfizer to do some good.

Finally, Bio companies make all kinds of products besides drugs – from diet drinks to lotions and pet vitamins to mouth wash. Pfizer, for instance, makes parasiticides, anti-infectives, biologicals, allergy, cancer, pain, metabolic disease, nutritionals, and food safety products *for animals*. Besides their pain management, dietary supplements, respiratory, topical, and gastrointestinal medicines for people, they have "a full line of infant formulas, follow-on formulas, growing-up milks, and prenatal and adult supplements."[37] So, they could use the Fair Trade Bio label on these products too.

Having different, e.g. gold and silver star, labels might help ensure that the Fair Trade Bio label does not just "rubber stamp" what may be genuinely bad behavior on the part of Bio companies.[38] Initially, even the best companies might not be doing enough to extend access to essential drugs and technologies to the poor.

Even in the absence of a complete account of companies' obligations or multiple labels, however, a Fair Trade Bio rating agency may not condone bad behavior. Just as it is possible to reward a generally bad employee or child for doing something right, it is possible to reward a generally bad company for good behavior. It is essential that everyone is clear about exactly what the Fair Trade Bio label does and does not mean.

It may be possible to keep companies from undermining the Fair Trade Bio label. Although some companies may lobby the rating agency or create counterfeit labels, there are also reasons for highly ranked companies to support that label. If the rating standards are transparent and simple, and consumers and health care professionals are educated about the Fair Trade Bio label, it might be widely trusted. If the label is well known, alternatives may be viewed with suspicion. This seems to be the case with

[36] For statistics see: Mullins et al., "Projections of Drug Approvals, Patent Expirations, and Generic Entry." Also see: *The Economist*, "Fair Enough," 33.

[37] Pfizer, "Diversified Business."

[38] Perhaps this consideration also tells in favor of a label that says something like *Extending Access* rather than *Fair Trade Bio* for companies that are just the best out of a bad lot. The Fair Trade Bio label might be reserved for companies that really are doing what they should.

many traditional Fair Trade labels, for instance.[39] Governments might even regulate use of the Fair Trade Bio label as the USA did, however imperfectly, with "Organic" labels.[40]

6.3.2 Fair Trade licensing

Having a Fair Trade certification system for Bio companies would open the door to all kinds of fruitful social activism. It might form the basis for a socially responsible investment campaign. Alternately, activists who believe, e.g. that people have a human right to essential drugs and technologies, might organize boycotts of (some) inessential medicines produced by companies that are not Fair Trade certified. Fair Trade Bio companies themselves could lobby insurance companies to include Fair Trade Bio products in their formularies. And so on. Such activism might positively impact the poor's access to essential drugs and technologies.

Fair Trade Bio might even encourage new kinds of social activism. An organization along the lines of Universities Allied for Access to Essential Medicines might create a campaign to get universities to develop "Fair Licensing" policies; they might launch a Fair Trade Bio licensing campaign.[41]

Bio companies rely, to a large extent, on university research and development. Universities have developed many drugs and technologies including vaccines, tests for osteoporosis and breast cancer, and the "gene splicing technology that initiated the biotechnology industry."[42] The big pharmaceutical companies probably license in or acquire a large percentage of their drug by purchasing small biotech companies from universities. "In 2002, for example, Pfizer licensed in 30 percent of its drugs, and Merck 35 percent."[43] All of Bristol-Myers Squibb's best-selling drugs

---

[39] TransFair USA, for instance, has never had to take anyone to court for misusing their label, a conversation usually suffices to either get companies to stop using the label or adhere to their standards for certification. Hassoun, Nicole, unpublished phone interview with Catherine Sinclair, Business Development Associate TransFair USA, 2009.

[40] Some worry that the agriculture lobby succeeded in lowering standards for calling something "organic." Even if the standards are not quite as good as one might like, the USDA does oversee the use of the pesticides and other farming practices that motivated the organic movement in the first place.

[41] I have discussed the proposal with the director of Universities Allied for Essential Medicines (UAEM). Hassoun, Nicole, unpublished phone interview with Ethan Guillan, Director UAEM, Palo Alto, California, 2009.

[42] Association of American Universities, "University Technology Transfer of Government-Funded Research Has Wide Public Benefits."

[43] Angell, *The Truth About the Drug Companies*.

in 2003 were licensed.[44] Pharmaceutical companies probably acquire even more of their most innovative drugs from universities.[45] Most cancer and HIV/AIDS medications come from university research sponsored by the National Institutes of Health.[46] In 2000, a US Senate report found that federal funding supported the development of 15 of the 21 most important drugs.[47] Most federally funded research is done at universities.[48]

On a conservative estimate, about a third of research and development (R&D) is done by universities in high-income countries (Figure 6.3). The percentage may be even greater as companies have a large incentive to over-report R&D and include marketing costs as R&D.[49]

This was not the case a few years ago. In 1980, Congress passed the Bayh-Dole Act. This act allowed universities to patent their research and to license it to third parties.[50] Before the act was passed, universities received less than 250 patents a year. In 1996, universities received over 2,000 patents, "executed nearly 2,200 licensing agreements, and received royalty

---

[44] Harris, "Will the Pain Ever Let Up for Bristol-Myers?" Section 3, 1. University technology transfer yielded around US$25 billion in 1996. Association of American Universities, "University Technology Transfer of Government-Funded Research Has Wide Public Benefits."

[45] On changing patterns in pharmaceutical company innovation, see: National Institute for Health Care Management Foundation, "Changing Pattern of Pharmaceutical Innovation."

[46] Angell, *The Truth About the Drug Companies.*

[47] These included captopril (Capoten), fluoxetine (Prozac), acyclovir (Zovirax), AZT, acyclovir, fluconazole (Diflucan), foscarnet (Foscavir), and ketoconazole (Nizoral). For more information, see: Joint Economic Committee, "The Benefits of Medical Research and the Role of NIH."

[48] Universities Allied for Essential Medicine, "Why Universities?" One might also get a sense of how much technology industry is licensing-in by considering how much of the research going into its products is coming from universities. "The NIH had selected the five top-selling drugs in 1995 (Zantac, Zonirax, Capoten, Vasotec, and Prozac) and found that sixteen of the seventeen key scientific papers leading to their discovery and development came from outside the industry. (Eli Lilly had sponsored one of the four key studies leading to the development of Prozac.) Looking at all the relevant published research, not just at the key studies, only 15 percent came from industry, whereas 55 percent came from NIH-funded laboratories and 20 percent from foreign academic institutions." Angell, *The Truth About the Drug Companies,*" 65. Furthermore, "a recent study published in the journal of *Health Affairs* reported that, in 1998, only about 15 percent of the scientific articles cited in patent applications for clinical medicine came from industry research, while 54 percent came from academic centers, 13 percent from government, and the rest from various other public and nonprofit institutions. Remember that these are patent applications for all new drugs and medical innovations, not simply for those ultimately judged to be clinically important. Had the data been limited to major breakthrough drugs, the industry's role would undoubtedly have been even smaller. An unpublished internal document produced by the NIH in February 2000, which was obtained by Public Citizen through the Freedom of Information Act, revealed similar percentages." Angell, *The Truth About the Drug Companies*, 64. See also: DiMasi, Hansen, and Grabowski, "The Price of Innovation," 151–85.

[49] Furthermore, a lot of funding for universities comes from government, so Figure 6.3 probably understates the government's role.

[50] Consumer Project on Technology, "The Bayh-Dole Act."

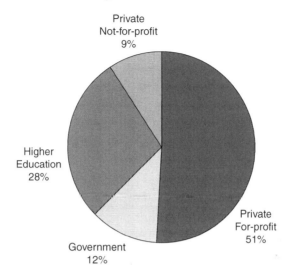

Figure 6.3 R&D in high-income countries. (Modified from: Global Forum for Health Research, "Monitoring Financial Flows for Health Research 2006," 41.)

income from licensing of US$242 million."[51] Between 1980 and 2007, over 1,500 start-up companies were formed from academic research.[52] In 2005, there were at least 28,349 active licenses.[53]

Furthermore, there is reason to believe pharmaceutical companies are coming to rely more and more on universities. Since the 1990s in-house pharmaceutical research has not been very productive.[54] In light of its dry pipeline, the pharmaceutical industry is "searching ever more

---

[51] Universities Allied for Essential Medicine, "Why Universities?"

[52] Ibid. The Stevenson-Wydler Act similarly allowed NIH-funded research to be patented and then licensed to drug companies. The companies market the drugs and then sometimes patent them for other uses. If a similar campaign could get the NIH to deal only with highly-rated Bio companies, this might help people access essential medicines and technologies as well. After all, the NIH has helped create essential drugs like AZT (which was developed by NIH in conjunction with Duke and then licensed to GlaxoSmithKline). Angell, *The Truth About the Drug Companies*, 57.

[53] Association of University Technology Managers, "AUTM U.S. Licensing Survey FY2005," 14. The Association of University Technology Managers licensing surveys provide information about almost 200 major universities' budgets, research expenditures, and licensing agreements as well as other useful information. See: Association of University Technology Managers, "FY 2005 AUTM U.S. Licensing Survey."

[54] National Institute for Health Care Management Foundation, "Changing Pattern of Pharmaceutical Innovation."

desperately for drugs to license from small biotechnology companies and universities."[55]

Because Bio companies depend to a great extent on universities' licenses, universities could, conceivably, influence these companies' policies. Suppose, for instance, universities require that Fair Trade Bio companies receive preferential access to their licenses. Companies will then have an incentive to abide by Fair Trade Bio standards.[56]

Universities might adopt a Fair Trade licensing policy voluntarily. Their technology transfer offices could agree to offer only Fair Trade licenses. At the University of Pittsburgh, for instance, the head of the Office of Technology Management has this decision-making capability.[57] He or she would probably also require the support of the chancellor if the policy negatively impacted the Office's ability to sell licenses.[58] Depending on how the Fair Trade Bio standards are set, the policy might not negatively impact the sale of university licenses. At least it is worth carrying out the requisite econometric analysis to determine the likely impact on all of the relevant stakeholders including universities and the poor.

Technology transfer offices already use some non-financial criteria when deciding to whom to license their products. The Bayh-Dole Act encourages universities to license to small, US companies. Universities comply without complaint.[59]

If the technology transfer offices at some universities are reluctant to sign on to voluntary programs, however, professors and researchers might

---

[55] Angell, *The Truth About the Drug Companies*, 236.

[56] It is important that universities' licenses include a clause requiring that those transferring their licenses, or selling technology derived from university licenses to others, give preference to Fair Trade Bio companies. Universities often create start-up companies or license to start-up companies that, being new, could not themselves be Fair Trade certified. These companies test and develop products using university technology. Eventually these companies are sold or sell their technology to larger companies that could be Fair Trade certified.

[57] Hassoun, Nicole, unpublished interview with Maria Vanegas, University of Pittsburgh Technology Licensing Associate, University of Pittsburgh Office of Technology Management, Pittsburgh, Pennsylvania, 2007.

[58] The University of Pittsburgh's Office of Technology Management alone generated US$7.1 million in revenue in 2007 from licensing revenue, equity cash-outs, and legal fee reimbursements from licensees. Licensing revenue alone was US$4.9 million and its equity in the start-up Novecea generated US$92,000; finally its spinout Stentor Inc. was sold for US$6.7 million: Office of Technology Management, "Annual Report 2007," 7–8.

[59] On average, 42.2 percent of university licenses go to small companies, while only 39.2 percent of US hospitals and research institutes license to small companies, and technology investment firms mostly license to large companies. Association of University Technology Managers, "AUTM U.S. Licensing Survey FY2005," 14. Also see: Association of University Technology Managers, "FY 2005 AUTM U.S. Licensing Survey," 32. Universities are likewise encouraged to license to US based companies and often do so without complaint. Association of American Universities, "University Technology Transfer of Government-Funded Research Has Wide Public Benefits."

have an impact. They sign agreements to allow universities to license patents resulting from research they create. Although some faculty at major
universities receive industry funding, only 7 percent of university research
is funded by industry.[60] Bio funding probably makes up only a portion of
the total.[61]

Universities might be receptive to the idea since:

…universities hold an avowed commitment to creating and disseminating knowledge for the public good, and they have pledged to see the technologies they
develop deployed to benefit the world. Campus decision makers are insulated
from lobbies that may dominate political arenas; they are expected to be responsive to students and faculty; and they operate in an environment where reasoned
debate, not power, is expected to be the currency.[62]

As the Association of University Technology Managers put it, universities
are not only concerned about monetary benefits. They want the new drugs
and technologies they develop to "be used to further the public good."[63]

Students could also encourage professors and universities to make the
necessary revisions. They might follow the lead of United Students Against
Sweatshops (USAS). USAS has helped convince campuses to buy "sweat-free"
clothing made at factories approved by the Worker Rights Consortium.[64]
Alternately, they could work with UAEM, which has convinced universities
to adopt Equitable Access (i.e. open access) licensing policies.[65]

---

[60] Association of University Technology Managers, "AUTM U.S. Licensing Survey FY2005," 14.
[61] About 20 percent of Stanford faculty members had industry funding in 2004. About 30 percent
of Stanford's faculty resided in the medical school. Ray Delgado, "Slow Growth Seen In Faculty
Ranks." Of course, not all of this funding would have been from pharmaceutical companies but
pharmaceutical companies probably fund some non-medical faculty so it might be reasonable to
suppose that 20 percent of the medical faculty had pharmaceutical funding at Stanford. If that
is right, then about 7 percent of Stanford's faculty were funded by pharmaceutical companies.
Another way of getting at the proportion of industry funding from pharmaceutical companies is
to suppose that the percentage of the medical faculty at Stanford receiving industry funding is
about the same as the percentage of medical faculty receiving industry funding on average. If it
is, then 25 percent of medical faculty at Stanford had industry funding. Again, other industries
may account for some of this funding but pharmaceutical companies may fund non-medical
faculty as well. So it seems reasonable to conclude (again) that about 7 percent of the Stanford
faculty had pharmaceutical funding. Stanford, however, has a large medical school and most
universities and colleges probably receive much less industry funding.
[62] Universities Allied for Essential Medicine, "Why Universities?"
[63] Association of University Technology Managers, "AUTM U.S. Licensing Survey FY2005," 14.
Also see: Association of University Technology Managers, "FY 2005 AUTM U.S. Licensing
Survey," 35.
[64] United Students Against Sweatshops, "About Ethical Contracting Campaigns."
[65] Universities Allied for Essential Medicine, "Our Proposals." The moral justification for this campaign would probably differ from USAS's since making goods that essentially and directly rely
on the labor of the poor is different to making goods that simply ignore the needs of the poor.

If a Fair Trade Bio licensing campaign was only as successful as USAS's campaign has been so far, this proposal could create US$840 million worth of incentive for Bio companies to become certified every year.[66] That is about the cost of developing a new drug on the highest estimates. This incentive might suffice to double the number of drugs produced for neglected diseases in 1975–1999 in a similar time-frame.

6.4 CREATING A GOOD RATING SYSTEM

The key to all aspects of the Fair Trade Bio proposal is developing a good rating system. Recall that there is reason to encourage Bio companies to do two things. First, improve access to existing drugs and technologies. Second, do more research on, and development of, new drugs and technologies that address the diseases of the poor. A good rating system should reward companies both for creating and helping poor people access essential drugs and technologies.

A rating system might be either input or output based. Input based systems reward companies based on the amount of resources they put into creating, and helping poor people access, essential drugs and technologies. Output based systems reward companies based on their actual impact on global health. If, for instance, the system just considered R&D and charity budgets, it would be rewarding companies based on their input. This is analogous to rewarding someone based on how much time or money they invest in a project. If, on the other hand, a system considered how a company's R&D and charitable donations impacted the health of the poor, it would be rewarding the company for its output. This is like paying someone for how much work they complete on a project.

There are some problems for an input measure. Companies rewarded for their investments might make it seem like they are investing more in

---

[66] This assumes 30 percent of pharmaceutical companies' research is done at universities, so that similar success would ensure that at least 2 percent of the research funds benefit the poor. Since US academic centers spent over US$42 billion in R&D in 2005, 2 percent of US$42 billion is US$840 million a year. Association of University Technology Managers, "FY 2005 AUTM U.S. Licensing Survey." As noted above, universities are only getting about US$240 million a year from licenses but they get more from the biotechnology companies they create. For instance, "Columbia University, which patented the technology used in the manufacture of Epogen and Cerezyme, collected nearly $300 million in royalties from more than thirty biotechnology companies over the seventeen-year life of the patent." Angell, *The Truth About the Drug Companies*, 71. Some of this incentive would presumably come from other downstream companies too. How much incentive companies will have will depend on how much the universities are willing to demand.

helping the poor than they are actually investing. This is just like someone who is rewarded for their time or monetary investment in a project making it seem like they are investing more time than they are actually investing. This is a real concern given that Bio companies may already be exaggerating their R&D costs.[67] It is also one of the problems with the (original) Access to Medicine Index. Furthermore, input measures may create other bad incentives for they provide the same reward to companies that produce little with their investments as to companies that make productive investments. If what is important is whether the poor can access essential drugs and technologies, it is probably better to reward companies based on how much their policies actually increase access.

Before considering how it is possible to measure the impact of companies' charitable and research activities on poor people's health, consider how a good rating system might be developed and administered. A good rating system should probably be developed and administered by an appropriately impartial and transparent rating organization. Perhaps a non-governmental group like the Fair Trade Labeling Organization would be willing to develop and oversee the label. Alternately, governments or international organizations might develop the label and provide the requisite oversight. Note that the US government exercises such oversight, albeit imperfectly, over the USDA Organic label and the International Organization for Standardization regulates the ISO 14000 environmental management standards.[68] Input from all the relevant stakeholders, including Bio companies, may be essential to creating a good and sustainable rating system. This will help insure that companies get credit for as many of the good things they are doing as possible and can help expose potential areas of abuse.

A good rating organization should probably also have a review panel to address unforeseen problems as they arise. This panel can hear objections to allowing a company to receive credit for a proposed project and alter the rating system as necessary.[69] It is impossible to foresee every problem. It may also be counter-productive to spend time worrying about problems that may not arise.

[67] Angell, *The Truth About the Drug Companies.*
[68] United States Department of Agriculture, "National Organic Program." International Organization for Standardization, "About ISO."
[69] A review panel could, for instance, create a mechanism to penalize companies for "dumping" drugs on developing country markets if donations do more harm than good for the poor because they are driving generic competitors out of business. This would insure that companies only receive credit for making donations on the condition that they are given in ways that will not have such consequences.

To evaluate companies, a rating agency might look at the number of disability-adjusted life-years (DALYs) each company is saving in developing countries.[70] It might maximize the positive impact on the poor to avoid just rewarding larger companies that have greater resources to invest in helping the poor secure essential drugs and technologies. If so, the agency might divide each company's impact by some measure of that company's size, e.g. their net worth or revenue. The details on this point have to be worked out carefully. The result would generate a final ranking of companies.

If it is too difficult to find verifiable information on the impact of companies' charitable or R&D endeavors, a rating agency could just start with the information it can secure. But the rating agency must keep in mind that the rating system, if effective, will create strong incentives for companies to do whatever it is that improves their rating.

Suppose, for instance, that to most improve poor people's access to existing drugs, the rating agency would have to look at how much good each company does for the poor with its (a) drug donations, (b) price reductions, and (c) approved and verifiable health projects (e.g. health-related infrastructure improvements in developing countries).[71] Suppose further that the agency lacked the information it needed to measure the impact of investments in good health projects so left this information out of its rating schema.[72] Then companies would have an incentive to cut their health-projects budgets and put their resources into drug donations and differential pricing instead. This may not, however, pose an ethical problem for the rating agency. It may be permissible for the agency to do what it can to encourage donations and price reductions.[73] This may just

---

[70] Different authors disagree about the merits of the available measures of an intervention's impact. Some, for instance, prefer to measure an intervention's impact on quality-adjusted life-years (QALYs). Given this disagreement, a good rating agency should consider the merits of the different measures for the task at hand.

[71] A good rating system need not measure every way in which Bio companies can improve health in developing countries. Still, Bio companies do invest in health infrastructure and rewarding them for these investments will help insure that they have incentives not only to cure illnesses but also to prevent them.

[72] Parts of the Access to Medicine Index may be useful here. Researchers should think carefully, however, before using it. The index is primarily input based as the index gives companies credit just for having good policies in place. As anyone familiar with Enron's official code of ethics knows, good policies do not guarantee good outcomes. Access to Medicine Foundation, "Access to Medicine Index."

[73] Because it is not entirely clear how much incentive companies would have to become Fair Trade Bio certified initially, it would be a good idea to include some things companies can do relatively cheaply to improve their ratings (e.g. donation programs). That way the poor could reap some

provide reason for other agencies to encourage appropriate health-related infrastructure investments. After all, the money that companies put into donation and price reduction programs need not come from their health-related infrastructure investment budgets. It could come from their non-essential drug budgets.

This point is a substantive philosophical one. Consider an analogy. Those who defend child labor often argue that if child labor is eliminated, children and their families will suffer. A child's next-best alternative might be prostitution. Even if this is true, however, it provides no reason to allow child labor. At least it provides no more reason to allow child labor than finding out that a child prostitute's next-best alternative is slavery provides to allow child prostitution. Rather, it provides reason to try to both eliminate child labor *and* provide better jobs for adults and schools for children.[74] None of this means, however, that it is impermissible for one group to open a school and another to expose child labor. The Fair Trade proposal advanced here is not a complete solution to the problems the poor face in meeting their basic health needs. Still, it may *help* the poor meet their basic health needs.

Once a rating agency has enough information to create some rating system, it may be easier for it to gather more information. The agency can make it a condition of being Fair Trade Bio certified in the future that companies provide access to the (verifiable) information the agency lacks. The initial rating system need not be perfect.

So consider, for instance, how a rating agency might estimate R&D output.[75] It would take a very long time to look at all the drugs each company produces, even in a given year. Fortunately, a rating agency might estimate companies' R&D output by looking at all the FDA approved "orphan" drugs and seeing how much each could improve poor people's health. Orphan drugs are those that Bio companies expect (or say they

---

benefits even if the incentive is not sufficient to convince countries to invest the kinds of money they would need to develop new drugs and technologies to benefit the poor.

[74] Of course, if there were good empirical evidence that all available alternatives to purchasing goods made with child labor would be worse for the children, it might be best to purchase the goods.

[75] To estimate the impact of health projects, an agency would have to transparently and systematically determine how much different investments in approved health projects help the poor. Perhaps the agency could induce companies to provide this information as a condition of certification. One place to start would be to evaluate the 126 health partnerships the pharmaceutical industry reported to the International Federation of Pharmaceutical Manufacturers & Associations in 2006 which have been verified by researchers at the London School of Economics. Global Forum for Health Research, "Monitoring Financial Flows for Health Research 2006."

expect) to have very small markets in the USA.[76] So the drugs and technologies for neglected diseases that Bio companies lack an incentive to
produce for the poor should be listed as orphan. (Bio companies already
have incentives to produce drugs and technologies for which there is
a large US market.)[77] Of course, some orphan drugs may not help the
poor. Further, there is an incentive for companies to get as many drugs
as possible listed as orphan because they get up to a 50 percent tax credit
for testing orphan drugs.[78] A rating agency might, however, just do an
effectiveness analysis on orphan drugs that address neglected diseases, to
estimate how much each of these drugs will help the poor.

Although there are different ways of doing effectiveness analysis and
the calculations can get quite complex, the basic idea is simple. First, look
at each drug's market price and the amount of need equivalent dosages of
each will fulfill in developing countries (e.g. in DALYs).[79] The amount of
need equivalent dosages of a drug will fulfill might be calculated using the
DALY information in the WHO's Global Burden of Disease study and
drug efficacy estimates from clinical trials or meta-analyses of such data.[80]
Suppose of the 34 million DALYs lost to malaria, 80 percent can be attributed to *Plasmodium falciparum* (the worst kind of malaria).[81] Quinine is
effective in about 9 percent of cases.[82] So, quinine would avert about 2.4
million DALYs if everyone had access to it. Then researchers can consider
each drug's availability to measure its actual impact. If half of the people
who need it can get quinine, it will save about 1.2 million DALYs.

The next step is to rate companies on the basis of their inventions'
impact – aggregating their individual inventions' impacts (in terms of

---

[76] More precisely, orphan drugs address rare diseases in the USA. The US Food and Drug
Administration "provides orphan status to drugs and biologics which are defined as those
intended for the safe and effective treatment, diagnosis or prevention of rare diseases/disorders
that affect fewer than 200,000 people in the U.S., or that affect more than 200,000 persons but
are not expected to recover the costs of developing and marketing a treatment drug." Food and
Drug Administration, "OOPD Program Overview."

[77] It might also be a good idea to provide more incentive for companies to develop drugs and technologies that will have a large impact on the poor even if they have a large market in developed
countries. If so, companies might also receive credit for producing drugs that address diseases on
the WHO's list of neglected diseases.

[78] Angell, *The Truth About the Drug Companies*.

[79] Once the rating system is up and running, the agency could make it a condition of being Fair
Trade Bio certified that companies provide verifiable data on the number of doses they sell by a
particular date.

[80] For some GBD data, see: World Health Organization, "The Global Burden of Disease."

[81] Ibid.

[82] World Health Organization, *Global Report on Antimalarial Drug Efficacy and Drug Resistance:
2000–2010*, 112.

DALYs averted). Suppose Pfizer has three drugs that avert the loss of 1.2 and 3.5 million DALYs, respectively. Suppose Bayer has two drugs that avert the loss of 2.2 and 2.4 million DALYs, respectively, Pfizer may be ranked above Bayer. Pfizer's drugs avert 4.7 million DALYs, while Bayer avert 4.6 million DALYs.

There may be good reasons to modify this kind of rating system. To insure that companies do not get too much credit for producing slight variations on standard drugs and technologies, it might be good to consider how much improvement each drug offers over the next best alternative.[83] To do this, it might suffice to simply subtract the expected benefit to the poor of the best old drug or technology from the expected benefit of the new drug or technology.[84] Companies would, however, receive credit if their products alleviate more disease because they have better pricing strategies, for instance, even if their drugs offer no new therapeutic improvements.[85]

The details of this schema would have to be worked out carefully and might diverge significantly from those suggested here. Economic analysis here may help to maximize the positive impact on the poor. It might be more difficult to capture the impact Bio companies are having on the poor than to create standards for good working conditions as the Workers Rights Consortium has tried to do. Still, it should be clear that it is possible to design and improve upon some such rating system, even if it is initially quite imperfect. The next section will set out some advantages of this proposal over some of the alternatives.

6.5 ADVANTAGES OF THE FAIR TRADE PROPOSALS AND RESPONSES TO OBJECTIONS

There are many ways of trying to restructure the incentives Bio companies face so that they do more to ensure that the poor secure essential drugs and technologies. The Fair Trade Bio proposals set out here have some advantages over, and avoid some of the problems with, the alternatives.

---

[83] This is because mefloquine is less effective than quinine, unless it offers some other therapeutic advantages over quinine. It is a synthetic analogue: There may be no reason to give credit to Roche Pharmaceuticals for the development of this drug.

[84] The agency might also consider the problems associated with drugs and technologies in estimating their net benefits (e.g. some drugs have pretty bad side effects that should probably be taken into account, others require difficult to implement treatment regimes).

[85] Taking into account companies' size will allow new or very small companies making only a few drugs to compete for good ratings. A rating agency might only rate large companies, however, if that is the best way to incentivize new R&D on drugs and technologies for the poor.

One advantage is that the proposals might both help the poor access existing drugs and technologies *and* encourage research on and development of new drugs and technologies that benefit the poor. Most of the alternatives address only one of these problems. The Fair Trade Bio labeling and licensing proposals also have other advantages over many of the alternatives. This section will make this case by considering just a few of the canonical alternatives. It is impossible to canvass every proposal in the literature here. There are many innovative licensing and intellectual property strategies.[86]

Consider, first, a few proposals that try to help the poor access existing drugs and technologies.[87] One way of lowering the cost of existing drugs and technologies is via differential pricing. Bio companies might offer drugs at different prices for different markets. Another option is compulsory licensing. Countries can issue licenses to produce and/or import these products without approval by the company holding the patent. Yet a third way of lowering the cost of existing drugs and technologies is to return to the pre-TRIPS situation where foreign patents are primarily recognized and enforced only in developed countries. Barring that, it may be possible to modify TRIPS to allow poor people to secure essential medicines at or below the marginal costs of production.[88]

Unfortunately, although Bio companies do some differential pricing, companies have also resisted differential pricing.[89] They have little

---

[86] Abramowicz, "Perfecting Patent Prizes," 114–236. Pharmaceutical R&D Policy Project, "The Landscape of Neglected Disease Drug Development." Faunce and Nasu, "Three Proposals for Rewarding Novel Health Technologies," 146–53. Berndt et al., "Advance Market Commitments for Vaccines Against Neglected Diseases," 491–511. Danzon and Towse, "Differential Pricing for Pharmaceuticals," 183–205. OHE Consulting, "A Review of IP and Non-IP Incentives for R&D for Diseases of Poverty."

[87] For a restatement of some part of what follows, see: Hassoun, "Pharmaceutical Justice."

[88] Although intellectual property rights encourage the development of new drugs and technologies, these rights may also prevent the poorest from securing existing drugs and technologies. The TRIPS Agreement requires WTO member countries to grant 20-year patent protection for new drugs and technologies. The so-called "TRIPS-Plus" provisions require countries to allow these patents to be "ever-greened" beyond the 20-year mark and discourage generic competition. Bio companies can apply for patents on many "trivial or irrelevant" aspects of their drugs and technologies like packaging or dosing regimen to extend protection beyond the life of their primary patent. They must then be notified before generics can be produced and get an automatic 30-month extension on their patent. Sometimes they try to extend protection further with legal action. See: Federal Trade Commission, "Generic Drug Entry Prior to Patent Expiration." Also see: National Institute for Health Care Management Foundation, "Changing Pattern of Pharmaceutical Innovation." Often generic drugs must be tested again before being put on the market even if they are basically equivalent to patented versions. This expensive testing can delay generic entry into the market. Pogge, "Intellectual Property Rights and Access to Essential Medicines." Lanjouw and Jack, "Trading Up."

[89] See: Kanavos, Costa-i-Font, Merkur, and Gemmill, "The Economic Impact of Pharmaceutical Parallel Trade in European Union Member States."

incentive to lower their prices for the poor. Companies argue that it is hard to prevent re-importation of cheaper versions of identical drugs across borders, even with different packaging.[90] They claim that Bio products are small and easy to hide.[91] So, it is not likely that differential pricing will be pursued to the extent required to protect global health.

Similarly, companies have resisted compulsory licensing. When South Africa passed its Medicines Act, many of the big pharmaceutical companies sued because the act encouraged generic competition for AIDS medicines.[92] It was only after protracted negotiations, and a great deal of negative media attention, that the pharmaceutical companies withdrew their lawsuit. Still, South Africa did not go on to import generic AIDS medicines.[93] At the behest of Bio companies, other countries have been singled out in the *301 Reports* of the US Trade Representative for not being aggressive enough in enforcing foreign intellectual property rights and have, thus, faced the threat of trade sanctions.[94] The USA has also used bilateral trade agreements and "diplomatic and political pressures to undermine countries that produce generic medicines and/or consider importing them."[95]

Worse, countries without their own manufacturing capacity may not be able to secure the drugs they need even if they do issue compulsory licenses.[96] Few poor countries have their own manufacturing capacity and, under TRIPS, it may become more difficult for those without manufacturing capacity to access generic drugs.[97] TRIPS requires countries like India, Brazil, and Thailand that export many generic drugs to developing countries to extend patent protection to essential drugs and technologies.

---

[90] Ibid.   [91] Ibid.

[92] Barnard, "In the High Court of South Africa," 159–74. "The combined worth of the world's top five drug companies is twice the combined GNP of all Sub-Saharan Africa." Global Health Watch, *Global Health Watch 2005–2006*, 103. In 2002, the ten largest pharmaceutical companies made over US$39 billion, more than half of the total profits of Fortune 500 companies. "With such profits at stake, it is no surprise Big Pharma invests a huge amount of money in protecting them." Global Health Watch, *Global Health Watch 2005–2006*, 103.

[93] Barnard, "In the High Court of South Africa," 159–74.

[94] Similarly, when Chile issued a compulsory license for efavirenz, an HIV/AIDS drug produced by Merck, the US government was displeased. See: Office of the United States Trade Representative, "Schwab Announces Results of Chile IPR Review." Also see: McDermott, "A Morality Tale on AIDS." For an account of Australia's difficulties in extending access to essential drugs and technologies to its population under TRIPS, see: Global Health Watch, *Global Health Watch 2005–2006*, 106.

[95] For an account of Australia's difficulties in extending access to essential drugs and technologies to its population under TRIPS, see: Global Health Watch, *Global Health Watch 2005–2006*, 106.

[96] Barnard, "In the High Court of South Africa," 159–74.

[97] Ibid. Steinbrook, "Closing the Affordability Gap for Drugs in Low-Income Countries," 1996–8.

Countries that want to export essential drugs and technologies will also have to issue compulsory licenses to do so. So far, only one country (Canada) has agreed to export drugs under a compulsory license.[98] Given the complexity of international and Canadian law, Canada was yet to export a single pill three years after issuing the license.[99]

Finally, there was a large social movement, backed even by the Pope, to prevent implementation of the TRIPS Agreement.[100] Ultimately, it failed.[101] Bio companies want control over the drugs they develop in every market. So a return to a pre-TRIPS situation, or even great modification, is unlikely.

Consider, next, alternatives to Fair Trade Bio that encourage R&D on essential drugs and medications for neglected diseases. Two such alternatives include prize funds and grants.[102] Agencies or individuals might, for instance, agree to buy a certain number of doses from any company that develops a malaria vaccine at a set price. Alternately, they might give grants for research on neglected diseases.[103]

Both alternatives have problems. Neither takes full advantage of the efficiency the free market offers. The agencies offering prize funds or grants have to decide what neglected diseases or problems they want to address and there may be better ways to help the poor. They also have to decide how much a given intervention is worth. "These decisions are likely to be associated with substantial inefficiencies due to incompetence, corruption, lobbying by companies and patient groups, and gaming."[104]

---

[98] World Trade Organization, "TRIPS and Public Health."

[99] Goodwin, "Right Idea, Wrong Result," 567–84.

[100] Martin, "Intervention by the Holy See at the World Trade Organization."

[101] The agreement was amended to make it easier to compulsory license essential drugs and technologies. World Trade Organization, "TRIPS and Public Health."

[102] A more recent alternative is another licensing and rating proposal – Universities Allied for Essential Medicines' (UAEM) Equal Access License (EAL) and their metric for rating university technology transfer offices. Their metric, however, looks only at technology transfer offices' policies rather than the impact of these policies. Hassoun, Nicole, unpublished phone interview with Ethan Guillan, Director UAEM, Palo Alto, California, 2009. Further, the EAL license is also a step in the right direction but may not do enough. It allows generic companies access to new research. It does nothing to help the poor secure access to existing drugs and technologies or encourage other Bio companies to do research on neglected diseases. Universities Allied for Essential Medicine, "Our Proposals."

[103] Such alternatives may be more cost-effective than prize funds. With prize funds, the prizes have to be large enough to compensate for the risk to companies of not being able to develop an acceptable invention or not being the first to do so. See: Kremer and Glennerster, *Strong Medicine*.

[104] Thomas Pogge, *World Poverty and Human Rights*, 243. Pogge also points out that a bidding system might provide a partial solution to this problem.

Hollis and Pogge's alternative is to create a second (voluntary) patent system. Under this system, Bio companies would not be given a limited monopoly for their inventions. Rather, inventors would be rewarded based on how much their inventions contribute to ameliorating the GBD. Inventors would have an incentive to invest in whatever R&D, infrastructure improvements, pricing systems, or donation programs would have the most impact on the GBD. They might even price their drugs below the marginal costs of production to capture a greater reward from this alternative patent scheme. The scheme would give inventors an incentive to collaborate with, rather than protest against, generic companies, country governments, and non-governmental organizations trying to alleviate the GBD. Hollis and Pogge's patent system would not create an incentive for companies to prefer drugs that treat the chronic diseases or disorders of affluent patients. Rather, companies would have an incentive to invest in those drugs that prevent the most death and alleviate the most suffering. Pogge says that the "cost of the plan might peak at around \$45-\$90 billion. With all the world's countries participating, \$45 billion amounts to 0.1 percent and \$90 billion to 0.2 percent of the global product."[105] In the proposal Pogge developed with Hollis, they advance a revised estimate of US\$6 billion.[106]

Hollis and Pogge's proposal would avoid some of the problems with prize funds. To offer a prize, someone other than the inventors must decide what is worth doing. Outside experts and bureaucrats may not know what can be done most efficiently with each company's resources. On Hollis and Pogge's proposal, companies would have a reason to invest in whatever research they believe will most cost-effectively reduce the GBD.

Unfortunately, Hollis and Pogge's proposal may also have a few problems. First, it is not clear how to correctly attribute reductions in the

[105] Thomas Pogge, "Intellectual Property Rights and Access to Essential Medicines," 18. It is not clear how they arrive at this estimate. Hollis and Pogge, "The Health Impact Fund, Making New Medicines Accessible for All." Pogge also seems to think that this way of incentivizing companies to do new R&D will be less expensive than prize funds which have to come up with big enough prizes to compensate companies for not being the first to develop a new drug or technology. This problem may be a general one for incentivizing companies to do new R&D, however. Presumably only one company can have a patent under Pogge's schema for a particular condition, so companies have to take into account the risk of doing R&D on a condition but not being the company to get the patent before deciding whether or not to do the R&D.

[106] Hollis and Pogge, "The Health Impact Fund, Making New Medicines Accessible for All." Their proposal is similar to some previous ones. See, for instance: Hubbard and Love, "A New Trade Framework for Global Healthcare R&D," e52.

GBD to an inventor's efforts. Granted a new drug or investment in infrastructure might help ameliorate a disease. Still, things non-governmental
organizations or other country governments are doing, independent of
the investor, may contribute more. It is not clear that Hollis and Pogge
are concerned to prevent investors from receiving undue credit and investors have incentive to claim credit where it is not due. Second, Hollis
and Pogge's current proposal relies on collecting a lot of *new* data by,
for instance, funding expensive clinical trials. They also want an accur-
ate estimate of potential impact. The necessary data is costly and hard to
collect.[107] Finally, their proposal is quite expensive and depends on the
goodwill of developed country taxpayers or donors who have historically
done little to help the global poor.[108] Unless it is well funded, it will not
generate a large enough incentive for companies to risk investing in new
drugs and technologies.[109]

There are probably ways of ameliorating the problems with some of
the proposals this chapter has canvassed, and each is likely to have
some positive impact. Nevertheless, the Fair Trade Bio proposals this
chapter has sketched avoid some of these problems. First, many Bio
companies have an incentive to support Fair Trade in Bio companies
while almost (if not) all Bio companies have an incentive to resist differential pricing, compulsory licensing, and a return to the pre-TRIPS
situation. Second, Fair Trade Bio labeling and licensing proposals
take full advantage of the free-market's efficiency. A Fair Trade rating agency need not decide what diseases or problems Bio companies
should address, nor need it determine how much inventions are worth
before they are created. Rather, a Fair Trade Bio rating agency would
reward companies based on how much their inventions and investments actually help the poor. Third, the Fair Trade Bio rating system
is output based and could be used to incentivize companies to not only
do R&D on neglected diseases but to extend access to existing drugs
and technologies to the poor. Fourth, it does not benefit companies
that do not help the poor.

This Chapter's Fair Trade proposals are supposed to capture only
what companies have already done. The way this chapter proposes to

---

[107] Selgelid, "A Full-Pull Program for the Provision of Pharmaceuticals," 1–12.
[108] It is not at all clear how Pogge estimates his program's cost but it might cost quite a bit more
than he imagines to really make an impact as drug companies report average R&D costs in the
hundreds of millions. Angell, *The Truth About the Drug Companies.*
[109] Buchanan and Keohane, "Justice in the Diffusion of Innovations."

evaluate companies' R&D, for instance, is by looking at what their drugs can do. It does not suggest collecting expensive new data or estimating the GBD.[110] It will consider only what portion of the GBD, as estimated by the WHO, companies' inventions alleviate. Furthermore, it only aims to rank companies ordinally and provide a constantly raising bar for companies to try to exceed. So it is much less data-intensive than Hollis and Pogge's alternative. Fifth, although the proposal is not as ambitious as Hollis and Pogge's, it has the advantage of being practical and relatively low cost. Although it will cost something to administer a trademark like Fair Trade Bio, those costs are nowhere near US$45–90 billion (or even US$6 billion).[111] The total revenue and support for TransFair USA, the primary Fair Trade labeling organization in the USA, was US$5,570,933 in 2006.[112] So, a reasonable estimate for the costs of the proposal would be in the millions rather than billions. This would not require taxpayer support. It could be developed in poor countries. Finally, Fair Trade Bio labeling and licensing campaigns might even be used in conjunction with some of the above alternatives to help the poor.

Even if the Fair Trade Bio proposals this chapter has sketched have some advantages over some of the main competitors, one might object that the opportunity costs of pursuing Fair Trade Bio labeling or licensing campaigns are too high. Perhaps there are better things Bio companies, universities, researchers, students, and consumers could be doing besides trying to extend access to essential drugs and technologies to the poor in the ways set out here. The greatest health problems facing the poor could not be ameliorated by better access to existing drugs and technologies or more research and development on diseases affecting the poor. War, natural disasters, dirty water, and inadequate food provide the biggest obstacles to health in developing countries. Prevention and poverty alleviation could do much more for the poor than pills. Some antiretrovirals, for

---

[110] The counter-factual relative to which something counts as an improvement should probably approximate the current situation as closely as possible. There are some other ways of dealing with any bad incentives this creates. For discussion see: Selgelid, "A Full-Pull Program for the Provision of Pharmaceuticals," 1–12.

[111] Hollis and Pogge, "The Health Impact Fund, Making New Medicines Accessible for All."

[112] TransFair USA, "2006 Annual Report," 36. They have never even had a lawsuit in defense of their label. They employ two people to help prevent abuse by contacting those who infringe on their copyright but they rely primarily upon their customer base for monitoring. Hassoun, Nicole, unpublished phone interview with Catherine Sinclair, Business Development Associate TransFair USA, 2009.

instance, are not effective in parts of Africa where people lack adequate nutrition.[113] Perhaps international institutions should just donate a part of their budgets to charity organizations. Perhaps researchers should spend most of their time trying to find ways of dealing with wars and natural disasters or helping people secure clean water. Maybe students and consumers should advocate for these kinds of changes or go to work for humanitarian aid organizations.[114]

Although there may be better things institutions or individuals could do for the poor besides supporting Fair Trade Bio, what is best cannot be decided a priori. We may do the most good for the poor by encouraging companies to do more R&D to benefit the poor. Fair Trade Bio campaigns might lead companies to come up with new antiretrovirals or treatment regimes that work in places like Africa. Even if there are other things that could, in principle, benefit the poor more, there may be room for those with different interests and talents to take different approaches to ameliorating poverty. Fair Trade Bio labeling and licensing campaigns are also compatible with doing many other things to help the poor as well. So it may be acceptable to pursue the Fair Trade Bio proposals suggested here as long as we do these other things too. Universities, companies, and individuals might both donate to good charities *and* support Fair Trade Bio labeling and licensing campaigns. The best need not be the enemy of the good.

Another worry is that companies might use the fact that they are highly rated to distract the public from their generally poor behavior in other arenas. Suppose, for instance, that another organization launched a campaign to get companies to stop fighting compulsory licensing in developing countries by lobbying US trade representatives. Companies might respond by holding a media event to promote their Fair Trade Bio status and undermine the campaign. Since companies control a lot of resources, they would probably win a battle in the press.[115]

This is a live possibility, but companies hardly need a label to hold a public relations event and undermine campaigns to get them to improve their practices. Companies can promote their charitable programs, or even start new programs to get good publicity. Those involved in the attempt to get Bio companies to improve their practices should not blame each other if companies abuse their efforts. Rather, they should stand

---

[113] Global Health Watch, *Global Health Watch 2005–2006.*
[114] I owe thanks to Jonathan Wolff for suggesting this objection.
[115] I owe thanks to Ethan Guillen and Johnathan Wolff for suggesting this objections.

together – those involved in the Fair Trade Bio movement might even create standards for revoking companies' licenses if they insist on acting poorly. A Fair Trade Bio rating agency's review panel might even create standards for reducing companies' high ratings if they find new ways of acting poorly. Although the Fair Trade Bio proposals this chapter has set out will not solve all the poor's health problems, they may make a significant difference in the lives of many poor people like Tamil.

Conclusion: Expanding obligations

SUMMARY

This book has focused on poverty-related suffering and death, the first avoidable and the second deferrable. The first half of this book defended a new argument for significant obligations to the global poor. Its first chapter laid the groundwork for this argument. It considered and reviewed some standard criticisms of one traditional way of grounding obligations to the global poor – in a concern for human rights. Following authors like James Nickel and James Griffin, it argued that everyone has a right to the necessary conditions for autonomy. On this account, legitimate states must ensure that their subjects secure the objects of their human rights. Other institutions and individuals have secondary obligations to ensure that people secure these things if states fail in their obligations. The first chapter, then, considered the objection that this account ignores the distinction between positive and negative rights. Positive rights are rights to assistance. Negative rights are rights that others not do certain kinds of things. The first chapter canvassed some plausible responses to critics. It suggested, however, that these responses would not appeal to some of those most concerned about individual freedom. So, it concluded that a new argument for positive rights was needed. In doing this, it also explained and defended some of the crucial concepts and claims relied upon in subsequent chapters. It described the kind of autonomy necessary to consent to coercive rules and institutions. It argued that most people need some food, water, shelter, education, health care, social support, and emotional goods to secure this autonomy.

Chapter 2 sketched the book's new argument for significant obligations to the global poor intended to appeal to liberals of many persuasions. It suggested that a negative right against coercion actually entails positive rights to things like adequate food, water, shelter, and so forth.

The second chapter argued that, to be legitimate, coercive institutions must do what they can to ensure that their subjects secure what they need for sufficient autonomy. Moreover, it suggested everyone is subject to many coercive international institutions and most people must be able to secure basic food, water, shelter, and so forth to secure this autonomy. So the second chapter concluded that, to be legitimate, these institutions must do what they can to ensure that these people secure these things.

Chapter 3 argued that right libertarians and actual consent theorists, in particular, have reason to accept significant obligations to the global poor. Most libertarians and actual consent theorists accept the second chapter's argument that coercive institutions must be legitimate. So, the third chapter started from this conclusion. It addressed libertarians who accept something like the following proposition: It is only legitimate to exercise coercive force over rights-respecting individuals to protect those individuals' liberty. The third chapter followed authors like John Simmons in arguing that libertarians who accept this much should accept actual consent theory; they should agree that coercive institutions are legitimate only if they secure their subjects' autonomous consent. It suggested that actual consent theorists, and hence these libertarians, should agree that legitimate coercive institutions have to ensure that most of their subjects secure adequate food, water, shelter, education, health care, social support, and emotional goods. So, libertarians have to agree that states, if not international institutions, must do what they can to ensure that these people secure these things. If they do so, almost everyone will be able to avoid severe poverty.

The second part of this book examined some of the institutions and rules guiding international development. Most of the people who cannot secure adequate food, water, shelter, medicine, and so forth live in the developing world. The second half of this book considered whether or not we have reason to believe that aid or trade is likely to ameliorate poverty. It argued that the case for some aid and trade is strong but that we must work to make free trade fair.

Chapter 4 started by noting that the biggest challenge to arguments for helping the global poor is the skeptical challenge that there is nothing those of us in the developed world can do for them. Almost all the philosophers who have considered the issue, for instance, question the claim that aid can ameliorate poverty. Most of these critics have come to this conclusion, at least in part, by discussing particular case studies that have not been rigorously evaluated. This chapter argued that this is a mistake.

It defended the kind of empirically based methodology used throughout the book that is particularly evident in the last chapters. Importantly, it found rigorous ways of figuring out when aid works and when it does not. Looking at rigorous data, it is clear that the case for giving at least some aid is strong.

Some argue, however, that free trade is a better way of helping the global poor than aid. So, Chapter 5 examined the case for the kind of free trade reforms the international financial institutions like the WTO, WB, and the IMF advocate. It found that there is no theoretical guarantee that free trade will ameliorate poverty. In theory, the most free trade reforms guarantee is that liberalized markets will reach a Pareto optimal state, that is, a state in which it is impossible to make anyone better off without making someone else worse off. Pareto optimality, under the relevant Kaldor–Hicks interpretation, tells us little about distribution. Even a situation in which one person has everything, and everyone else is poor, can be Pareto optimal if no one can be made better off without making someone else worse off. In practice, the case for free trade was even less clear. Even if the aggregate benefits of free trade for the poor are large, that alone does not tell us whether or not to support trade. We need to pay attention to the details of different trade reforms to take trade's distributional impacts into account in practice. Most reforms probably have mixed effects. So, this chapter concluded that we should consider ways of capturing the benefits of free trade for the poor while avoiding the costs. It then sketched some possible reforms including linkage, trade barriers, trade-related adjustment assistance programs, and the Fair Trade movement.

Finally, Chapter 6 presented a concrete proposal for helping the poor secure some of the things that they need – in particular essential drugs and technologies. It proposed and defended a package of Fair Trade strategies to encourage pharmaceutical and biotechnology companies to improve poor people's access to these things. The idea was to rate pharmaceutical and biotechnology companies based on how their policies impact poor people's access to essential drugs and technologies. The best companies, in a given year, will be Fair Trade certified and be allowed to use a Fair Trade label on their products. Highly rated companies, then, have an incentive to use the label to garner a larger share of the market as those engaged in trade and investment often prefer to purchase Fair Trade goods and invest in Fair Trade companies. If even a small percentage of consumers or doctors would prefer Fair Trade products, the incentive to use this label could be substantial. Socially responsible investment companies could also include in their portfolio Fair Trade certified companies. Finally, having a Fair Trade certification system for pharmaceutical and biotechnology companies would open the door to all kinds of fruitful social activism including boycotts of poorly rated companies, lobbying of insurance companies to include Fair Trade products in their formularies, and so forth. After considering some of the details of the Fair Trade certification scheme, Chapter 6 considered one kind of activism using the scheme that might benefit the poor – a Fair Trade licensing campaign. Pharmaceutical and biotechnology companies rely, to a large extent, on university research and development. If universities only allow companies that agree to use Fair Trade practices to benefit from their technology, companies will have an incentive to abide by Fair Trade standards. If universities are reluctant to require this much of their clients, researchers and students might have an impact. Researchers sign agreements to allow universities to license patents resulting from research they create. Students have been successful in convincing their campuses to participate in other Fair Trade licensing campaigns. The Fair Trade proposals this chapter defends will not solve all of the poor's problems. Still, the book concludes as long as one can see the good we can do for some, even if we cannot completely ameliorate poverty immediately, there is reason for optimism. There is a lot that we can and must do now.

Bibliography

Abizadeh, Arash, "Cooperation, Pervasive Impact, and Coercion: On the Scope (not Site) of Distributive Justice," *Philosophy and Public Affairs*, 35 (2007), 318–58

Abramowicz, Michael, "Perfecting Patent Prizes," *Vanderbilt Law Review*, 56 (2003), 114–236

Access to Medicine Foundation, "Access to Medicine Index" (2008). Available at: www.nytimes.com/2008/06/17/health/17glob.html?_r=1&ref=health&oref=slogin

Adams Jr., R., "Economic Growth, Inequality, and Poverty: Estimating the Growth Elasticity of Poverty," *World Development*, 32 (2004), 1989–2014

African Development Bank Group, "Poverty Reduction Strategy Papers" (2010). Available at: www.afdb.org/en/documents/project-operations/poverty-reduction-strategy-papers/

Aiken, W. and H. La Follette (eds.), *World Hunger and Moral Obligation* (Englewood Cliffs, NJ: Prentice-Hall, 1977)

Alexander, Lawrence, "Zimmerman on Coercive Wage Offers," *Philosophy and Public Affairs* 12 (1983), 160–64. Available at http://philpapers.org/s/ (Lawrence A. Alexander)

Amanthis, Judith, "Niger: The IMF and World Bank's Invisible War on Africans," Global Policy Forum. Available at: www.globalpolicy.org/socecon/bwi-wto/imf/2005/0901invisible.htm

Amponsah, William A., "Analytical and Empirical Evidence of Trade Policy Effects of Regional Integration: Implications for Africa," Preliminary Draft, Africa Development Forum III (2002). Available at: www.uneca.org/adfiii/docs/afrdevforpapf02.pdf

Anderson, James, "The Relative Inefficiency of Quotas," *The Journal of Economic Education*, 19 (1988), 65–81

Anderson, Kym, "Agricultural Trade Reform and Poverty Reduction in Developing Countries," Policy Research Working Paper No. 3396, World Bank (2004). Available at: http://papers.ssrn.com/sol3/papers.cfm?abstract_id=625273

Anderson, Scott, "Coercion," *Stanford Encyclopedia of Philosophy* (2006). Available at: http://plato.stanford.edu/entries/coercion/

Ang, Adrian U-Jin and Dursun Peksen, "When Do Economic Sanctions Work? Asymmetric Perceptions, Issue Salience, and Outcomes," *Political Research Quarterly*, 60 (2007), 135–45

Angell, Marcia, *The Truth About the Drug Companies: How They Deceive Us and What To Do About It* (New York, NY: Random House, 2004)

Arbache, J.S., A. Dickerson, and F. Green, "Trade Liberalization and Wages in Developing Countries," *The Economic Journal*, 114 (2004), 73–96

von Arnim, Rudiger and Lance Taylor, "World Bank CGE Macroeconomics and the Doha Debate," New School for Economic Research (2007)

Ashraf, Nava, Dean Karlan, and Wesley Yin, "Female Empowerment: Impact of a Commitment Savings Product in the Philippines," Working Paper No. 106, Center for Global Development (2006)

Asian Development Bank, "Smokey Mountain Remediation and Development Project" (2010). Available at: www.adb.org/Projects/PEP/phi-smokey.asp

Association of American Universities, "University Technology Transfer of Government-Funded Research Has Wide Public Benefits" (1998). Available at: www.aau.edu/research/TechTrans6.3.98.html

Association of University Technology Managers, "AUTM U.S. Licensing Survey FY2005" (2005). Available at: www.autm.net/events/File/US_LS_05Final(1).pdf

"FY 2005 AUTM U.S. Licensing Survey" (2007). Available at: www.autm.net/about/dsp.Detail.cfm?pid=194

Ayadi, O. Felix, Esther O. Adegbite, and Funso S. Ayadi, "Structural Adjustment, Financial Sector Development and Economic Prosperity in Nigeria," *International Research Journal of Finance and Economics*, 15 (2008), 318–331. Available at: www.eurojournals.com/irjfe%2015%20felix.pdf

Bacon, Christopher, "Confronting the Coffee Crisis: Can Fair Trade, Organic, and Specialty Coffees Reduce Small-Scale Farmer Vulnerability in Northern Nicaragua?" *World Development*, 33 (2004), 497–511

Baker, Lucy, "The World Bank and Human Rights," Bretton Woods Project (2007). Available at: www.ifiwatchnet.org/sites/ifiwatchnet.org/files/The_World_Bank_and_human_rights-%20at%20issue.pdf

Baker, P., "Russia Backs Kyoto to Get on Path to Join World Trade Organization," *Washington Post*, 10 (2004), A15

Bandara, Jayatilleke S. and Wusheng Yu, "How Desirable is the South Asian Free Trade Area? A Quantitative Economic Assessment," *World Economy*, 26 (2003), 1293–323

Banerjee, Abhijit and Ester Duflo, "The Experimental Approach to Development Economics," Abdul Laff Jameel Poverty Action Lab Working Paper, Massachusetts Institute of Technology (2009)

Banerjee, Abhijit, Shawn Cole, Esther Duflo, and Leigh Linden, "Improving the Quality of Education in India: Evidence from Three Randomized Experiments," mimeo, Massachusetts Institute of Technology (2003)

Bannister, Geoffrey J. and Kamau Thugge, "International Trade and Poverty Alleviation," Working Paper No. 01/54, IMF (2001). Available at: http://papers.ssrn.com/Sol3/papers.cfm?abstract_id=270440##

Barnard, David, "In the High Court of South Africa, Case No. 4138/98: The Global Politics of Access to Low-Cost AIDS Drugs in Poor Countries," *Kennedy Institute of Ethics Journal*, 12 (2002), 159–74

Barry, Christian and Sanjay Reddy, *Just Linkage: International Trade and Labor Standards* (New York, NY: Columbia University Press, 2005)

Bauer, Peter, *Dissent on Development* (Cambridge, MA: Harvard University Press, 1972)

"N. H. Stern on Substance and Method in Development Economics," *Journal of Development Economics*, 2 (1975), 387–405

Bayles, Michael D., "Coercive Offers and Public Benefits," *The Personalist*, 55 (1974), 139–44

BCC Research, "The U.S. Market for Prescription Allergy Treatment and Management," Report Code: PHM026A (2002). Available at: www.bccresearch.com/report/PHM026A.html

Beaton, David B., "Effects of Stress and Psychological Disorders on the Immune System," Working Paper, Rochester Institute of Technology (2003)

van Beers, Cees, "International Trade, Environment, and Sustainable Development," in M. Cogoy and K. Steininger (eds.), *Economics of Sustainable Development: International Perspectives* (Cheltenham: Edward Elgar, 2006)

Beitz, Charles, *Political Theory and International Relations* (Princeton University Press, 1979)

Bello, Walden, "Structural Adjustment Programs: 'Success for Whom?'," in J. Mander and E. Goldsmith (eds.), *The Case Against the Global Economy and for a Turn Toward the Local* (San Francisco, CA: Sierra Club Books, 1996)

Benditt, Theodore, "Threats and Offers," *The Personalist*, 58 (1979), 382–4

Beran, Harry, *The Consent Theory of Political Obligation* (New York, NY: Croom Helm, 1987)

Berman, Mitchell, "The Normative Functions of Coercion Claims," *Legal Theory*, 8 (2002), 45–89

Berndt, Ernst, Rachel Glennerster, Michael Kremer, Jean Lee, Ruth Levine, Georg Weizsacker, and Heidi Williams, "Advance Market Commitments for Vaccines against Neglected Diseases: Estimating Costs and Effectiveness," *Health Economics*, 16 (2007), 491–511

Besley, Timothy and Louise Cord, *Delivering on the Promise of Pro-Poor Growth: Insight and Lessons from Country Experiences* (New York, NY: Palgrave Macmillan, 2007)

Bhagwati, Jagdish, "Revisiting the 1930s," in *Termites in the Trading System* (Oxford University Press, 2008). Available at: www.international-economy.com/TIE_W09_Bhagwati.pdf

Bhutta, Mahmood F., "Fair Trade for Surgical Instruments," *British Medical Journal*, 333 (2006), 297–9. Available at: www.ncbi.nlm.nih.gov/pmc/articles/PMC1526950/pdf/bmj33300297.pdf/?tool=pmcentrez

Bigsten, Arne and Jorgen Levin, "Growth, Income Distribution, and Poverty: A Review," in A. Shorrocks and R. van der Hoeven (eds.), *Growth, Inequality, and Poverty* (Oxford University Press, 2004, Ch. 12)

Black, Richard and Howard White (eds.), *Critical Perspectives on the Millennium Development Goals* (London: Routledge, 2004)

Blake, Michael, "Distributive Justice, State Coercion, and Autonomy," *Philosophy and Public Affairs*, 30 (2001), 257–96

Blossner, Monika and Mercedes de Onis, *Malnutrition: Quantifying the Health Impact at National and Local Levels* (Geneva, Switzerland: World Health Organization, 2005)

Blum, Larry, *Moral Perception and Particularity* (Cambridge University Press, 1994)

Blustein, Paul, *The Chastening: Inside the Crisis that Rocked the Global Financial System and Humbled the IMF* (New York, NY: Public Affairs, 2001)

Boaz, David, *Libertarianism: A Primer* (New York, NY: Free Press, 1997)

Bobonis, Gustavo, Edward Miguel, and Charu Sharma, "Iron Supplementation and Early Childhood Development: A Randomized Evaluation in India," mimeo, University of California, Berkeley (2002)

Boone, Peter, "Politics and the Effectiveness of Foreign Aid," *European Economic Review*, 40 (1996), 289–329

Bourguignon, François, Anne-Sophie Robilliard, and Sherman Robinson, *Representative versus Real Households in the Macro-Economic Modeling of Inequality* (Washington, DC: World Bank, 2004)

Bourguignon, François, Jaime de Melo and Akiko Suwa-Eisenmann, "Distributional Effects of Adjustment Policies: Simulations for Two Archetype Economies," *The World Bank Economic Review*, 5 (1991), 339–66

Bourne, Compton, "Poverty and Its Alleviation in the Caribbean," Alfred O. Heath Distinguished Speakers' Forum, University of the Virgin Islands (2005)

BRAC, *BRAC at a Glance: Alleviation of Poverty and Empowerment of the Poor* (Bangladesh: BRAC, 2005)

Braintree Laboratories, "Products" (2010). Available at: www.braintreelabs.com/products-suprep.htm

Bratman, Michael, "Planning Agency, Autonomous Agency," in J. S. Taylor (ed.), *New Essays on Personal Autonomy and its Role in Contemporary Moral Philosophy* (Cambridge University Press, 2005), 33–57

British Broadcasting Corporation, "Argentina Blames IMF for Crisis" (2004). Available at: http://news.bbc.co.uk/2/hi/americas/3941809.stm

"WTO Approves Banana Sanctions" (1999). Available at: http://news.bbc.co.uk/2/hi/business/322938.stm

Brock, Gillian, *Cosmopolitan Justice and Patriotic Concern* (Oxford University Press, 2009)

"Egalitarianism, Ideals, and Cosmopolitan Justice," *The Philosophical Forum*, 36 (2005), 1–30

Global Justice: A Cosmopolitan Account (Oxford University Press, 2009)

"Liberal Nationalism versus Cosmopolitanism: Locating the Disputes," *Public Affairs Quarterly*, 16 (2002), 307–27

Brock, Gillian and Darrel Moellendorf, *Current Debates in Global Justice: Studies in Global Justice* (Norwell, MA: Springer, 2005)

Brock, Karen, "'It's Not Only Wealth that Matters it's Peace of Mind Too': Review of Participatory Work on Poverty and Illbeing" (Birmingham: Institute of Development Studies, 1999)

Buchanan, Allen, *Ethics, Efficiency, and the Market* (Lanham, MD: Rowman and Littlefield Publishers, 1985)

Justice, Legitimacy, and Self-Determination: Moral Foundations for International Law (Oxford University Press, 2004)

"Justice as Reciprocity vs. Subject-Centered Justice," *Philosophy and Public Affairs*, 19 (1990), 227–52

"Political Legitimacy and Democracy," *Ethics*, 112 (2002), 697–8

Buchanan, Allen and Dan Brock, *Deciding for Others – The Ethics of Surrogate Decision Making* (Cambridge University Press, 1989)

Buchanan, Allen and Robert O. Keohane, "Justice in the Diffusion of Innovations," Conference Paper, University of Washington (2009)

"The Legitimacy of Global Governance Institutions," *Ethics and International Affairs*, 20 (2006), 405–37

Buffie, Edward F. and Manoj Atolia, "Trade Policy, Poverty, and Development in a Dynamic General Equilibrium Model for Zambia," Working Paper, Florida State University (2008). Available at: ftp://econpapers.fsu.edu/RePEc/fsu/wpaper/wp2008_11_04.pdf

Burnside, Craig and David Dollar, "Aid, Policies and Growth," *American Economic Review*, 90 (2000), 847–68

Busse, Matthias, Axel Borrmann, and Harald Großmann, "The Impact of ACP/EU Economic Partnership Agreements on ECOWAS Countries: An Empirical Analysis of the Trade and Budget Effects," Discussion Paper, Hamburg Institute of International Economics (2004). Available at: www.econstor.eu/bitstream/10419/19266/1/294.pdf

Calo, Muriel and Timothy A. Wise, "Revaluing Peasant Coffee Production: Organic and Fair Trade Markets in Mexico," Global Development and Environment Institute, Tufts University (2005)

Caney, Simon, "Cosmopolitan Justice and Equalizing Opportunities," *Metaphilosophy*, 32 (2001), 113–34

Justice Beyond Borders – A Global Political Theory (New York, NY: Oxford University Press, 2005)

"Survey Article: Cosmopolitanism and the Law of Peoples," *The Journal of Political Philosophy*, 10 (2002), 95–133

Carens, Joseph H., "Who Should Get in? The Ethics of Immigration Admissions," *Ethics and International Affairs*, 17 (2003), 95–110. Available at: http://onlinelibrary.wiley.com/doi/10.1111/j.1747–7093.2003. tb00421.x/abstract;jsessionid=0466F9C8F1C97F5D180F306B05BA4462. d02t02

Cashin, Paul, Paolo Mauro, Catherine Pattillo, and Ratna Sahay, "Macroeconomic Policies and Poverty Reduction: Stylized Facts and an Overview of Research," Working Paper 135, International Monetary Fund (2001)

Cassen, Robert, *Does Aid Work?* (Oxford: Clarendon Press, 1986)

Cato Unbound, "Can the Resource Curse Be Lifted?" (2008). Available at: www. cato-unbound.org/issues/can-the-resource-curse-be-lifted/

Cavallero, Eric, "Coercion, Inequality and the International Property Regime," *The Journal of Political Philosophy*, 18 (2009), 16–31

Center for Global Development, "Making It Pay to Stay in School," Center for Global Development Notes (2005)

Centers for Disease and Development, "World TB Day, March 24th 2005," Division of Tuberculosis Elimination (2005). Available at: www.cdc.gov/nchstp/tb/WorldTBDay/2005/resources_progress_elimination.htm

Centers for Disease Control and Prevention, "Vector Control" (2007). Available at: www.cdc.gov/malaria/control_prevention/vector_control.htm

Cernea, Michael, "Involuntary Resettlement in Development Projects: Policy Guidelines in World Bank-Financed Projects," World Bank Technical Paper No. 80 (1998). Available at repository.forcedmigration.org/show_metdata.jsp?pid=fmo:2823

Chain Drug Review, "Internal Analgesic Tablets" (2010). Available at: http://findarticles.com/p/articles/mi_hb3007/is_4_31/ai_n31414841

Charcon, Oscar, Laura Carlsen, Michael Collins, Paula Alvarez, Ricardo Verdum, and Christopher Loperena. "Inter-American Development Bank Megaprojects: Displacement and Forced Migration," CIP America (2010). Available at: www.cipamericas.org/archives/2421

Chatterjee, Dean K. (ed.), *The Ethics of Assistance: Morality and the Distant Needy* (Cambridge University Press, 2004)

Chen, Shaohua and Martin Ravallion, "How Have the World's Poorest Fared since the Early 1980s?" *World Bank Research Observer*, 19 (2004), 141–69. Available at: http://wbro.oupjournals.org/cgi/content/abstract/19/2/141

Cheong, David, "Methods for Ex Ante Economic Evaluation of Free Trade Agreements," Working Paper on Regional Economic Integration 52, Asian Development Bank (2010). Available at: http://aric.adb.org/pdf/working-paper/WP52_Ex_Ante_Economic_Evaluation.pdf

Christiaensen, Luc, "Revisiting the Global Food Architecture – Lessons from the 2008 Food Crisis," Discussion Paper No. 2009/04, World Institute for Development Economics Research (2009). Available at: http://ideas.repec.org/p/unu/wpaper/2009–04.html

Christiano, Thomas, "Authority," *Stanford Encyclopedia of Philosophy* (2004). Available at: http://plato.stanford.edu/entries/authority/

The Rule of the Many: Fundamental Issues in Democratic Theory (Boulder, CO: Westview Press, 1996)

Cicoweiz, Martin and Adrianna Conconi, "Linking Trade and Pro-poor Growth: A Survey," in J. Cockburn and P. Giordano (eds.), *Trade and Poverty in the Developing World* (Inter-American Development Bank/Poverty and Economic Policy Network, 2008), 7–30

Clemens, M., S. Radelet, et al., "Counting Chickens when they Hatch: The Short Term Effect of Aid on Growth," Working Paper Number 44, Center for Global Development (2011)

Cockburn, J. and P. Giordano (eds.) *Trade and Poverty in the Developing World* (Inter-American Development Bank/Poverty and Economic Policy Research Network, 2008). Available at: www.pep-net.org/fileadmin/medias/pdf/promotionnal_material/Proceedings_TradePoverty.pdf

Cohen, Jessica and Pascaline Dupas, "Free Distribution or Cost-Sharing? Evidence from a Randomized Malaria Prevention Experiment," Brooking Global Economy and Development Working Paper 11 (2007)

Collier, Paul and David Dollar, "Development Effectiveness: What Have We Learnt?" *The Economic Journal*, 114 (2004), F244–71

Committee on Economic, Social and Cultural Rights, "The Nature of States Parties' Obligations," General Comment 3, Fifth Session (1990)

Conroy, M.E., "Can Advocacy-Led Certification Systems Transform Global Corporate Practices?" University of Massachusetts, Political Economy Research Institute, Amherst (2001)

Consumer Project on Technology, "The Bayh-Dole Act" (2005). Available at: www.cptech.org/ip/health/bd/

Cordella, Tito and Giovanni Dell-Ariccia, "Budget Support versus Project Aid," Working Paper 03/88, International Monetary Fund (2003)

Corong, Erwin L., Rachel C. Reyes, and Angelo B. Taningco, "Poverty Impacts of Preferential and Multilateral Trade Liberalization on the Philippines: A Computable General Equilibrium Analysis," Pr-MPIA-0470 Working Paper Version (2009). Available at: www.pep-net.org/fileadmin/medias/pdf/files_events/reyes.pdf

Cororaton, C., J. Cockburn, and E. Corong, "Doha Scenarios, Trade Reforms, and Poverty in the Philippines: A CGE Analysis," in T. Hertel and A. Winters (eds.), *Putting Development Back into the DOHA Agenda: Poverty Impacts of a WTO Agreement* (Washington, DC, World Bank, 2005, Ch. 13). Available at: http://siteresources.worldbank.org/INTRANETTRADE/Resources/Topics/285683–1109974429289/Chapter13_Philippines_final.pdf

Craig, David and Doug Porter, "Poverty Reduction Strategy Papers: A New Convergence. What Does it Miss, and What Can Be Done About It?" Background Paper, Regional Conference on National Poverty Reduction Strategies, World Bank, UNDP, IMF and ADB (2001). Available at: www.adb.org/poverty/prs_paper_30_nov.pdf

Cullen, Michelle and Harvey Whiteford, "Inter-relations of Social Capital with Health and Mental Health," Discussion Paper, Commonwealth Department of Health and Aged Care (2001)

Cullity, Garrett, *The Moral Demands of Affluence* (Oxford: Clarendon Press, 2004)

Dagdeviren, Hulya, Rolph van der Hoeven, and John Weeks, "Redistribution Does Matter: Growth and Redistribution for Poverty Reduction," in A. Shorrocks and R. van der Hoeven (eds.), *Growth, Inequality, and Poverty* (Oxford University Press, 2004)

Dalgaard, Carl-Johan, Henrik Hansen, and Finn Tarp, "On the Empirics of Foreign Aid and Growth," *The Economic Journal*, 114 (2004), F191–F216

Danzon, Patricia and Adrian Towse, "Differential Pricing for Pharmaceuticals: Reconciling Access, R&D and Patents," *International Journal of Health Care Finance and Economics*, 3 (2003), 183–205

Deaton, Angus, "Counting the World's Poor: Problems And Possible Solutions," Research Program in Development Studies Working Paper, Princeton University (2000)

    "Instruments for Development: Randomization in the Tropics, and the Search for the Elusive Keys to Economic Development," The Keynes Lecture, British Academy (2008)

Decreux, Yvan, and Lionel Fontagné, "A Quantitative Assessment of the Outcome of the Doha Development Agenda," Working Papers 2006–10, CEPII Research Centre (2006)

Delgado Cabrera, Eng. Miguel, Observatorio Ciudadano de Servicios Públicos, "Incidencia de Calidad de los Servicios en el Brote de Hepatitis A en el Suburbio Oeste de Guayaquil" (July, 2005)

Delgado, Ray, "Slow Growth Seen in Faculty Ranks; Challenges Remain in Hiring Minorities, Women," Stanford Report (2005). Available at: http://news-service.stanford.edu/news/2005/may4/faculty-050405.html

Devarajan, Shantayanan and Dani Rodrik, "Trade Liberalization in Developing Countries: Do Imperfect Competition and Scale Economies Matter?" *American Economic Review*, 79 (1989), 283–7

DiMasi, Joseph, Ronald Hansen, and Henry Grabowski, "The Price of Innovation: New Estimates of Drug Development Costs," *Journal of Health Economics*, 22 (2002), 151–85

Doane, Deborah, "Taking Flight: The Rapid Growth of Ethical Consumerism," in *The Ethical Purchasing Index 2001. New Economics Foundation Report for The Co-operative Bank* (Manchester: The Co-operative Bank, 2001)

Dollar, David, "Outward Oriented Developing Countries Really Do Grow More Rapidly: Evidence from 95 LDCs, 1976–85," *Economic Development and Cultural Change*, 40 (1992), 523–44

Dollar, David and A. Kraay, "Growth is Good for the Poor," Policy Research Working Paper Number 2587 (2000). Subsequently published as: D. Dollar and A. Kraay, "Growth is Good for the Poor," *Journal of Economic Growth*, 7 (2001), 195–225

Dorsey, Dale, "Three Arguments for Perfectionism," *Nous*, 44 (2010), 59–79

Doyle, Rodger, "Calculus of Happiness: Assessing Subjective Well-being Across Societies," *Scientific American* (2002), 280–32

Dreher, Axel, "The IMF and Economic Growth: The Effect of Programs, Loans, and Compliance with Conditionality," Thurgau Institute of Economics

Working Paper, University of Konstanz (2004). Available at: http://econstor. eu/bitstream/10419/19804/1/Dreher.pdf

Duflo, Esther and Michael Kremer, "Use of Randomization in the Evaluation of Development Effectiveness," World Bank Operations Evaluation Department Conference on Evaluation and Development Effectiveness, World Bank (2003)

Duflo, Esther, Rachel Glennerster, and Michael Kremer, "Using Randomization in Development Economics Research: A Toolkit," Working Paper 6059, Center for Economic Policy Research (2007)

Duflo, Ester, Michael Kremer, and Jonathan Robinson, "Nudging Farmers to Use Fertilizer: Evidence from Kenya," MIT Working Paper (2009)

Dupas, Pascaline, "Relative Risks and the Market for Sex: Teenagers, Sugar Daddies and HIV in Kenya," Dartmouth College Working Paper (2006)

Easterly, William, "Can Foreign Aid Buy Growth?" *Journal of Economic Perspectives*, 17 (2003), 23–48

The White Man's Burden: Why the West's Efforts to Aid the Rest Have Done so Much Ill and so Little Good (New York, NY: Penguin Press, 2006)

The Economist, "Fair Enough," 378 (2006), 33

Eden, Benjamin, "Efficient Barriers to Trade: A Sequential Trade Model With Heterogeneous Agents," *Journal of International Economics*, 77 (2009), 234–44

EFTA, *Fair Trade in Europe* (Maastricht: EFTA, 2001)

European Commission, "The EU and Eastern Caribbean Bananas" (2007). Available at: www.delbrb.ec.europa.eu/en/winban/overview.htm

European Union, "Economic Partnership Agreements and Free Trade – Myths and Reality," *EU-Uganda News: A Quarterly News Letter of the Delegation of the European Commission in Uganda* (2004)

"U.S. Congress Repeals Byrd Amendment but Allows for a Transition Period," No. 128/05 (2003). Available at: www.eurunion.org/News/press/2005/2005128.htm

Expreso de Guayaquil, "Hepatitis Se Expande Hacia Ocho Escuelas" (June 21, 2005)

Fairtrade Foundation, "What is Fairtrade?" (2008). Available at: www.fairtrade.org.uk/about_standards.htm

Fairtrade Labelling Organizations International, "Facts and Figures" (2009). Available at: www.fairtrade.net/facts_and_figures.html?&L=&scale=0

Farer, Tom J., "Political and Economic Coercion in Contemporary International Law," *American Journal of International Law*, 79 (1985) 405–413. Available at: www.questia.com/googleScholar.qst;jsessionid=E401E2B53DB6A11F8A8C61FEBD14929B.inst3_1b?docId=79259239

FATF, "High-risk and Non-Cooperative Jurisdictions" (2010). Available at: www.fatf-gafi.org/pages/0,3417,en_32250379_32236992_1_1_1_1,00.html

Faunce, Alured and Hitoshi Nasu, "Three Proposals for Rewarding Novel Health Technologies Benefiting People Living in Poverty: A Comparative Analysis of Prize Funds, Health Impact Funds and a Cost-effectiveness/Competitive

Tender Treaty," *Public Health Ethics*, 1 (2008), 146–53 Available at: http://phe.oxfordjournals.org/cgi/reprint/phn013v1

Federal Trade Commission, "Generic Drug Entry Prior to Patent Expiration: An FTC Study" (2002). Available at: www.ftc.gov/os/2002/07/genericdrugstudy.pdf

Feinberg, Joel, "Collective Responsibility," *Journal of Philosophy*, 65 (1968), 674–88

    Harm to Self (Oxford University Press, 1986)

    Social Philosophy (New Jersey: Prentice-Hall Inc., 1973)

Flory, James and Philip Kitcher, "Global Health and the Scientific Research Agenda," *Philosophy and Public Affairs*, 32 (2004), 36–65

Flower, Barnaby, Darius Armstrong-James, Claire Dance, Fion Bremner, and Tom Doherty, "Blind, Breathless, and Paralysed from Benign Malaria," *Lancet*, 377 (2011), 438

Food and Agriculture Organization, "The State of Food Insecurity in the World" (2010). Available at: ftp://ftp.fao.org/docrep/fao/012/i0876e/i0876e01a.pdf

Food and Drug Administration, "OOPD Program Overview" (2008). Available at: www.fda.gov/ForIndustry/DevelopingProductsforRareDiseasesConditions/default.htm

Fowler, Mark, "Coercion and Practical Reason," *Social Theory and Practice*, 8 (1982), 329–55

Frank, Richard, "The Ongoing Regulation of Generic Drugs," *New England Journal of Medicine*, 357 (2007), 1993–6

Frankel, J. and D. Romer, "Does Trade Cause Growth?" *American Economic Review*, 89 (1999), 379–99

Frankfurt, Harry, "Coercion and Moral Responsibility," in T. Honderich (ed.), *Essays on Freedom of Action* (London: Routledge & Kegan Paul, 1973), 65–86

Freeman, Samuel, *Justice and the Social Contract: Essays on Rawlsian Social and Political Philosophy* (Oxford University Press, 2007)

G24, "Heavily Indebted Poor Country (HIPC) Initiative," G-24 Secretariat Briefing Paper (2003). Available at: www.g24.org/hipc.pdf

Ganuza, Enrique, Ricardo Paes de Barros, and Rob Vos, "Labour Market Adjustment, Poverty and Inequality during Liberalisation," in R. Vos and R. Paes de Barros (eds.), *Economic Liberalisation, Distribution and Poverty: Latin America in the 1990s* (Cheltenham: Edward Elgar Publishers, 2002), 54–88

Gauci, Adrian and Stephen N. Karingi, "Trade and Poverty: the Little We Know on the Effect in Africa and Possibly Why," in J. Cockburn and P. Giordano (eds.), *Trade and Poverty in the Developing World* (Inter-American Development Bank/Poverty and Economic Policy Network, 2008), 87–108

Gaus, Gerald, "Liberal Neutrality: A Compelling and Radical Principle," in S. Wall and G. Klosko (eds.), *Perfectionism and Neutrality: Essays in Liberal Theory* (New York, NY: Rowman and Littlefield Publishers, 2003), 137–66

"The Place of Autonomy within Liberalism," in J. Christman and J. Anderson (eds.), *Autonomy and the Challenges To Liberalism: New Essays* (New York, NY: Cambridge University Press, 2005), 272–306

Gertler, Paul J. and Simone Boyce, "An Experiment in Incentive-Based Welfare: The Impact of PROGRESA on Health in Mexico," mimeo, University of California, Berkeley (2001)

Gewirth, Alan, *The Community of Rights* (University of Chicago Press, 1996)

Gilbert, John, "Trade Policy, Poverty and Income Distribution in Computable General Equilibrium Models: An Application to the South Asia Free Trade Agreement," Working Paper, Utah State University (2008). Available at: www.unescap.org/tid/publication/tipub2526_chap6.pdf

Global Forum for Health Research, "Monitoring Financial Flows for Health Research 2006: The Changing Landscape of Health Research for Development," A. de Francisco and S. Matlin (eds.) (2006)

The Global Fund to Fight AIDS, Tuberculosis and Malaria, "REDTM Generates Landmark $US150 Million for The Global Fund" (2011) Available at: www.theglobalfund.org/en/pressreleases/?pr=pr_100601

Global Health Watch, *Global Health Watch 2005–2006: An Alternative World Health Report* (New York, NY: Zed Books, 2005)

Gomanee, Karuna and Oliver Morrissey, "Evaluating Aid Effectiveness Against a Poverty Reduction Criterion," DESG Conference (2002)

Gomanee, Karuna, Sourafel Girma, and Oliver Morrissey, "Aid and Growth in Sub-Saharan Africa: Accounting for Transmission Mechanisms," CREDIT Research Paper No. 02/05, Center for Research in Economic Development and International Trade, University of Nottingham (2002)

Goodwin, Paige, "Right Idea, Wrong Result – Canada's Access to Medicines Regime," *American Journal of Law & Medicine*, 34 (2008), 567–84

Gorr, Michael, "Toward a Theory of Coercion," *Canadian Journal of Philosophy*, 16 (1986), 383–406

Gosselin, Abigail, *Global Poverty and Individual Responsibility* (Lanham, MD: Rowman & Littlefield Publishers, 2009)

Green, Michael, "Institutional Responsibility for Global Problems," *Philosophical Topics*, 30 (2002), 79–96

Griffin, James, *Human Rights: The Incomplete Idea*, Working Draft, Corpus Christi College (2006), Subsequently published in Griffin, James, *Human Rights: The Incomplete Idea* (Oxford University Press, 2008)

Haksar, Vinit, "Coercive Proposals [Rawls and Gandhi]," *Political Theory*, 4 (1976), 65–79

Hansen, Henrik and Finn Tarp, "Aid Effectiveness Disputed," CREDIT Research Papers, University of Nottingham (2011)

"Aid and Growth Regressions," *Journal of Development Economics*, 64 (2001), 547–70

"The Effectiveness of Foreign Aid," Development Economics Research Group mimeo, University of Copenhagen (1999)

Harris, Gardiner, "Will the Pain Ever Let Up for Bristol-Myers?" *New York Times* (2003), Section 3, 1

Harrison, Ann and Gordon Hanson, "Who Gains from Trade Reform? Some Remaining Puzzles," *Journal of Development Economics*, 59 (1999), 125–54. Available at: www.nber.org/papers/w6915.pdf

Hart, H.L.A., "Are There Any Natural Rights?" *The Philosophical Review*, 64 (1954), 175–91

The Concept of Law, 2nd edn. (Oxford: Clarendon Press, 1994)

Hassoun, Nicole, "Another Mere Addition Paradox: Some Reflections on Variable Population Poverty Measurement," Working Paper, The United Nations' University's World Institute for Development Economics Research (forthcoming). Available at: www.wider.unu.edu/publications/working-papers//2010en_GB/wp2010-120/

"Coercion, Legitimacy, and Global Justice," Working Paper, Carnegie Mellon University (2009). Available at: www.hss.cmu.edu/philosophy/hassoun/papers.php

"Consumption: Achieving a Realistic Utopia," in H. Widdows and D. Moellendorf (eds.), *Handbook of Global Ethics* (forthcoming)

"Empirical Evidence and the Case for Foreign Aid," *Public Affairs Quarterly*, 24 (2010), 1–20

"Fair Trade," in D. Chaterjee (ed.), *The Encyclopedia of Global Justice* (Oxford University Press, 2011)

"Free Trade and the Environment," *Environmental Ethics*, 31 (2009), 51–66

"Free Trade, Poverty, and the Environment," *Public Affairs Quarterly*, 22 (2008), 353–80

"Free Trade, Poverty, and Inequality," *The Journal of Moral Philosophy*, 8 (2011), 5–44

"Global Health Impact: A Basis for Labeling and Licensing Campaigns?" *Developing World Bioethics* (forthcoming)

"Global Poverty," in D. Chaterjee (ed.), *The Encyclopedia of Global Justice* (Oxford University Press, 2011)

"Ideal Theory and Practice," Working Paper, Carnegie Mellon University (2011)

"Making Free Trade Fair," in V. Hendricks and D. Pritchard (eds.), *New Waves in Ethics* (London: Palgrave and Macmillan, 2011) "Making the Case for Foreign Aid," *Public Affairs Quarterly*, 24 (2010), 1–20

"Meeting Need," *Utilitas*, 21 (2008), 250–75

"Pharmaceutical Justice," in D. Chaterjee (ed.), *The Encyclopedia of Global Justice* (Oxford University Press, 2011)

"Raz on the Right to Autonomy," *European Journal of Philosophy* (forthcoming). Available at: http://onlinelibrary.wiley.com/doi/10.1111/j.1468-0378.2011.00473.x/abstract

"World Bank Rules for Aid Allocation," Carnegie Mellon University Working Paper (2010). Available at: www.hss.cmu.edu/philosophy/hassoun/papers.php

"World Poverty and Individual Freedom," *American Philosophical Quarterly*, 45 (2008), 191–8

Hassoun, Nicole and Matt Frank, "Are Debt-for-Nature Swaps Morally Permissible?" Working Paper, Carnegie Mellon University (2010). Available at: www.hss.cmu.edu/philosophy/hassoun/papers.php

Hassoun, Nicole and S. Subramanian, "An Aspect of Variable Population Poverty Comparisons," Working Paper, The United Nations' University's World Institute for Development Economics Research (2010). *Journal of Development Economics*. Available at: www.sciencedirect.com/science/article/pii/S0304387811000794

Hayter, Teresa, *Aid as Imperialism* (London: Pelican Books, 1971)

Hayter, Teresa and Catherine Watson, *Aid: Rhetoric or Reality?* (London: Pluto Press, 1985)

Headey, Derek and Shenggen Fan, "Reflections on the Global Food Crisis: How Did It Happen, How Has It Hurt, And How Can We Prevent the Next One?" Research Monograph 165, International Food Policy Research Institute (2010). Available at: www.ifpri.org/sites/default/files/publications/rr165.pdf

Healey, Richard, *Gauging What's Real: the Conceptual Foundations of Contemporary Gauge Theories* (Oxford University Press, 2009)

Held, David, *Democracy and the Global Order: From the Modern State to Cosmopolitan Governance* (Stanford University Press, 1995)

Held, Virginia, "Can a Random Collection of Individuals Be Morally Responsible?" *Journal of Philosophy*, 67 (1970), 471–81

"Coercion and Coercive Offers," in J.R. Pennock and J. Chapman (eds.), *Coercion* (Chicago, IL: Aldine Atherton, 1972), 49–62

Heltberg, Rasmus, "The Growth Elasticity of Poverty," in A. Shorrocks and R. van der Hoeven (eds.), *Growth, Inequality, and Poverty* (Oxford University Press, 2004)

"The Poverty Elasticity of Growth," Discussion Paper, WIDER (2002). Available at: www.wider.unu.edu/publications/working-papers/discussion-papers/2002/en_GB/dp2002–21

Hertel, T., D. Hummels, M. Ivanic, and R. Keeney, "How Confident Can We Be in CGE-Based Assessments of Free Trade Agreements?" Working Paper 10477, National Bureau of Economic Research (2004). Available at: www.nber.org/papers/w10477

Hill Jr., Thomas E., "The Kantian Conception of Autonomy," in J. Christman (ed.), *The Inner Citadel: Essays on Autonomy* (Oxford University Press, 1989), 91–108

Hoekema, David, *Rights and Wrongs: Coercion, Punishment and the State* (Susquehanna University Press, 1986)

Hoekman, Bernard and Michel M. Kostecki, *The Political Economy of the World Trading System: From GATT to WTO* (Oxford University Press, 1995)

Hollis, Aidan and Thomas Pogge, "The Health Impact Fund, Making New Medicines Accessible for All: A Report of Incentives for Global Health"

(2008). Available at: www.keionline.org/blogs/2008/11/27/trade-off-innov-access/

Hopkins, R., "Impact Assessment Study of Oxfam Fair Trade," unpublished paper prepared for Oxfam/GB (2000)

Hubbard, T. and J. Love, "A New Trade Framework for Global Healthcare R&D," *PLoS Biology*, 2 (2004), e52. Available at: www.plosbiology.org/article/info:doi/10.1371/journal.pbio.0020052

Hudson, Christopher G., "Socioeconomic Status and Mental Illness: Tests of the Social Causation and Selection Hypotheses," *American Journal of Orthopsychiatry*, 75 (2005), 3–18

Hume, David, *A Treatise of Human Nature* (New York, NY: Penguin Books, 1969); originally published 1739–40

Hurrell, Andrew, "Global Inequality and International Institutions," *Metaphilosophy*, 32 (2001), 34–57

ILO, "Accelerating Action Against Child Labour," Global Report Under the Follow-up to the ILO Declaration on Fundamental Principles and Rights at Work (2010). Available at: www.ilo.org/ipec/Informationresources/lang–en/index.htm

IMF, "About the IMF" (2010). Available at: www.imf.org/external/about.htm

"Factsheet: Debt Relief Under the Heavily Indebted Poor Countries (HIPC) Initiative" (2010). Available at: www.imf.org/external/np/exr/facts/hipc.htm

"Factsheet: The IMF and World Bank" (2010). Available at: www.imf.org/external/np/exr/facts/imfwb.htm

"Joint Statement by Heads of IMF, World Bank and WTO" (2003). Available at: www.imf.org/external/np/sec/pr/2003/pr0368.htm

"Poverty Reduction Strategy Papers" (2010). Available at: www.imf.org/external/np/prsp/prsp.asp

"Tanzania Poverty Reduction Strategy Paper Progress Report," IMF Country Report No. 03/96 (2004). Available at: http://siteresources.worldbank.org/INTPRS1/Resources/Country-Papers-and-JSAs/cr0396.pdf

"Zambia: Enhanced Structural Adjustment Facility Policy Framework Paper" (1999). Available at: www.imf.org/external/np/pfp/1999/zambia/

IMF and World Bank, "ESAF Policy Framework Paper" (1998). Available at: www.imf.org/external/np/pfp/bolivia/index.htm

"Heavily Indebted Poor Countries (HIPC) Initiative" (1999). Available at: www.imf.org/external/np/hipc/modify/hipc.htm

Imhof, Sandra and Andrew Lee, "Assessing the Potential of Fair Trade for Poverty Reduction and Conflict Prevention: A Case Study of Bolivian Coffee Producers," Working Paper, University of Basel (2007)

Independent Evaluation Group, "The World Bank's Country Policy and Institutional Assessment" (2009). Available at: http://siteresources.worldbank.org/EXTCPIA/Resources/cpia_full.pdf

Ingco, Merlinda and John D. Nash, "What's at Stake? Developing–Country Interests in the Doha Development Round," in *Agriculture and the WTO:*

Creating a Trading System for Development (Oxford University Press, 2004), 1–22

Inter-American Development Bank, *Privatization for the Public Good?* A. Chong (ed.) (Cambridge, MA: Harvard University Press, 2008)

"Programs of Conditional Cash Transfers Seen as Effective in Reducing Poverty and Exclusion," Press Release (2006)

International Comparison Program, "Global Purchasing Power Parities and Real Expenditures" (2008). Available at: http://siteresources.worldbank.org/ICPINT/Resources/icp-final.pdf

International Fair Trade Association, "What is Fair Trade?" (2008). Available at: www.ifat.org/index.php?option=com_content&task=blogcategory&id=11&Itemid=12

International Institute for Environment & Development, "Fair Trade: Overview, Impact, Challenges," Unpublished paper prepared for Department for International Development (2000)

International Organization for Standardization, "About ISO" (2010). Available at: www.iso.org/iso/about.htm

International Security Assistance Force, "About ISAF" (2011). Available at: www.isaf.nato.int/history.html

International Trade Administration, "An Introduction to US Trade Remedies" (2011). Available at: http://ia.ita.doc.gov/intro/index.html

Isbam, Jonathan, Deepa Narayan, and Lant Pritchett, "Does Participation Improve Project Performance: Project Performance in the Rural Water Supply Projects Establishing Causality," Policy Research Working Paper 1357, World Bank (1994)

Jamieson, Dale, "Duties to the Distant: Aid, Assistance, and Intervention in the Developing World," *The Journal of Ethics*, 9 (2005), 151–70

Jansen, Hans G.P., Sam Morley, and Maximo Torero, "The Impact of the Central America Free Trade Agreement on Agriculture and the Rural Sector in Five Central American Countries," Working Paper, RUTA (2007). Available at: www.ruta.org/admin/biblioteca/documentos/361_EN.pdf

Jigsaw, "Braintree Laboratories Inc. Company Information" (2011). Available at: www.spoke.com/info/c494unR/BraintreeLaboratoriesInc

"Hoechst Marion Roussel Company Information" (2007). Available at: www.jigsaw.com/id150236/aventis_hoechst_marion_roussel_company.xhtml

"Romark Laboratories Lc Company Information" (2010). Available at: www.jigsaw.com/id2028996/romark_laboratories_lc_company.xhtml

Joiner, Emily, "Murky Waters: A Look at the Perpetual Puzzle of Water and Sanitation Services in Guayaquil, Ecuador," ILASSA Student Conference Proceedings Archive (2007). Available at: http://lanic.utexas.edu/project/etext/llilas/ilassa/2007/joiner.pdf

Joint Economic Committee, "The Benefits of Medical Research and the Role of NIH" (2000). Available at: http://hsc.utoledo.edu/research/nih_research_benefits.pdf

Julius, A. J., "Basic Structure and the Value of Equality," *Philosophy and Public Affairs*, 31 (2003), 321–55

Kalorama Information, "The U.S. Market for Over-the-Counter Allergy and Asthma Products" (2001). Available at: www.marketresearch.com/product/display.asp?ProductID=521895

Kanavos, Panos, J. Costa-i-Font, S. Merkur, and M. Gemmill, "The Economic Impact of Pharmaceutical Parallel Trade in European Union Member States," Special Research Paper LSE Health and Social Care, London School of Economics and Political Science (2004)

Kanbur, R., "Structural Adjustment, Macroeconomic Adjustment and Poverty: A Methodology for Analysis," *World Development*, 16 (1988)

Kant, Immanuel, *On the Common Saying: What is True in Theory Does Not Work in Practice* (Cambridge University Press, 1970)

Karlan, Dean and Nathanel Goldberg, "Impact Evaluation for Microfinance: Review of Methodological Issues," Innovations for Poverty Action Working Paper, Yale University (2007)

Kehler, Al, "Humanitarian Exchange," Humanitarian Policy Group No. 27, Overseas Development Institute (2004)

Kekes, John, "Ought Implies Can and Two Kinds of Morality," *Philosophical Quarterly*, 34 (1984), 459–67

Kesselheim, Aaron S., "Think Globally, Prescribe Locally: How Rational Pharmaceutical Policy in the U.S. Can Improve Global Access to Essential Medicines," *American Journal of Law & Medicine*, 34 (2008), 125–39

Kinsella, N. Stephan, "Against Intellectual Property," *Journal of Libertarian Studies*, 15 (2001), 1–53

Knight, Jack and James Johnson, "What Sort of Political Equality Does Deliberative Democracy Require?" in J. Bohman and W. Reh (eds.), *Deliberative Democracy* (MIT Press, Cambridge, MA, 1997), 279–319

Kremer, Michael, "The Role of Randomized Evaluations in Making Progress towards Universal Basic and Secondary Education," Working Paper, American Academy of Arts and Sciences (2005)

Kremer, Michael and Rachel Glennerster, *Strong Medicine* (Princeton University Press, 2004)

Kukathas, Chandran, *The Liberal Archipelago: A Theory of Diversity and Freedom* (Oxford University Press, 2003)

Kuper, Andrew, "More Than Charity: Cosmopolitan Alternatives to the 'Singer Solution'," *Ethics and International Affairs*, 16 (2002), 107–20

"Redistributing Responsibilities: The UN Global Compact with Corporations," in A. Follesdal and T. Pogge (eds.), *Real World Justice: Grounds, Principles, Human Rights and Social Institutions* (Dordrecht: Springer, 2005), 359–80

Kutz, Christopher, *Complicity: Ethics and Law for a Collective Age* (Cambridge University Press, 2000)

Kymlicka, Will, "The Rights of Minority Cultures: Reply to Kukathas," *Political Theory*, 20 (1992), 140–6

Landenson, Robert, "In Defense of a Hobbesian Conception of Law," *Philosophy and Public Affairs*, 9 (1980), 134–59

Lanjouw, Jean and William Jack, "Trading Up: How Much Should Poor Countries Pay to Support Pharmaceutical Innovation," Center for Global Development (2004). Available at: www.cgdev.org/content/publications/detail/2842

Leathers, Howard and Phillips Foster, *The World Food Problem: Tackling the Causes of Undernutrition in the Third World* (Colorado: Lynne Rienner Publisher, 2004)

Lipsey, Richard and Kelvin Lancaster, "The General Theory of Second Best," *The Review of Economic Studies*, 24 (1956–7), 11–32

Lipson, Molly and Peter Vallentyne, "Child Liberationism and Legitimate Interference," *Journal of Social Philosophy*, 23 (1992), 5–15

   "Libertarianism, Autonomy, and Children," *Public Affairs Quarterly*, 5 (1991), 333–52

List, Christian and M. Koenig-Archibugi, "Can There Be a Global Demos? An Agency-Based Approach," *Philosophy and Public Affairs*, 38 (2010), 76–110

Loayza, Norman and Claudio Raddatz, "The Composition of Growth Matters for Poverty Alleviation," Working Paper 4077, World Bank Policy Research (2006). Available at: www.wds.worldbank.org/servlet/WDSContentServer/WDSP/IB/2006/12/05/000016406_20061205152514/Rendered/PDF/wps4077.pdf

Locke, John, *Second Treatise on Civil Government*, C.B. MacPherson (ed.) (Indianapolis, IN: Hackett, 1990)

Lomasky, Loren, "Liberalism Beyond Borders," *Peace Research Abstracts Journal*, 44 (2007), 206

   Persons, Rights, and the Moral Community (New York, NY: Oxford University Press, 1987)

Long, Roderick and Tibor Machan, *Anarchism/Minarchism: Is a Government Part of a Free Country?* (London: Ashgate Press, 2008)

Lyons, Daniel, "Welcome Threats and Coercive Offers," *Philosophy*, 50 (1975), 425–36

Machan, Tibor, "The Perils of Positive Rights," *The Freeman: Ideas on Liberty*, 51 (2001)

   "Sterba on Machan's 'Concession'," *Journal of Social Philosophy*, 32 (2002), 241–3

MacIntyre, Alaisdair, *Whose Justice, Which Rationality?* (Notre Dame University Press, 1988)

Mahecha, Laura A., "Outlook: Rx-to-OTC Switches: Trends and Factors," *Nature Reviews Drug Discovery*, 5 (2006), 380–6. Available at: www.nature.com/nrd/journal/v5/n5/fig_tab/nrd2028_F3.html

MailOnline, "Copyright Laws Should Be Extended to Protect Ageing Artists, Say MPs" (2007). Available at: www.dailymail.co.uk/news/article-455284/Copyright-laws-extended-protect-ageing-artists-say-MPs.html

Mangels, Reed, "How Many Vegetarians Are There?" National Harris Interactive Survey Question, Vegetarian Resource Group, *Vegetarian Journal* (2003). Available at: http://findarticles.com/p/articles/mi_m0FDE/is_3_22/ai_10642231

Marmot, Michael, *Status Syndrome: How your Social Standing Directly Affects your Health and Life Expectancy* (London: Bloomsbury, 2004)

Martin, H.E. Msgr. Diarmuid, "Intervention by the Holy See at the World Trade Organization" (2002). Available at: www.vatican.va/roman_curia/secretariat_state/documents/rc_seg-st_doc_20021220_martin-wto_en.html

Masud, Nadia and Boriana Yontcheva, "Does Foreign Aid Reduce Poverty? Empirical Evidence from Nongovernmental and Bilateral Aid," Working Paper, International Monetary Fund (2005)

Mavrotas, George, "Assessing Aid Effectiveness in Uganda: An Aid-Disaggregation Approach," Oxford Policy Management, Oxford University

Max Havelaar Belgium. "Cafe" (2002). Available at: http://www2.maxhavelaar.com/fr/koffie/resultaten.html

May, Larry, "Symposia Papers: Collective Inaction and Shared Responsibility," *Noûs*, 24 (1990), 269–77

May, Larry and Stacey Hoffman, *Collective Responsibility: Five Decades of Debate in Theoretical and Applied Ethics* (Lanham, MD: Rowman and Littlefield, 1991)

Mayer, Jorg, "Implications of New Trade and Endogenous Growth Theories for Diversification Policies of Commodity-Dependent Countries," Discussion Paper No. 122, UNCTAD (1996). Available at: www.unctad.org/en/docs/dp_122.en.pdf

McCormick, Michael J. "A Primer on the European Union and its Legal System," The Army Lawyer. Superintendent of Government Documents, 358 (2002), 1–12

McCulloch, Neil, L. Alan Winters, and Xavier Cirera, *Trade Liberalization and Poverty: A Handbook* (London: Department for International Development, 2001)

McDermott, Jim, "A Morality Tale on AIDS" (2006), Address by Congressman Jim McDermott. US House of Representatives June 20, 2006. Available at: www.house.gov/mcdermott/sp060619.shtml

McGregor, Joan, "Bargaining Advantages and Coercion in the Market," *Philosophy Research Archives*, 14 (1988–9), 23–50

McMahon, Patrick, "'Cause Coffees' Produce a Cup with an Agenda," *USA Today*, 2001, A1–2

Medical Fair and Ethical Trade Group, "Contact Us" (2009). Available at: http://mfetg.wordpress.com/contact-us-2/

Michalopoulos, C. and V. Sukhatme, "The Impact of Development Assistance: A Review of the Quantitative Evidence," in A.O. Krueger (ed.), *Aid and Development* (Baltimore, MD: Johns Hopkins University Press, 1989), 111–24

Miguel, Edward and Michael Kremer, "Worms: Identifying Impacts on Education and Health in the Presence of Treatment Externalities," *Econometrica*, 72 (2004), 159–217

Milanovic, B., "The Two Faces of Globalization: Against Globalization as We Know It," *World Development*, 31 (2003), 667–83

Milford, Anna, "Coffee, Co-operatives and Competition: The Impact of Fair Trade," Chr. Michelsen Institute (2004)

Mill, John Stuart, *On Liberty* (New York, NY: P.F. Collier & Son, 1917), vol. XXV, 1909–14; originally published 1859

Miller, David, *National Responsibility and Global Justice* (New York, NY: Oxford University Press, 2007)

   On Nationality (Oxford: Clarendon Press, 1995)

Miller, Richard, "Cosmopolitan Respect and Patriotic Concern," *Philosophy and Public Affairs*, 27 (1998), 202–24

   Globalizing Justice: The Ethics of Poverty and Power (Oxford University Press, 2010)

Moellendorf, Darrel, *Cosmopolitan Justice* (Cambridge: Westview Press, 2002)

   Global Inequality Matters (New York, NY: Palgrave Macmillan, 2009)

   "World Trade Organization and Egalitarian Justice," *Metaphilosophy*, 36 (2005), 145–62

Morduch, Jonathan, "Does Microfinance Really Help the Poor? New Evidence from Flagship Programs in Bangladesh," Working Paper, Harvard University Department of Economics (1998)

Morgenthau, Hans and Kenneth W. Thompson, *Politics Among Nations: The Struggle for Power and Peace*, 6th edn. (New York, NY: Alfred A. Knopf, 1985)

Mortished, Carl, "What Happens When a Country Goes Bust?" *The Sunday Times* (2008). Available at: http://business.timesonline.co.uk/tol/business/economics/article5031413.ece

Mosley, Paul, John Hudson, and Sara Horrell, "Aid, the Public Sector and the Market in Less Developed Countries," *The Economic Journal,* 97 (1987), 616–41

Mosley, Paul, John Hudson, and Arjan Verschoor, "Aid, Poverty Reduction and the 'New Conditionality'," *The Economic Journal*, 114 (2004) F217–43

Moyo, Dambisa, *Dead Aid: Why Aid is Not Working and How There is Another Way for Africa*, With a Foreword by Niall Ferguson (London: Allen Lane, 2009)

Mullins, C. Daniel, Francis Palumbo, and Bruce Stuart, "Projections of Drug Approvals, Patent Expirations, and Generic Entry From 2000 To 2004," Background Report Prepared for The Department of Health and Human Services' Conference on Pharmaceutical Pricing Practices, Utilization and Costs, University of Maryland School of Pharmacy and University of Maryland Center on Drugs and Public Policy (2000). Available at: http://

aspe.hhs.gov/health/reports/Drug-papers/Mullins-Palumbo%20paper-final.htm

Murray, Douglas, Laura T. Raynolds, and Peter Leigh Taylor, "One Cup at a Time: Poverty Alleviation and Fair Trade Coffee in Latin America," Fair Trade Research Group, Colorado State University (2003). Available at: www.usaid.gov/our_work/environment/compliance/ane/workshops/Jordan2007/day3/S/FairTradeandPovertyReductionStudy.pdf

Nagel, Thomas, "The Problem of Global Justice," *Philosophy and Public Affairs*, 33 (2005), 113–47

Narveson, Jan, *The Libertarian Idea* (Philadelphia: Temple University Press, 1988)

Narveson, Jan and James P. Sterba, *Are Liberty and Equality Compatible?* (Cambridge University Press, 2010)

National Institute for Health Care Management Foundation, "Changing Pattern of Pharmaceutical Innovation" (2002). Available at: www.nihcm.org/final-web/innovations.pdf

NATO, "What's on NATO's Agenda?" (2007). Available at: www.nato.int/#

New York Times, "Analgesic Makers in a Battle" (February 18, 1986). Available at: http://query.nytimes.com/gst/fullpage.html?sec=health&res=9A0DE7D91F31F93BA25751C0A960948260

Nickel, James, "A Defense of Welfare Rights as Human Rights," in T. Christiano and J.P. Christman (eds.), *Contemporary Debates in Political Philosophy* (Wiley-Blackwell, 2009)

"How Human Rights Generate Duties to Protect and Provide," *Human Rights Quarterly*, 15 (1993), 77–86

"A Human Rights Approach to World Hunger," in W. Aiken and H. LaFollette (eds.), *World Hunger and Morality* (Upper Saddle River, NJ: Prentice-Hall, 1995), 171–85

Making Sense of Human Rights (Oxford University Press, 2006)

Nozick, Robert, *Anarchy, State, and Utopia* (New York, NY: Basic Books, 1974)

"Coercion," in S. Morgenbesser, P. Suppes, and M. White (eds.), *Philosophy, Science, and Method: Essays in Honor of Ernest Nagel* (New York, NY: St. Martin's Press, 1969), 440–72

Nussbaum, Martha, *Women and Human Development: The Capabilities Approach* (Cambridge University Press, 2000)

OECD, "Aid Statistics, Recipient Aid Charts" (2010). Available at: www.oecd.org/countrylist/0,3349,en_2649_34447_25602317_1_1_1_1,00.html

Office of Technology Management, "Annual Report 2007," University of Pittsburgh, 7–8

Office of the United Nations High Commissioner for Human Rights, "Optional Protocol to the International Covenant on Civil and Political Rights," General Assembly Resolution 2200A, XXI (1966). Available at: www2.ohchr.org/english/law/ccpr-one.htm

Office of the United States Trade Representative, "Schwab Announces Results of Chile IPR Review, Cites Deteriorating Performance," press release (2007). Available at: www.ustr.gov/Document_Library/Press_Releases/2007/January/Schwab_Announces_Results_of_Chile_IPR_Review,_Cites_Deteriorating_Performance.html

OHE Consulting, "A Review of IP and Non-IP Incentives for R&D for Diseases of Poverty: What Type of Innovation is Required and How Can We Incentivise the Private Sector to Deliver It?" Final Report for the WHO Commission on Intellectual Property Rights, Innovation and Public Health, London Office of Health Economics (2005)

O'Neill, Onora, *Bounds of Justice* (Cambridge University Press, 2000)
  "The Dark Side of Human Rights," *International Affairs*, 81 (2005), 427–39
  Faces of Hunger: An Essay on Poverty, Justice and Development (London: Allen and Unwin, 1986)

Owens, Trudy and John Hoddinott, "Investing in Development or Investing in Relief: Quantifying the Poverty Tradeoffs Using Zimbabwe Household Panel Data," Working Paper 99–4, Centre for the Study of African Economies, Department of Economics, Oxford University (1999)

Oxfam, "Food Aid or Hidden Dumping? Separating Wheat from Chaff," Oxfam Briefing Paper 71, Oxfam GB (2005)

Parekh, Bikhu, *Rethinking Multiculturalism: Cultural Diversity and Political Theory* (Basingstoke: Macmillan, 2000)

Patten, Alan, "Should We Stop Thinking about Poverty in Terms of Helping the Poor?" *Ethics and International Affairs*, 19 (2005), 19–27.

Pattillo, Catherine, Jacques Polak, and Joydeep Roy, "Measuring the Effect of Foreign Aid on Growth and Poverty Reduction or the Pitfalls of Interaction Variables," IMF Working Paper, International Monetary Fund (2007)

Pauwelyn, Joost, "Bridging Fragmentation and Unity: International Law as a Universe of Inter-connected Islands," *Michigan Journal of International Law*, 25 (2004), 903–16

Pfizer, "Diversified Business" (2010). Available at: http://pfizer.com/research/licensing/diversified_business.jsp
  "Pfizer Reports Fourth-Quarter and Full-Year 2008 Results and 2009 Financial Guidance" (2009). Available at: http://media.pfizer.com/files/investors/presentations/q4performance_january012609.pdf

Pharmaceutical R&D Policy Project, "The Landscape of Neglected Disease Drug Development," Wellcome Trust and London School of Economics (2005)

The Philippine Christian Foundation, "What We Do" (2010). Available at: http://pcf.ph/what_we_do/index.php

Pitt, Mark, "Reply to Jonathan Morduch's 'Does Microfinance Really Help the Poor?' New Evidence from Flagship Programs in Bangladesh," Working Paper, Brown University Department of Economics (1999)

Pogge, Thomas, "Eradicating Systemic Poverty: Brief for a Global Resources Dividend," *Journal of Human Development*, 2 (2001), 59–77

"Human Rights and Global Health: A Research Program," *Metaphilosophy*, 36 (2005), 182–209

"Intellectual Property Rights and Access to Essential Medicines," Global Policy Innovations, Carnegie Council for International Affairs (2007). Available at: http://siteresources.worldbank.org/INTDECINEQ/Resources/Intellectual PropRts.pdf.

"Introduction," *Ethics and International Affairs*, 19 (2005), 9–18

Realizing Rawls (Ithaca, NY: Cornell University Press, 1989)

"Severe Poverty as a Human Rights Violation," in T. Pogge (ed.), *Freedom from Poverty as a Human Right: Who Owes What to the Very Poor?* (Oxford University Press, 2007), 11–54

World Poverty and Human Rights: Cosmopolitan Responsibilities and Reforms, 2nd edn (Polity Press, 2007)

Pogge, Thomas and Sanjay Reddy, "Unknown: The Extent, Distribution, and Trend of Global Income Poverty," Working Paper Version 3.4 (2003). Available at: www.etikk.no/globaljustice/papers/GJ2003_Thomas_Pogge_with%20Sanjay_Reddy._Unknown_-_The_Extent,_Distribution_and_Trend_of_Global_Income_Poverty.pdf

Polaski, S., "Winners and Losers: Impact of the Doha Round on Developing Countries," Carnegie Endowment for International Peace (2006)

Public Citizen, "Water Privatization Case Study: Cochabamba, Bolivia" (2001). Available at: www.citizen.org/documents/Bolivia_(PDF).PDF

Pyarelal, *Mahatma Gandhi: The Last Phase*, Vol. 2 (India: Navajivan Press, 1958)

Rajan, Raghuram G. and Arvind Subramanian, "Aid and Growth: What Does the Cross-Country Evidence Really Show?" Working Paper 127, International Monetary Fund (2004)

Ravallion, Martin, "Looking beyond Averages in the Trade and Poverty Debate," Working Paper 3461, World Bank Policy Research (2004). Available at: www-wds.worldbank.org/servlet/WDSContentServer/WDSP/IB/2004/12/15/000012009_20041215104739/Rendered/PDF/wps3461.pdf

Ravallion, Martin and S. Chen, "Measuring Pro-Poor Growth," *Economics Letters*, 78 (2003), 93–9

Ravallion, Martin and G. Datt, "Why has Economic Growth Been More Pro-Poor in Some States of India than Others?" *Journal of Development Economics*, 68 (2002), 381–400

Ravallion, Martin and M. Lokshin, "Gainers and Losers from Trade Reform in Morocco," Working Paper 3368, The World Bank Policy Research (2004)

Rawlings, Laura and Gloria Rubio, "Evaluating the Impact of Conditional Cash Transfer Programs," *The World Bank Observer*, 20 (2005), 29–56

Rawls, John, *Justice as Fairness: A Restatement* (Cambridge, MA: Harvard University Press, 2003)

"Kantian Constructivism in Moral Theory," *Journal of Philosophy*, 88 (1980), 520–32

Law of Peoples (Cambridge, MA: Harvard University Press, 1999)

Political Liberalism (New York, NY: Columbia University Press, 1993)

A Theory of Justice (Cambridge, MA: Belknap Press, 1971)

Raworth, Kate and David Stewart, "Critiques of the HDI," in S.F. Parr and A.K. Shiva Kumar (eds.), *Readings in Human Development: Concepts, Measures and Policies for a Development Paradigm* (Oxford University Press, 2003)

Raynolds, Laura, "Poverty Alleviation Through Participation in Fair Trade Coffee Networks: Existing Research and Critical Issues," The Ford Foundation (2002)

Raz, Joseph, *The Morality of Freedom* (Oxford: Clarendon Press, 1998)

Red Cross, "American Red Cross Urges Public Health Precautions" (2007). Available at: www.redcross.org/pressrelease/0,1077,0_172_4554,00.htm

Reddy, Sanjay and Thomas Pogge, "How Not to Count the Poor," in S. Anand and J. Stiglitz (eds.), *Measuring Global Poverty* (Oxford University Press, 2006)

Reed, D., *Structural Adjustment, The Environment and Sustainable Development* (London: Earthscan Publications, 1996)

Respect Fair Trade Sports, "Gear Shop" (2008). Available at: www.fairtrade-sports.com/gearshop/

Rhodes, Michael, *Coercion: A Nonevaluative Approach* (Amsterdam: Rodopi, 2002)

Rieff, David, *A Bed for the Night: Humanitarianism in Crisis* (New York, NY: Simon & Schuster, 2002)

Risse, Mathias, "Do We Owe the Poor Assistance or Rectification?" *Ethics and International Affairs*, 19 (2005), 9–18

"Fairness in Trade," Working Paper, Harvard University (2006). Available at: http://ksghome.harvard.edu/~mrisse/docs/cv0306.pdf

"How Does the Global Order Harm the Poor?" *Philosophy and Public Affairs*, 33 (2005), 9–10

"On the Morality of Immigration," *Ethics and International Affairs*, 22 (2008), 25–33

"What to Say about the State," *Social Theory and Practice*, 32 (2006), 671–98

Risse, Mathias and Michael Blake, "Immigration and Original Ownership of the Earth," *Notre Dame Journal of Law, Ethics, and Public Policy*, 23 (2009), 133–67

Risser, David, "Collective Moral Responsibility," *Internet Encyclopedia of Philosophy* (2009), Available at: www.iep.utm.edu/collecti/#H1

Roberts, Adam, "United Nations," in J. Krieger (ed.), *The Oxford Companion to Politics of the World* (New York, NY: Oxford University Press, 2001)

Rodriguez, Francisco and Dani Rodrik, "Trade Policy and Economic Growth: A Skeptic's Guide to Cross-National Evidence," Working Paper No. 7081, NBER (1999). Available at: www.nber.org/papers/w7081

Rodrik, Dani, "Globalization, Growth and Poverty: Is the World Bank Beginning to Get It?" (2001). Available at: http://ksghome.harvard.edu/~drodrik/shortpieces.html

"Imperfect Competition, Scale Economies, and Trade Policy in Developing Countries," in R. E. Baldwin (ed.), *Trade Policy Issues and Empirical Analysis* (University of Chicago Press, 1988), 109–44. Available at: www.nber.org/chapters/c5849.pdf

"Is There a New Washington Consensus?" Project Syndicate (2008). Available at: www.project-syndicate.org/commentary/rodrik20/English

"The New Development Economics: We Shall Experiment, But How Shall We Learn?" in J. Cohen and W. Easterly (eds.), *What Works in Development? Thinking Big and Thinking Small* (Washington, DC: Brookings Institution Press, 2009)

Ronchi, Loraine, "Fair Trade in Costa Rica: An Impact Report," Economics Subject Group, University of Sussex (2000)

Rosser, Andrew, "The Political Economy of the Resource Curse: A Literature Survey," Working Paper 268, Institute of Development Studies (2006)

Roth, Abraham Sesshu, "Shared Agency," *Stanford Encyclopedia of Philosophy* (2010). Available at: http://plato.stanford.edu/entries/shared-agency/#MutObl

Ruben, Ruerd, *The Impact of Fair Trade* (Wageningen, Netherlands: Wageningen Academic Publishers, 2008)

Sachs, Jeff, "Alternative Approaches to Financial Crises in Emerging Markets," *Revisita de Economia Politica*, 16 (1996), 40–52. Available at: www.earthinstitute.columbia.edu/sitefiles/file/about/director/documents/jrnrepo696.pdf

The End of Poverty: Economic Possibilities of Our Time (New York, NY: Penguin Press, 2005)

Saez, Emmanuel, "Direct or Indirect Tax Instruments for Redistribution: Short-run versus Long-run," *Journal of Public Economics*, 88 (2004), 503–18

Sala-i-Martin, X., "The World Distribution of Income: Falling Poverty and... Convergence, Period," *The Quarterly Journal of Economics*, CXXI (2006), 375

Schabbel, Christian, *The Value Chain of Foreign Aid: Development, Poverty Reduction, and Regional Conditions* (Heidelberg: Physica-Verlag, 2007)

Schmidtz, David, "Islands in a Sea of Obligation: Limits of the Duty to Rescue," *Law and Philosophy*, 19 (2000), 683–705

Selgelid, M.J., "A Full-Pull Program for the Provision of Pharmaceuticals: Practical Issues," *Public Health Ethics*, 1 (2008), 1–12

Sen, Amartya, *Development as Freedom* (New York, NY: Anchor Books, 1999)

On Ethics and Economics (Oxford: Basil Blackwell, 1987)

"Global Justice: Beyond International Equity," United Nations Development Programme (1999). Available at: http://them.polylog.org/3/fsa-en.htm

"Human Development Index," in D.A. Clark (ed.), *The Elgar Companion to Development Studies* (Cheltenham: Edward Elgar, 2006), 256–9

Shue, Henry, *Basic Rights: Subsistence, Affluence, and U.S. Foreign Policy* (Princeton University Press, 1980)

Shultz, T. Paul, "School Subsidies for the Poor: Evaluating the Mexican PROGRESA Poverty Program," *Journal of Development Economics*, 74 (2004), 199–250

Simmons, John, "Consent Theory for Libertarians," *Social Philosophy and Policy*, 22 (2005), 330–56

    "Justification and Legitimacy," *Ethics*, 109 (1999), 770

    Moral Principles and Political Obligations (Princeton University Press, 1979)

Singer, Peter, "Famine, Affluence, and Morality," *Philosophy and Public Affairs*, 1 (1972), 229–43

Skoufias, Emmanuel et al., "Is PROGRESA Working? Summary of the Results of an Evaluation by IFPRI," FCND Discussion Paper No. 118, The International Food Policy Research Institute (2001)

Smiley, Marion, "Collective Responsibility," *Stanford Encyclopedia of Philosophy* (2010). Available at: http://plato.stanford.edu/entries/collective-responsibility/

Steinbrook, Robert, "Closing the Affordability Gap for Drugs in Low-Income Countries," *New England Journal of Medicine*, 357 (2007), 1996–8

Steiner, H. and P. Alston, *International Human Rights in Context*, 2nd edn. (Oxford University Press, 2008)

Stenger, Robert L., "Exclusive or Concurrent Competence to Make Medical Decisions for Adolescents in the United States and United Kingdom," *Journal of Law and Health*, 7 (1999), 209–41. Available at: http://findarticles.com/p/articles/mi_hb3048/is_2_14/ai_n28756516

Sterba, James, *From Liberty to Equality: Justice for Here and Now* (Cambridge University Press, 1998)

    "Progress in Reconciliation: Evidence from Right and Left," *Journal of Social Philosophy*, 28 (1997), 101–16

    The Triumph of Practice Over Theory in Ethics (Oxford University Press, 2005)

Stern, Nicholas and Francisco Ferreira, "The World Bank as 'intellectual actor'," in Devesh Kapur, J. P. Lewis, and Richard Webb (eds.) *The World Bank: its first half century. Volume 2: perspectives* (Washington, DC: Brookings Institution, 1997), pp. 523–609

Stevens, Robert, "Coercive Offers," *Australasian Journal of Philosophy*, 66 (1988), 83–95

Stiglitz, Joseph, *Globalization and Its Discontents* (New York, NY: W.W. Norton & Co, 2003)

Stuckler, David, Lawrence P. King, and Sanjay Basu, "International Monetary Fund Programs and Tuberculosis Outcomes in Post-Communist Countries," *PLoS Medicine*, 5 (2008), 1079–90

Stuckler, David, Lawrence King, and M. McKee, "Mass Privatisation and the Post-Communist Mortality Crisis: A Cross-National Analysis," *Lancet*, 373 (2009), 399–407

Tan, Kok-Chor, *Justice Without Borders: Cosmopolitanism, Nationalism, and Patriotism* (Cambridge University Press, 2004)

Tarp, Finn, "Aid and Development," *Swedish Economic Policy Review*, 13 (2006), 9–61

Tasioulas, John, "The Moral Reality of Human Rights," UNESCO Poverty Project (2004). Available at: http://portal.unesco.org/shs/en/ev.php-URL_ID=4333&URL_DO=DO_TOPIC&URL_SECTION=201.html

Taylor, Charles, "The Dynamics of Democratic Exclusion," *Journal of Democracy*, 9 (1998), 153

    Philosophy and Human Sciences: Philosophical Papers 2 (Cambridge University Press, 1985), Ch. 7

    Sources of the Self: The Making of Modern Identity (Cambridge, MA: Harvard University Press, 1988)

Taylor, Peter Leigh, "Poverty Alleviation Through Participation in Fair Trade Coffee Networks: Synthesis of Case Study Research Question Findings," Report Prepared for Project Funded by the Community and Resource Development Program, Colorado State University (2002)

Temple, J., "The New Growth Evidence," *Journal of Economic Literature*, 37 (1999), 112–56

Teson, Fernando, "Global Justice, Socioeconomic Rights, and Trade," Draft prepared for the Georgetown Law Center International Human Rights Colloquium (2005)

    "On Trade and Justice," *Theoria*, 104 (2004), 192

Teson, Fernando and Jonathon Klick, "Global Justice and Trade: A Puzzling Omission," Public Law Research Paper No. 285, FSU College of Law (2007). Available at: http://ssrn.com/abstract=1022996

TransFair USA, "TransFair USA" (2002). Available at: www.transfairusa.org

    "2006 Annual Report" (2006). Available at: http://transfairusa.org/content/shop/products.php

    "Wake Up the World" (2011). Available at: www.transfairusa.org

Trouiller, Patrice, Els Torreele, Piero Olliaro, Nick White, Susan Foster, Dyann Wirth, and Bernard Pécoul, "Drugs for Neglected Diseases: A Failure of the Market and a Public Health Failure?" *Tropical Medicine and International Health*, 6 (2001), 945–51

UNAIDS, "World AIDS Day 2004: Women, Girls, HIV and AIDS," AIDS Epidemic Update (2004). Available at: www.unaids.org/wad2004/report.html

UNICEF, "Millennium Development Goals: Combat AIDS/HIV, Malaria, and other Diseases" (2005). Available at: www.unicef.org/mdg/disease.html

United Human Rights Council, "Genocide in Rwanda" (2009). Available at: www.unitedhumanrights.org/Genocide/genocide_in_rwanda.htm

United Nations, "Article 56" (1945). Available at: www.un.org/aboutun/charter/

    "Conference at Bretton Woods," United Nations Monetary and Financial Conference (1944). Available at: www.ibiblio.org/pha/policy/1944/440722a.html

    The Millennium Development Goals Report (New York, NY: United Nations, 2006)

    "Overview of the UN Global Compact" (2010). Available at: www.unglobalcompact.org/aboutthegc/

"Report of the Secretary-General Pursuant to General Assembly Resolution 53/35," United Nations General Assembly (1999). Available at: www.un.org/peace/srebrenica.pdf

"Security Council Seeks Expansion of Role of International Effort in Afghanistan, to Extend Beyond Kabul," Press Release SC/7894, Security Council 4840th Meeting (2003). Available at: www.un.org/News/Press/docs/2003/sc7894.doc.htm

"United Nations Member States," Press Release ORG/1469 (2006). Available at: www.un.org/News/Press/docs/2006/org1469.doc.htm

United Nations' Treaty Collection (Geneva: United Nations, 2010). Available at: http://treaties.un.org/

United Nations Development Program, *Human Development Report* (Oxford University Press, 2005)

United Nations Educational, Scientific and Cultural Organization, "Education in India," UNESCO Institute for Statistics (2006)

United States Department of Agriculture, "National Organic Program" (2010). Available at: www.ams.usda.gov/AMSv1.0/nop

United Students Against Sweatshops, "About Ethical Contracting Campaigns" (2007). Available at: www.studentsagainstsweatshops.org//index.php?option=com_content&task=view&id=20&Itemid=67

Universities Allied for Essential Medicine, "Our Proposals" (2009). Available at: www.essentialmedicine.org/our-proposals/

"Why Universities?" Available at: www.essentialmedicine.org/?page_id=97

Van De Veer, Don, "Coercion, Seduction, and Rights," *The Personalist*, 58 (1979), 374–81

Villanueva, Daniel and A. Mirakhor, "Interest Rate Policies in Developing Countries," *Finance & Development*, 30 (1993), 31–7

Vos, Rob, "What We Do and Don't Know About Trade Liberalization and Poverty Reduction," in J. Cockburn and P. Giordano (eds.), *Trade and Poverty in the Developing World* (Inter-American Development Bank/Poverty and Economic Policy Network, 2008)

Wade, Robert, "Is Globalization Reducing Poverty and Inequality?" *World Development*, 32 (2004), 567–89

Waldron, Jeremy, "Theoretical Foundations of Liberalism," *Philosophical Quarterly*, 37 (1987), 132–46

Wallach, Lori, "Slow Motion Coup d'Etat: Global Trade Agreements and the Displacement of Democracy," *Multinational Monitor*, 26 (2005). Available at: http://multinationalmonitor.org/mm2005/012005/wallach.html

Walgreens, "Search Results" (2010). Available at: www.walgreens.com/search/results.jsp?Ntt=advil+pm&x=0&y=0

WE International Inc., "Programs" (2010). Available at: www.weinternational.org.ph/programs/

Wenar, Leif, "Accountability in International Development Aid," Working Paper, Carnegie Council on Ethics and International Affairs (2006). Available at: www.cceia.org/media/5344_20.1_Wenar.pdf

"The Basic Structure as Object: Institutions and Humanitarian Concern," *Canadian Journal of Philosophy*, 31 (2007), 253–78

"Poverty is No Pond: Challenges for the Affluent," in P. Illingworth, T. Pogge, and L. Wenar (eds.), *Giving Well: The Ethics of Philanthropy* (Oxford University Press, 2010)

"Property Rights and the Resource Curse," *Philosophy and Public Affairs*, 36 (2008), 2–32

"Responsibility for Severe Poverty: Human Rights and Severe Poverty," UNESCO Working Paper, United Nations (2004), subsequently published in T. Pogge (ed.), *Freedom from Poverty as a Human Right* (Oxford University Press, 2007)

Wertheimer, Alan, *Coercion* (Princeton University Press, 1987)

White, Howard, "The Macroeconomic Impact of Development Aid: A Critical Survey," *Journal of Development Studies*, 28 (1992), 163–240

White, Howard and Michael Bamberger, "Introduction: Impact Evaluation in Official Development Agencies," *IDS Bulletin*, 39 (2008), 1–11

Winters, Alan, Neil McCulloch and Andrew McKay, "Trade Liberalization and Poverty: The Evidence So Far," *Journal of Economic Literature*, 42 (2004), 72–115

Wolf, M., *Why Globalization Works* (New Haven, CT: Yale University Press, 2004)

Wolf, Susan, *Freedom within Reason* (Oxford University Press, 1990)

Woolcock, Michael, "The Place of Social Capital in Understanding Social and Economic Outcomes," *Canadian Journal of Policy Research*, 2 (2001), 11–17

World Bank, "About Us" (2010). Available at: http://go.worldbank.org/3QT2 P1GNH0

Assessing Aid: What Works, What Doesn't and Why (Oxford University Press, 2004)

"Country Lending Summaries – Philippines" (2011). Available at: http://web. worldbank.org/WBSITE/EXTERNAL/PROJECTS/0,,pagePK:64392398 ~piPK:64392037~theSitePK:40941~countrycode:PH~menuPK:64820000,0 0.html

"Financing Instruments" (2005). Available at: http://web.worldbank.org/WBSITE/ EXTERNAL/PROJECTS/0,,contentMDK:20120721~menuPK:232467!piP K:51533~theSitePK:40941,00.html

Globalization, Growth, and Poverty (Washington, DC: The World Bank, 2001)

"The Impact of Conditional Cash Transfer Programs: A Review of Evaluation Results," Second International Workshop on Conditional Cash Transfer Panel 3, World Bank (2004)

"International Development Association Articles of Agreement" (2011). Available at: http://go.worldbank.org/TSLNEK1XT0

"Partners" (2011). Available at: http://go.worldbank.org/987 TFNNAT0

"Povcalnet" (2007). Available at: http://web.worldbank.org/WBSITE/ EXTERNAL/EXTDEC/EXTRESEARCH/EXTPROGRAMS/

EXTPOVRES/EXTPOVCALNET/0,,contentMDK:21867101~pagePK:64
168427~piPK:64168435~theSitePK:5280443,00.html

Pro-Poor Growth in the 1990s: Lessons and Insights from 14 Countries (New
York, NY: The World Bank, 2005)

"PRSP Sourcebook: Chapter and Annexes" (2010). Available at: http://
web.worldbank.org/WBSITE/EXTERNAL/TOPICS/EXTPOVERTY/
EXTPRS/0,,contentMDK:22404376~pagePK:210058~piPK:210062~theS
itePK:384201~isCURL:Y,00.html

"World Bank Guarantee Catalyzes Private Sector Investment for Uch Power
Project in Pakistan." (1996) Available at: siteresources.worldbank.org/
INTGUARANTEES/Resources/UchPower_PFG_Note.pdf.

"World Bank's Loans to Japan" (2011). Available at: http://web.worldbank.org/
WBSITE/EXTERNAL/COUNTRIES/EASTASIAPACIFICEXT/JAPANE
XTN/0,,contentMDK:20647268~menuPK:1685599~pagePK:1497618~piPK:217
854~theSitePK:273812,00.html

World Development Indicators 2002 (Washington, DC: The World Bank,
2002)

World Health Organization, "10 Facts on Preventing Disease Through Healthy
Environments" (2007). Available at: www.who.int/features/factfiles/
environmental_health/en/index.html

"The Global Burden of Disease: 2004 Update" (2004). Available at: www.
who.int/healthinfo/global_burden_disease/en/index.html

Global Report on Antimalarial Drug Efficacy and Drug Resistance: 2000–2010
(Geneva: World Health Organization, 2010)

"Investing in Health Research and Development," Report of the Ad Hoc
Committee on Health Research Relating to Future Intervention Options
(1996), Figure S.2

"Malaria is Alive and Well and Killing More Than 3000 African Children
Every Day" (2003). Available at: www.who.int/mediacentre/news/
releases/2003/pr33/en/

"The Top 10 Causes of Death" (2007). Available at: www.who.int/mediacentre/
factsheets/fs310/en/

World Health Report 2004 (Geneva: World Health Organization, 2004)

World Malaria Report 2009 (Geneva: World Health Organization, 2009).
Available at: www.who.int/malaria/world_malaria_report_2009

World Trade Organization, "Committee on Agriculture: Report to the General
Council by the Vice-Chairman," Committee on Agriculture (2001). Available
at: www.wto.int/english/tratop_e/agric_e/implementation2001_e.pdf

"Committee Settles Three Implementation Issues" (2001). Available at: www.
wto.int/english/tratop_e/agric_e/implementation2001_e.htm

"The General Agreement on Tariffs and Trade (General Agreement on Tariffs
and Trade 1947)" in *Legal Texts: General Agreement on Tariffs and Trade
1947* (Geneva: World Trade Organization, 2006), Article III (Sections 1, 2,
and 4)

"Heads of International Agencies Agree to Work Together to Implement the WTO's Doha Development Agenda" (2002). Available at: www.wto.org/english/news_e/pres02_e/pr275_e.htm

"Intergovernmental Organizations Working with the WTO Secretariat" (2010). Available at: www.wto.org/english/thewto_e/coher_e/igo_divisions_e.htm

"Marrakesh Agreement Establishing the World Trade Organization," WTO Analytical Index. Available at: www.wto.org/english/res_e/booksp_e/analytic_index_e/wto_agree_01_e.htm

"Members and Observers" (2010). Available at: www.wto.org/english/theWTO_e/whatis_e/tif_e/org6_e.htm

"Mexico etc. vs. US: 'Tuna Dolphin'" (2010). Available at: www.wto.org/english/tratop_e/envir_e/edis04_e.htm

"Regionalism: Friends or Rivals?" in *Understanding the WTO: Cross-Cutting and New Issues* (Geneva. World Trade Organization, 2007)

"TRIPS and Public Health: Canada is First to Notify Compulsory License to Export Generic Drug" (2007). Available at: www.wto.org/english/news_E/news07_E/trips_health_notif_oct07_E.htm

"Work with Other International Organizations: The WTO and the United Nations" (2010). Available at: www.wto.org/english/thewto_e/coher_e/wto_un_e.htm

"The World Trade Organization in Brief" (2010). Available at: www.wto.org

WTO Watch, "NGOs Call on Trade Ministers to Reject Closed WTO Process," Global Policy Forum (2002). Available at: www.globalpolicy.org/component/content/article/177/31586.html

Zaman, Hassan, "Poverty and BRAC's Microcredit Programme: Exploring Some Linkages," Working Paper Number 18, BRAC (1997)

Zhuang, Juzhong, Herath M. Gunatilake, Yoko Niimi, Muhammad Ehsan Khan, Yi Jiang, Rana Hasan, Niny Khor, Anneli Lagman Martin, Pamela Bracey, and Biao Huang, "Financial Sector Development, Economic Growth, and Poverty Reduction: A Literature Review," Working Paper Series No. 173, Asian Development Bank Economics (2009). Available at: http://ssrn.com/abstract=1617022

Zimmerman, David, "Coercive Wage Offers," *Philosophy and Public Affairs*, 10 (1981), 121–45

Index

Made in the USA
San Bernardino, CA
03 February 2015